Maths Progress

Depth Book

Series editors: Dr Naomi Norman and Katherine Pate
Author: Caroline Locke

Second Edition

3

Pearson

Published by Pearson Education Limited, 80 Strand, London, WC2R 0RL.

www.pearsonschoolsandfecolleges.co.uk

Text © Pearson Education Limited 2019
Project managed and edited by Just Content Ltd
Typeset by PDQ Digital Media Solutions Ltd
Original illustrations © Pearson Education Limited 2019
Cover illustration by Robert Samuel Hanson

The rights of Nick Asker, Jack Barraclough, Sharon Bolger, Lynn Byrd, Andrew Edmondson, Bobbie Johns, Caroline Locke, Catherine Murphy, Naomi Norman, Mary Pardoe, Katherine Pate, Harry Smith and Angela Wheeler to be identified as authors of this work have been asserted by them in accordance with the Copyright, Designs and Patents Act 1988.

First published 2019

22 21 20 19
10 9 8 7 6 5 4 3 2 1

British Library Cataloguing in Publication Data
A catalogue record for this book is available from the British Library.

ISBN 978 1 292 28000 4

Printed in Italy by L.E.G.O S.p.A

Note from the publisher
Pearson has robust editorial processes, including answer and fact checks, to ensure the accuracy of the content in this publication, and every effort is made to ensure this publication is free of errors. We are, however, only human, and occasionally errors do occur. Pearson is not liable for any misunderstandings that arise as a result of errors in this publication, but it is our priority to ensure that the content is accurate. If you spot an error, please do contact us at resourcescorrections@pearson.com so we can make sure it is corrected.

Contents

Maths Progress Second Edition

Confidence at the heart

Maths Progress Second Edition is built around a unique pedagogy that has been created by leading mathematics educational researchers and Key Stage 3 teachers in the UK. The result is an innovative structure, based around 10 key principles designed to nurture confidence and raise achievement.

Pedagogy – our 10 key principles

- Fluency
- Problem-solving
- Reflection
- Mathematical Reasoning
- Progression
- Linking
- Multiplicative Reasoning
- Modelling
- Concrete - Pictorial - Abstract (CPA)
- Relevance

This edition of Maths Progress has been updated based on feedback from thousands of teachers and students.

The Core Curriculum

Textbooks with tried-and-tested differentiation

Core Textbooks *For your whole cohort*

Based on a single, well-paced curriculum with built-in differentiation, fluency, problem-solving and reasoning so you can use them with your whole class. They follow the unique unit structure that's been shown to boost confidence and support every student's progress.

Support Books
Strengthening skills and knowledge

Provide extra scaffolding and support on key concepts for each lesson in the Core Textbook, giving students the mathematical foundations they need to progress with confidence.

Depth Books
Extending skills and knowledge

Deepen students' understanding of key concepts, and build problem-solving skills for each lesson in the Core Textbook so students can explore key concepts to their fullest.

Welcome to Maths Progress Second Edition Depth Books!

Building confidence with depth of understanding

Pearson's unique unit structure in the Core Textbooks has been shown to build confidence. The Depth Books take elements of this structure and help students continue to grow in confidence.

Master → **Extend**

1 In the **Master** section of the Depth books, students can deepen their understanding of the key concepts introduced in the Core Textbooks through rich tasks involving problem-solving and reasoning.

2 Students who have developed fluency and a solid understanding of key concepts throughout the Depth unit can **extend** their learning.

Master

Deepen understanding of key mathematical concepts.

Reasoning questions allow students to:
- practice constructing multiple chains of reasoning
- interpret and explain results
- understand how and why to apply certain mathematical processes.

Unit opener
Lesson opener outlines lesson objectives.

A wealth of problem-solving questions encouraging students to:
- think in different ways
- translate contextual information
- make choices about the best method or strategy (e.g. work backwards, draw a diagram).

Investigation

Rich, problem-solving tasks to encourage deep thinking and exploring mathematical concepts at students' own pace.

Hints
Guide students to help build problem-solving strategies throughout the course.

Reflect Metacognitive questions that relate to the key concepts drawn out in each lesson, encouraging students to examine their thinking and understanding.

Extend

Students can take their understanding even further by applying what they have learned in different situations, and linking topics together.

This Depth Book is designed to give the right level of additional problem-solving content to help strengthen students' understanding of key concepts. It can be used as further stretch for students who are comfortable with the work in the Core Textbook Unit.
Students who would benefit from additional scaffolding for key concepts can use the Support Book.

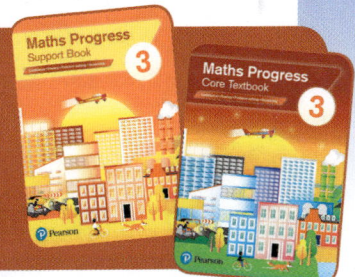

Progress with confidence!

This innovative Key Stage 3 Mathematics course builds on the first edition KS3 Maths Progress (2014) course, drawing on input from thousands of teachers and students, and a 2-year study into the effectiveness of the course. All of this has come together with the latest cutting-edge approaches to shape Maths Progress Second Edition.

Take a look at the other parts of the series

ActiveLearn Service

The *Active*Learn service enhances the course by bringing together your planning, teaching and assessment tools, as well as giving students access to additional resources to support their learning. Use the interactive Scheme of Work, linked to all the teacher and student resources, to create a personalised learning experience both in and outside the classroom.

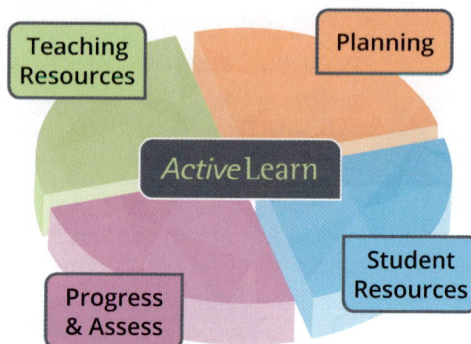

Teaching Resources

Planning

*Active*Learn

Progress & Assess

Student Resources

What's in ActiveLearn for Maths Progress?

- ☑ **Front-of-class student books** with links to PowerPoints, videos, animations and homework activities

- ☑ **96 new KS3 assessments and online markbooks,** including end-of-unit, end-of-term and end-of-year tests

- ☑ **Over 500 editable and printable homework worksheets** linked to each lesson and differentiated for Support, Core and Depth

- ☑ **Online, auto-marked homework activities**

- ☑ **Interactive Scheme of Work** makes re-ordering the course easy by bringing everything together into one curriculum for all students with links to Core, Support and Depth resources, and teacher guidance

- ☑ **Student access to videos, homework and online textbooks**

ActiveLearn Progress & Assess

The Progress & Assess service is part of the full ActiveLearn service, or can be bought as a separate subscription. It includes assessments that have been designed to ensure all students have the opportunity to show what they have learned through:

- a 2-tier assessment model
- approximately 60% common questions from Core in each tier
- separate calculator and non-calculator sections
- online markbooks for tracking and reporting
- mapped to indicative 9–1 grades

New *Assessment Builder*

Create your own classroom assessments from the bank of Maths Progress assessment questions by selecting questions on the skills and topics you have covered. Map the results of your custom assessments to indicative 9–1 grades using the custom online markbooks. *Assessment Builder* is available to purchase as an add-on to *Active*Learn Service or Progress & Assess subscriptions.

Purposeful Practice Books

Over 3,750 questions using minimal variation that:

- ☑ build in small steps to consolidate knowledge and boost confidence
- ☑ focus on strengthening skills and strategies, such as problem-solving
- ☑ help every student put their learning into practice in different ways
- ☑ give students a strong preparation for progressing to GCSE study.

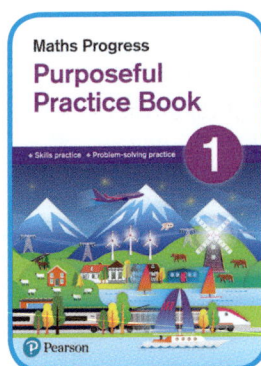

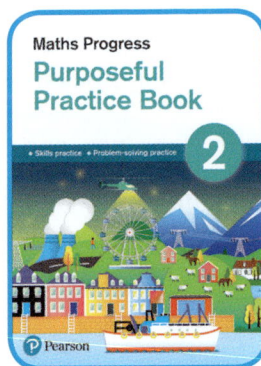

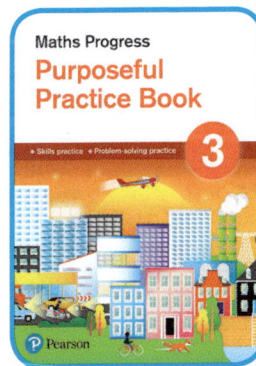

Maths Progress
Purposeful Practice Book 1
• Skills practice • Problem-solving practice
Pearson

Maths Progress
Purposeful Practice Book 2
• Skills practice • Problem-solving practice
Pearson

Maths Progress
Purposeful Practice Book 3
• Skills practice • Problem-solving practice
Pearson

1 Indices and standard form

Master   **Extend p9**

1.1 Indices

> - Calculate combinations of indices, fractions and brackets, including square brackets
> - Use index laws to simplify expressions

1 a Work out

    i $(-2)^4$ **ii** $(-2)^5$ **iii** $(-2)^6$ **iv** $(-2)^7$

  b **i** What do you notice about the signs of the answers?

    ii Write a rule that tells you the sign of a power of a negative number.

  c Test your rule works for other negative numbers and powers.

2 P-S Copy and complete the calculation in three different ways.

$(-10)^\square = -\square$

3 P-S / R $5 \times 6 + 3^2$

  a What is the answer to this calculation?

  b Insert a single pair of brackets into the calculation to make the largest possible answer.

  c Insert brackets, if needed, to make the smallest possible answer.

  d What is the mean of the largest and smallest possible answers?

  e Sophie says:

    'You can change one number in the original calculation to give the same answer as part **d**'.
    Which number must change, and what must it change to?

4 P-S Insert brackets so each calculation gives the target number.
If necessary, use square brackets for outer brackets.

  a $3 \times 2 + 3^2$ Target 75

  b $10 - 5 - 3^2$ Target 64

  c $2 \times 6 - 2^2 - 2$ Target 28

  d $2\sqrt{81} - \sqrt{25}$ Target 8

  e $5\sqrt{49} + 3 - 2$ Target 40

  f $3 \times 4 + 2 \times 6 + 8$ Target 252

> **Q4d hint** $2\sqrt{81} = 2 \times \sqrt{81}$

5 The diameter of Saturn is approximately 2^{17} km. The diameter of the dwarf planet, Ceres, is approximately 2^{10} km.

How many times larger is the diameter of Saturn than the diameter of Ceres?

6 Copy and complete the number patterns.

a **i** $2^2 = 4$

$2^2 + 2^2 = \square$

$2^2 + 2^2 + 2^3 = \square$

$2^2 + 2^2 + 2^3 + 2^4 = \square$

$2^2 + 2^2 + 2^3 + 2^4 + 2^5 = \square$

ii $2^2 = 4$

$2^3 = \square$

$2^4 = \square$

$2^5 = \square$

$2^6 = \square$

b What do you notice about the answers to part **a i**?

c What do you notice about the answers to part **a i** and **ii**?

d Write the missing numbers in this statement.

$2^2 + 2^2 + 2^3 + 2^4 + 2^5 + 2^6 = \square = 2^{\square}$

e Use your answer to part **d** to write down the value of

$2^1 + 2^2 + 2^3 + 2^4 + 2^5 + 2^6$

> **Q6e hint** Compare
> $2^1 + 2^2 + 2^3 + 2^4 + 2^5 + 2^6$ with
> $2^2 + 2^2 + 2^3 + 2^4 + 2^5 + 2^6$

f Copy and complete:

$2^1 + 2^2 + 2^3 + 2^4 + 2^5 + 2^6 = 2^{\square} - 2$

$2^1 + 2^2 + 2^3 + 2^4 + 2^5 + 2^6 + 2^7 = 2^{\square} - 2$

$2^1 + 2^2 + 2^3 + 2^4 + \ldots + 2^x = 2^{\square} - 2$

7 **P-S** $\dfrac{1}{8} \div \left(\dfrac{1}{4}\right)^2 - \dfrac{1}{4} \div \left(\dfrac{1}{2}\right)^3$

> **Q7a hint** $\left(\dfrac{1}{4}\right)^2 = \dfrac{1}{4} \times \dfrac{1}{4}$

a What is the answer to the calculation?

b Insert a set of brackets so the calculation gives an answer of 14.

8 Write each of these as a simplified product of powers.

a $6^4 \times 2^3 \times 3^2$ **b** $15^3 \times 3^2 \times 5^4$ **c** $12^2 \times 2^4 \times 3^3$ **d** $6^{-2} \times 3^4$

9 **P-S** The diagram shows a cuboid and two cubes. Which of these calculations does *not* give the total volume of the three solids?

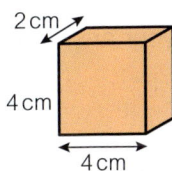

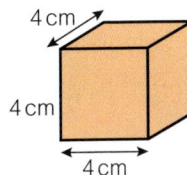

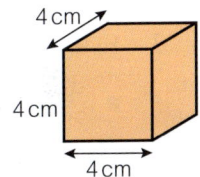

a 5×2^5 **b** $4^2 \times 3 \times 32$ **c** $2(4^2 + 4^3)$ **d** $2^5 + 2^6 + 2^6$

10 Work out each of these. Give your answer in its simplest form, as a mixed number or a fraction.

a $\dfrac{(2 \times 5)^2}{15 \times 2^3}$ **b** $\dfrac{(3 \times 7)^3}{21 \times 14}$ **c** $\dfrac{6 \times 5^2}{(4 \times 3)^3}$ **d** $\dfrac{(3 \times 2 \times 4)^3}{9 \times (6 \times 2)^2}$

11 **P-S** Use the digits 1, 2, 2, 3, 3, 4, 4, 5, 5 to make this statement true.

$$\dfrac{(\square \times \square)^{\square}}{\square\square} = \dfrac{\square \times \square^{\square}}{\square}$$

12 In Q4 you were asked to insert brackets so that each calculation gave a target number. What steps did you use to work out the place for the brackets? Did you use the same steps for every part of the question? Explain.

1.2 Calculations and estimates

- Calculate combinations of powers, roots, fractions and brackets
- Estimate answers to calculations

1 a Work out

    i $\sqrt{2^4}$ and 2^2

    ii $\sqrt{2^6}$ and 2^3

    iii $\sqrt{2^8}$ and 2^4

> **Q1a i hint** Work out 2^4 first. Then the square root.

  b i What do you notice?

    ii Write a rule for finding the square root of an even power of 2.

    iii Test that your rule works for even powers of other numbers.

2 The diagram shows the floor plan of a building made using three squares.

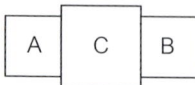

Rooms A and B each have an area of $50\,m^2$.

Room C has an area of $120\,m^2$.

Which one of the following expressions gives the length of the building?

a $\sqrt{2 \times 50 + 120}$ **b** $2 \times \sqrt{50 + 120}$ **c** $2 \times \sqrt{50} + \sqrt{120}$ **d** $\sqrt{2 \times 50} + \sqrt{120}$

3 Evaluate these calculations. Give your answers as fractions.

a $\dfrac{3^4}{25}$ **b** $\left(\dfrac{3}{2}\right)^4$ **c** $\left(\dfrac{3^2}{2^2}\right)^2$

d $\dfrac{\sqrt{16}}{25}$ **e** $\sqrt{\dfrac{16}{25}}$ **f** $\left(\sqrt{\dfrac{16}{25}}\right)^2$

4 P-S / R Marco says:

'The square root of a number is always smaller than the original number'.

Give an example to show Marco is incorrect.

5 P-S / R Jean says:

'The cube root of a number is always smaller than the square root'.

Give an example to show Jean is incorrect.

6 a Write these in order of size:

    2^3, 3^2, 3^4, 4^3, 5^6, 6^5

  b R Using your answer to part **a**, explain which is more likely to be larger, a^b or b^a, where a and b are both positive integers and $a < b$.

7 **R**

    a Estimate the answers to the calculations.

      i $\dfrac{\sqrt{15}+5.365}{\sqrt[3]{26}}$ **ii** $\dfrac{\sqrt{17}+5.365}{\sqrt[3]{28}}$ **iii** $\dfrac{\sqrt{15}+5.365}{\sqrt[3]{28}}$

    b Predict whether your answers are overestimates or underestimates.

    c Use a calculator to work out each answer and compare it with your estimate.
      Was it an overestimate or an underestimate?

    d For each calculation, state whether an estimate would be an overestimate or
      an underestimate.

      i $\dfrac{\sqrt{80}-7.2}{\sqrt[3]{7}}$ **ii** $\dfrac{\sqrt{83.2}-7.134}{\sqrt[3]{9}}$ **iii** $\dfrac{\sqrt{79.1}-7.342}{\sqrt[3]{11}}$

    e Estimate the answers to the calculations in part **d**.

    f Use a calculator to work out each answer and compare it with your estimate.
      Were your expectations of overestimates and underestimates correct?

8 **P-S** Complete this calculation in three different ways so that each estimated answer is 8.

    $\dfrac{\square^{\square}}{\square\sqrt{\square}}$

9 **P-S / R**

    a Give values for a and b so that this statement is true.

    $\sqrt[3]{\dfrac{a}{b}} > \left(\dfrac{a}{b}\right)^3$

    b Is there only one pair of values for a and b that works? Explain.

> **Key point**   A square root is a root of **degree** 2 and a cube root is a root of degree 3.
> Roots of higher degree are called **fourth roots**, **fifth roots**, **sixth roots**, ...

10 What is the sixth root of one million?

> **Q10 hint** $\square^6 = 1\,000\,000$

11 Copy and complete:

    a $2^4 = 16$, so $\sqrt[4]{16} = \square$ **b** $2^5 = 32$, so $\sqrt[5]{32} = \square$

    c $\sqrt[6]{64} = \square$ **d** $\sqrt[7]{128} = \square$

    e $\sqrt[8]{\square} = 2$

12 **P-S** Jamie is thinking of a number.
    The square root of the number is equal to 9 multiplied by the fourth root of 625.
    What is Jamie's number?

13 **R** By writing each decimal as a fraction, explain why 0.16 has an exact square root,
    but 1.6 and 0.016 do not.

> **Reflect**
>
> **14** In this lesson, you have worked with powers and roots of fractions.
>   Write three new things you have learned about powers and roots of fractions.

1.3 More indices

- Understand numbers written in index form that are raised to a power
- Understand negative and zero indices
- Use powers of 10 and their prefixes

1 **a** **i** Work out $(2 \times 5)^{-2}$ as a fraction.

    ii Work out $2^{-2} \times 5^{-2}$ as a fraction.

    iii What do you notice?

  b **i** Work out $(2 \times 5)^{-3}$

    ii Work out $2^{-3} \times 5^{-3}$

    iii What do you notice?

  c **i** Write a rule for calculating a negative power of a product.

    ii Use a calculator to test if the rule works for other negative powers of products.

2 **P-S / R** Use integers greater than 1 to copy and complete:

$(\Box \times \Box)^{-2} = \dfrac{1}{36}$

3 **R** Which of these numbers have the same value?

$(0.5)^3$	8^{-2}	$\left(\frac{1}{4}\right)^2$	$\left(\frac{1}{2}\right)^3$	2^{-3}	$(2 \times 4)^{-3}$	$\left(\frac{1}{8}\right)^0$

4 A sheet of newspaper is approximately 100 000 nanometres thick.
Write this measure

  a as a power of 10 metres

  b in millimetres.

5 **R** People who practise homeopathy claim that very tiny amounts of a substance can treat illness.

  a One drop of the substance is mixed with 9 drops of water to make a Potency 1 remedy. What fraction of the Potency 1 remedy is not water?
Write your answer as a power of 10.

  b To make a Potency 2 remedy, one drop of Potency 1 remedy is mixed with 9 drops of water. What fraction of the Potency 2 remedy is not water? Write your answer as a power of 10.

  c What fraction of these remedies is not water?
Write each answer as a power of 10.

    i Potency 5   **ii** Potency 10   **iii** Potency 100

  d People who practise homeopathy claim that the more times a remedy is diluted, the more effective it becomes. There are about 1.7×10^{22} molecules in 10 drops of a remedy.
Is it likely that a Potency 100 remedy contains any molecules of the original substance?
Explain your answer.

6 **P-S** In this spider diagram, the four calculations give the answer in the middle.

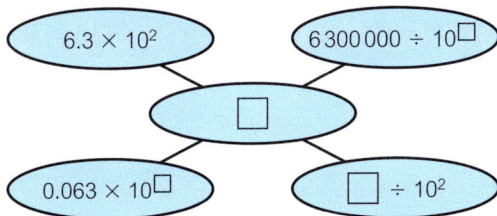

Work out the missing numbers.

7 Write each of these as a single power of the smallest possible integer.

a $(7^3)^{33}$ **b** $[(13^5)^3]^4$ **c** $10\,000^{12}$ **d** $(27^6)^5$

8 The table shows the dimensions of some small organisms.

Name of organism	Length	Width
dust mite	0.42 millimetres	0.25 millimetres
bacteria	2 micrometres	0.5 micrometres
virus	0.3 micrometres	15 nanometres

a Write all the dimensions in metres.

b Which organism has the greatest length?

c Which organism has the smallest width?

d How can you work out parts **b** and **c** without writing the dimensions as ordinary numbers?

> **Q8a hint** The dimensions of an object are its measurements.

9 **R** An atom is the smallest object that we can see with an electron microscope. The width of an atom is about 0.1 nanometres. What is this distance in millimetres?

Investigation

10 Place the digits 1 to 6 in the boxes to give:

a the smallest possible answer   **b** the largest possible answer.

$$\Box^{-\Box} + \Box^{\Box} - \Box^{-\Box}$$

Reflect

11 How did your knowledge of negative indices help you with answering Q10?

1.4 Standard form

- Write large and small numbers using standard form
- Enter and read standard form numbers on a calculator
- Order numbers written in standard form

1 Write these numbers using standard form.

   a 7.2 million   **b** 295 thousand   **c** 0.62 million

   d 17 millionths   **e** 32 thousandths   **f** 350 billion

   g 1.9 trillion   **h** 24 billionths   **i** 32 trillionths

> **Q1c hint** Watch out!
> $0.62 \times 10^{\square}$ is not in standard form.

2 Put the answers to these calculations in order, from smallest to largest.

   A $(2.3 \times 10^{-3}) \times (7.4 \times 10^{-2})$

   B $(1.3 \times 10^{-2})^2$

   C $(5.3 \times 10^{-2}) \div (3.2 \times 10^2)$

   D $(1.091 \times 10^{-4}) + (6 \times 10^{-5})$

   E $(1.8 \times 10^{-4}) - (1.8 \times 10^{-5})$

3 The populations of Bangladesh, China, India and Pakistan are shown in the table.

   a Write the countries in order of population size, from smallest to largest.

   b What is the difference between the population of India and China?

Country	Population in 2014
Bangladesh	1.556×10^8
China	1.366×10^9
India	1.247×10^9
Pakistan	1.880×10^8

   c How many times larger is the population of India than that of Pakistan?

   d What is the total population of these four countries?

   The world population is 7.183×10^9.

   e What proportion of the world's population lives in China or India?

4 The table shows the approximate populations and areas of five countries.

   a Copy the table, writing all the numbers as ordinary numbers.

   b The population density of a country is calculated using this formula:

   $$\text{Population density} = \frac{\text{population of country}}{\text{area of country}}$$

Country	Population	Area (km²)
China	1.36×10^9	9.57×10^6
Hong Kong	7.11×10^6	1.05×10^3
Iceland	3.17×10^5	1.00×10^5
USA	3.19×10^8	9.16×10^6
Vietnam	9.34×10^7	3.10×10^5

   Calculate the population density of each country in the table. Give your answers to the nearest whole number.

> **Q4b hint** The population density is the number of people per square kilometre.

   c Which country has

      i the highest population density

      ii the lowest population density?

5 **P-S** Light travels at 299 792 458 metres per second (m/s) and sound travels at 3.4×10^2 m/s.
What is the ratio of the speed of light to the speed of sound?
Give your answer in the form $n : 1$, to 2 decimal places, where n is in standard form.

6 **R**
a Use a calculator to work out $(9.6 \times 10^7) \times (6.41 \times 10^3)$.
b For part **a**, Clare says,
'You can calculate 9.6×6.41 first, and then multiply by 10^{10}.'
Is Clare correct? Explain.
c Clare is working out $(9.6 \times 10^7) + (6.41 \times 10^3)$.
Does her method, calculating $9.6 + 6.41$ first and then multiplying by 10^{10}, still work?
Explain.
d Clare rewrites $(9.6 \times 10^7) + (6.41 \times 10^3)$ like this:

$$(9.6 \times 10^4 \times 10^3) + (6.41 \times 10^3) = (96\,000 \times 10^3) + (6.41 \times 10^3)$$
$$= 10^3 \times (96\,000 + 6.41)$$

   i Look carefully at Clare's working. Is it correct?
   ii Use a calculator to check your answer to part **i**.

> **Q6d ii hint** Use a calculator to check the answer to the original calculation and the final line of Clare's working.

7 a Rewrite the calculations in a simpler way.
   i $6.75 \times 10^{-4} + 4.25 \times 10^{-4}$
   ii $8.88 \times 10^4 - 8.37 \times 10^4$
   iii $3.9 \times 10^7 + 4.2 \times 10^4$
   iv $7.02 \times 10^{-3} - 6.1 \times 10^{-4}$
b Work out the answers to your rewritten calculations in part **a**.

8 The wavelengths in the visible light spectrum extend from 3.8×10^{-7} m to 7.5×10^{-7} m.
What is the range of wavelengths in the visible light spectrum?

9 **P-S** The number of app downloads in July 2008 was 1.0×10^7.
There were 10 times as many in September 2008 and 10 times as many again in April 2009.
In June 2014 there were 7.5×10^{10} app downloads.
a How many downloads were there in April 2009?
b What was the increase from July 2008 to June 2014?

> **Reflect**
>
> **10** In Q7 you added and subtracted numbers in standard form.
> When is it possible to add or subtract numbers in standard form without changing any of them to ordinary numbers? Explain.

1 Extend

Investigation

1   6 is exactly halfway between 3 and 3^2.

   a What number is exactly halfway between 2 and 2^2?

   b What number is exactly halfway between 4 and 4^2?

   c Continue this until you have found the halfway numbers up to 10.

   d What pattern do you see?

   e Predict the halfway number between 11 and 11^2, and then check it.

   f Try the investigation again for numbers and their cubes.

2   **R**   The smallest size the human eye can see is 10^{-4} m.
   The diameter of a virus particle is 170 nm.
   Could you see a group of 1 million virus particles with the naked eye? Explain your answer.

3   **P-S / R**   A science museum wants
   to make a scale model of the
   Solar System.
   The diagram shows the real
   distances between the Earth,
   Moon and Sun.
   In the model the Earth and the Moon
   are 10 cm apart.
   How far away from the Earth will the Sun need to be?
   Is this a good scale for the model? Suggest some distances that might work better.

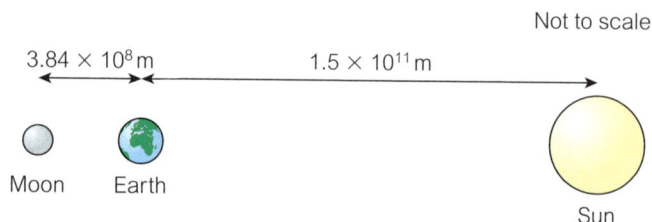

   Not to scale

   3.84×10^8 m 1.5×10^{11} m

   Moon   Earth   Sun

4   **R**   State which of each pair is greater:

   a A $3^2 - 2^3$ **B** $2^3 - 3^2$

   b A $4^3 - 3^4$ **B** $3^4 - 4^3$

   c A $(-4)^3 - 3^{-4}$ **B** $3^{-4} - (-4)^3$

   d A $x^y - y^x$ **B** $y^x - x^y$ where $x > 2$ and $y > 2$ and $x > y$

   e A $x^y - y^x$ **B** $y^x - x^y$
   where $x < 0$ and y is an odd number greater
   than 2, and the **absolute value** of x is greater
   than the absolute value of y.

   f A $x^y - y^x$ **B** $y^x - x^y$
   where $x < 0$ and y is an even number greater
   than 2, and the absolute value of x is greater
   than the absolute value of y.

   > **Key point**   **Absolute value** refers
   > to the distance between the number
   > and zero without considering signs.
   > For example, the absolute value of
   > −5 is 5.

5   **P-S / R**   Is it possible to choose positive integers x and y that are both less than 100 so
   that $\sqrt[y]{x} > \sqrt[x]{y}$ and both $\sqrt[y]{x}$ and $\sqrt[x]{y}$ are integers?

6 **R** How many times in total will 302^2 appear under the square root to make the statement true?
$\sqrt{302^2 \times 302^2 \times ... \times 302^2} = 302^{16}$

7 **R** What root would make the statement true?
$\sqrt[\square]{302^2 \times 302^2 \times 302^2} = 302^2$

8 **P-S** Use any digits 1 to 9 in this calculation to make the statement true.
$4^{\square} = \square^2 + \square$

9 **a** **P-S / R** Janine says that half of 2^{16} is 2^8. Explain why she is wrong.
  b Janine says that half of 3^{16} must be 3^{15}. She is wrong. What fraction of 3^{16} is 3^{15}?
  c What fraction of 4^{16} is 4^{14}?

10 **P-S / R** Poppy is thinking of a number.
The cube root of the number is double the sixth root of the number and is half the square root of the number.
What is Poppy's number?

11 **P-S** A number can be written as $\dfrac{\square^{\square}}{\square}$, and $\frac{3}{8}$ of the number is 2^6. What is the number?

12 **P-S** A parsec is 3.26 light years. A light year is 9.4607×10^{12} km.
A spaceship pilot claims that a particular journey was 23 parsecs.
  a How far did she fly? Give your answer correct to 2 decimal places.
  b She was flying at 0.8 times the speed of light (3×10^8 m/s).
  How long did her journey take? Give your answer correct to 2 decimal places.

Investigation

13 Standard form involves writing a number as units multiplied by a power of 10.
This works because our number system is in base 10 and uses the digits 0 to 9.
It is possible to use bases other than 10. For example, base 4 uses the digits 0, 1, 2, 3.
When working in base 4:
  4 is written as 10 ('one zero'), as it is one lot of 4 and zero 1s.
  5 is written as 11 ('one one'), as it is one lot of 4 and one 1, and so on.
This means that base 4 would count like this:
  1, 2, 3, 10, 11, 12, 13, 20, etc.
16 is written as 100 in base 4.

  a Write each of these numbers, written in base 10, in base 4: 12, 17, 20, 64.

  b Write each number from part **a** using standard form in base 4.

  c Try some calculations using base 4. How do multiplying and dividing work?
    In base 4, is it easier to work in standard form, or writing the numbers in full?

Reflect

14 In this lesson, you have looked at indices and standard form.
  a Standard form is sometimes called 'standard index form'. Explain why.
  b Scientists often call standard form 'scientific notation'. Why do you think this is?

2 Expressions and formulae

Master   **Extend p23**

2.1 Solving equations

- Write and solve equations with fractions
- Write and solve equations with the unknown on both sides

1   **R**   Kerry and Alice are both solving the equation $3g - 2 = 10g - 8$.
Kerry writes:

$$3g - 2 = 10g - 8$$
$$-2 = 7g - 8$$
$$6 = 7g$$
$$\frac{6}{7} = g$$

Alice says that Kerry is wrong, because you should always start by dealing with the number-only terms.

  a   **i** Solve the equation Alice's way, dealing with the constant terms first.

      ii Which way do you prefer and why?

Jake solves the same equation and says the solution is $g = \frac{6}{7} = 0.857$ (3 d.p.).

  b Check Kerry and Jake's solutions by substitution.
     Which solution is better and why?

2   **P-S**   A bag of paintballs is divided equally between four players.
Karen has used three paint balls and has two left.
Write and solve an equation to find the number of paintballs in the bag.

> **Q2 hint** Let n be the number of paintballs in the bag.

3   Solve the equations:

  a $2e + 5 = 5e - 7$ **b** $3(b - 2) = 4(b - 3)$ **c** $12 - 5m = m$ **d** $28 - 4m = 3m$

  e $2p = 12 - 2p$ **f** $15 - 3n = 7 - n$ **g** $7 - 2s = 10 - 5s$ **h** $2(3 - a) = a$

  i $\dfrac{3d + 11}{4} = d + 2$ **j** $7 - z = \dfrac{8z - 1}{3}$

4   **R**

  a Show that you can solve the equation $3x + 6 = 5x - 2$ by first

      i subtracting $3x$ from both sides   **ii** subtracting $5x$ from both sides.

  b Did you find one way easier than the other? Explain.

  c Show that you can solve the equation $10 - 2x = 13 - 3x$ by first

      i adding $3x$ to both sides   **ii** adding $2x$ to both sides.

  d Did you find one way easier than the other? Explain.

5 **P-S** Renting a motorcycle from Company A costs £50 plus £8.30 an hour.
Renting from Company B costs £37 plus £10.90 an hour.
How many hours' rental would cost the same for Company A and Company B?

6 Alek goes on holiday to a country where he does not speak the language.
In a shop, he buys three sandwiches and a can of drink.
The next day, he goes back to the shop and buys two cans of drink and a sandwich.
He knows the sandwiches cost €2.43 each, but does not know how much the cans
of drink cost. On both days he paid the same amount of money in total.
  a How much does a can of drink cost?
  b R Why is it better to give your answer as a decimal rather than as a fraction?

7 **P-S** Aaron and Fiona are thinking of the same number.
Aaron multiplies it by 3, then adds 5.
Fiona multiplies it by 12, subtracts 3, then divides the
result by 3.
They both get the same answer.
What number did they start with?

> **Q7 hint** Use a letter to represent the number. Write expressions for Aaron's and Fiona's calculations.

8 **P-S / R** The diagram shows an equilateral triangle.
  a Work out the perimeter of the triangle.
  b Does it matter which two sides of the triangle you used?
     How can you check your answer is correct?

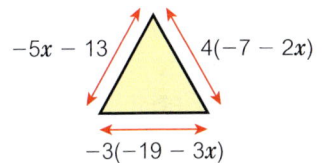

9 **R** Humphrey says that the area
of the L-shape is equal to the
area of the triangle.
By finding the value of x, explain
why Humphrey is wrong.

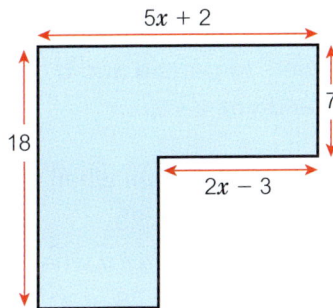

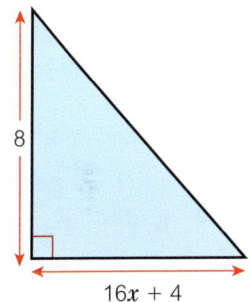

Investigation

10 a A triangle has side lengths of $(x + 2)$, $(2x - 3)$ and $(5x - 7)$.
Is it an equilateral triangle?
  b Create expressions for the sides of a triangle that would be equilateral.

Reflect

11 a The solution to an equation is $\frac{3}{4}$ or 0.75.
Is one of these more accurate than the other? Explain.
  b Is it always best to write a non-integer solution to an equation as a fraction?
Use examples from this lesson to explain.

2.2 Substituting into expressions

- Use the priority of operations when substituting into algebraic expressions
- Substitute values into expressions involving powers and roots

1 **a** $a = \sqrt{b^2 + c^2}$

Find the value of a when

   i $b = 3$ and $c = 4$

   ii $b = 30$ and $c = 40$

   iii $b = 7$ and $c = 9$, correct to 1 decimal place.

b $d = \sqrt{a^2 + b^2 + c^2}$

Find the value of d when

   i $a = 1$, $b = 2$ and $c = 2$

   ii $a = 2$, $b = 6$ and $c = 9$

   iii $a = 3.4$, $b = 2.7$ and $c = 5.1$, correct to 3 decimal places.

2 **a** Find the value of the expression $\sqrt{m + n}$ when

   i $m = 4$, $n = 9$ **ii** $m = 16$, $n = 25$.

b Find the value of the expression $\sqrt{m} + \sqrt{n}$ when

   i $m = 4$, $n = 9$ **ii** $m = 16$, $n = 25$.

c **R** What do your answers to parts **a** and **b** demonstrate about the values of $\sqrt{m + n}$ and $\sqrt{m} + \sqrt{n}$?

> **Q2c hint** You can complete a proof of this in the Extend lesson.

3 **a** Find the value of the expression $\sqrt{mn}$ when

   i $m = 4$, $n = 9$ **ii** $m = 16$, $n = 25$.

b Find the value of the expression $\sqrt{m}\,\sqrt{n}$ when

   i $m = 4$, $n = 9$ **ii** $m = 16$, $n = 25$.

c **R** What do your answers to parts **a** and **b** demonstrate about the values of $\sqrt{mn}$ and $\sqrt{m}\,\sqrt{n}$?

> **Q3c hint** You can complete a proof of this in the Extend lesson.

4 **R** The length L cm of a Dover sole fish can be estimated from its mass m grams using the formula $L = \sqrt[3]{10m}$.

a Estimate the length of a Dover sole with a mass of 100 g.

b Work out the value of L when $m = 20$ g is:

   i correct to the nearest cm

   ii correct to 2 decimal places

   iii as accurately as possible.

c Pris says that the most accurate way to write the answer to part **b** is $\sqrt[3]{200}$. Is she correct? Explain your answer.

5 **P-S** The simple interest £I earned in a year on an investment of £A at a rate of r% interest is given by the formula $I = \dfrac{rA}{100}$.

    a Fauzia invested £250 and earned £20 interest.
Substitute these amounts into the formula.

    b Work out the rate of interest.

    c Jack earned £8.50 in a year with a 2% interest rate.
What was his investment?

6 **P-S**

    a Match each lettered expression with the correct numbered answer.
Use the value of the letters given in the table.

a	b	c	d	e	f	g	h	i
3	−2	−5	16	25	−27	−4	4	12

A $4a^2 - \sqrt{e}$ **D** $\dfrac{hi}{3} + 3b^2c$

B $b(\sqrt{d} + \sqrt{ai})$ **E** $\dfrac{b^2 + g^2}{h}$

C $\sqrt[3]{f} - 8c$ **F** $\sqrt[3]{dh} - 2c^2$

1	−44	**5**	31
2	−20	**6**	5
3	37	**7**	12
4	−46		

    b One answer card has not been used. Write an expression for this answer card. Use at least three of the letters from the table, and include a power or a root in your expression.

7 **R** Carlos is substituting values into the expression $3x^2y + z^3$. The values he uses for x, y and z are always negative. Carlos says, 'The value of my expression will never be a positive number.' Is he correct? Explain your answer.

> **Q7 hint** Substitute different negative number values for x, y and z into the expression.

8 Substitute $a = -2$ and $b = -4$ into each expression and simplify the answer.

    a $a^4 - b^3$ **b** $\sqrt{a^6}$ **c** $\sqrt[3]{b^2 - 2a^2}$ **d** $ab^2 - a^2b - (ab)^2$

    e $\left(\dfrac{5}{2}b\right)^2$ **f** $\left(\dfrac{a}{b}\right)^3$ **g** $\dfrac{a^2b^2}{a^2 + b^2}$ **h** $\dfrac{\sqrt[3]{ab} + ab}{a^2 - b^2}$

Reflect

9 **a** How can you use substitution to demonstrate whether two expressions are equivalent?

    b Why is this not a proof?

2.3 Writing and using formulae

- Write and use formulae

1 You can use this formula to work out the distance, s, travelled by an object.

$$s = \frac{(u + v)t}{2}$$

Where:

s = distance travelled (metres, m)
u = starting speed (metres per second, m/s)
v = finishing speed (metres per second, m/s)
t = time (seconds, s)
Work out the value of s when

a $u = 0$, $v = 20$ and $t = 8$
b $u = 12$, $v = 25$ and $t = 5$

> **Q1a hint**
>
> $$s = \frac{(0 + 20) \times 8}{2}$$

2 Scientists use this formula to work out the coefficient of restitution, e, of two objects that collide.

$$e = \frac{v - V}{U - u}$$

Where:

e = coefficient of restitution
U = starting speed of first object (m/s)
V = finishing speed of first object (m/s)
u = starting speed of second object (m/s)
v = finishing speed of second object (m/s).
Work out the value of e when

a $U = 15$, $V = 4$, $u = 5$ and $v = 6$ b $U = 30$, $V = 2$, $u = 12$ and $v = 8$

3 **P-S**   There is a linear relationship between the amount of pocket money P that Alice receives per week and her age a.
When Alice was 8 she received £6 a week.
Now that Alice is 14 she receives £15 a week.

a Work out an equation in the form $P = ma + c$.

b How much pocket money will Alice receive per week when she is 16?

4 The force F newtons on an object is equal to its mass m multiplied by its acceleration a m s^{-1}. Acceleration can be calculated by the difference between the initial speed u and the final speed v, divided by the time taken t.

a Write a formula for force.

b Write a formula for acceleration.

c An object of mass 5 kg starts moving at 3 m s^{-1}.
   After 6 seconds it is moving at 15 m s^{-1}.

   i What is the acceleration?
   ii What is the size of the force acting on the object?

5   **P-S / R**   A company's profit P is calculated by subtracting the costs from the revenue.
Revenue is calculated by multiplying the selling price S by the number of units of
product sold U.
Cost is calculated by adding the fixed costs F to the manufacturing costs, which are the cost
of producing each unit of product, C, multiplied by the number of units sold.
  a Write a formula linking profit to the number of units sold and the costs.
  b The fixed costs of a firm are £300.
    The unit cost is £3.50.
    The unit selling price is £5.00.
      i What is the equation of the line linking the profit to the number of units sold?
      ii How did you calculate the gradient of the line?
      iii What does the y-intercept of the line show?
      iv Will the y-intercept ever be positive?
  c The equation of the line linking profit and number of units sold for a different firm is
    $P = 7U - 82$, where P is profit and U is number of units sold.
      i What is the fixed cost for this firm?
      ii The cost to produce each unit is £2.20.
        What is the selling price for each unit?
      iii The firm sells 20 units.
        What percentage of its revenue is profit?

6   **R**   Afridi spends 2 hours in the garden at the weekend and finds 3 snails.
The next weekend, he spends 4 hours in the garden and finds 7 snails.
  a Write an equation linking the number of snails Afridi finds, S, and the amount of time he
    spends in the garden, h.
  b Explain what the y-intercept and gradient mean in this context.
  c What is the problem with using this model to predict the number of snails Afridi might
    find in the garden?

Investigation

7   a A line is plotted through $(0, 5)$ and $(5, 8)$.
    What is the equation of the line?
  b A second line is plotted through $(0, 8)$ and $(5, 11)$.
    What is the equation of this line?
  c A third line is plotted through $(3, 5)$ and $(8, 8)$.
    What is the equation of this line?
  d A fourth line is plotted through $(3, 8)$ and $(8, 11)$.
    What is the equation of this line?
  e What is the impact of adding the same number to the x- or the y-coordinates of points
    on line? Test your theory by adding a different number and finding the new equations.

Reflect

8   For a car hire company, the graph of hire cost H against time t is a straight line.
How could you find the formula that links hire cost and time?

2.4 Using and rearranging formulae

- Change the subject of a formula

1 The formula for converting between temperatures in Fahrenheit (°F) and Celsius (°C) is
$$F = + \frac{9C}{5} + 32$$
a Work out each temperature in Fahrenheit.
   i 20°C   ii 100°C   iii 0°C
b Work out each temperature in Celsius.
   i 59°F   ii 212°F   iii 32°F
c Make the Celsius temperature (C) the subject of the formula.

2 Make x the subject of each formula.
   a $5x = kx + p$ b $mx + t = x + 10$
   c $xy - 5 = 12 + 4x$ d $r^2x = m^2x + mr$

3 In an experiment, Gareth works out the speed of two balls after they collide.
This is one of the formulae that he writes:
   $6eu - ev = 2v + u$
a Make u the subject of this formula.
b Work out the value of u when $v = 4$ and $e = 0.5$.

4 The formula to work out the force (F) acting on an object is
   $F = ma$
where m is the mass and a is the acceleration of the object.
   a i Make a the subject of the formula.
      ii Work out the value of a when $F = 24$ and $m = 3$.
   b i Make m the subject of the formula.
      ii Work out the value of m when $F = 35$ and $a = 10$.

> **Q4a i hint**
> $F = m \times a$
> $m \times a = F$
> $a = \dfrac{\square}{\square}$

5 Make x the subject of each formula.
   a $y = 2x + 3$
   b $t = 5x - 9$
   c $v = 3x + 8m$

> **Q5a hint**
> $y - 3 = 2x$
> $x = \dfrac{y - 3}{\square}$

6 The equation of a straight line can be written in the form $y = mx + c$.
Write these equations of lines in the form $y = mx + c$.
   a $y - 5x = 12$
   b $y + 4x - 11 = 0$
   c $2y - 6x = 18$

7 **P-S** The diagrams show three different trapezia.

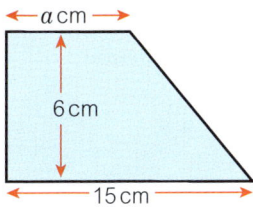
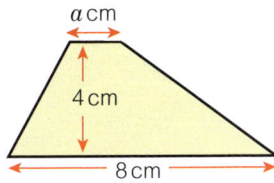
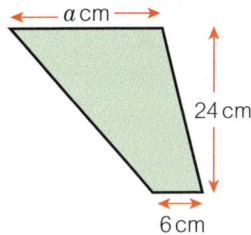

Area = 72 cm²   Area = 18 cm²   Area = 432 cm²

  a Write the formula for the area of a trapezium.

  b Work out the top length of each trapezium.

8 This formula is used to work out the distance, d, travelled by an object that starts from rest.

$$d = \frac{at^2}{2}$$

a = acceleration and t = time taken.

  a Rearrange the formula to make a the subject.

  b Work out the acceleration when $d = 100$ and $t = 8$

  c Work out the time taken when $a = 25$ and $d = 50$

9 **P-S / R** The volume of a sphere can be found from the formula
   $V = \frac{4}{3}\pi r^3$

  a Write a formula showing the volume of a hemisphere.

  b Make r the subject of your formula from part **a**.

  c Adjust your formula from part **b** so that it gives the radius of a quarter sphere.

> **Q9 hint** The greek letter π (pronounced 'pi') represents the number 3.141 529 6...
> You will learn more about this number in Unit 7.

10 Look at this formula: $P^2 = T^2 + ag^2$

  a Make T the subject.   b Make a the subject.   c Make g the subject.

  d **R** Is P the subject of the original formula? Explain.

11 The areas of these two rectangles are equal.

  a Write a formula linking the two areas.

  b Make y the subject of the formula.

  c Make x the subject of the formula.

  d **R** Which do you think is larger, x or y?
      Use your answers to parts **b** and **c** to decide.

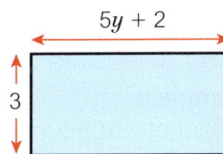
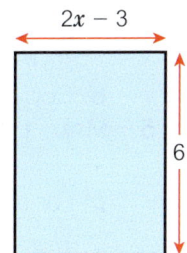

Reflect

12 When you were converting Fahrenheit to Celsius in Q1 parts **a** and **b**, you had to solve several equations.

  a In part **c**, you made Celsius the subject of the formula.
      How would that have helped you in part **b**?

  b Look back at your answers to Q4 and Q7.
      Is it always more efficient to rearrange the formula first?

2.5 Index laws and brackets

- Use the rules for indices for multiplying and dividing
- Simplify expressions involving brackets
- Factorise an expression by taking out an algebraic common factor

1 Copy and complete:

 a $x^4 \times x^5 = x^{\square}$ **b** $x^3 \times x^2 = x^{\square}$ **c** $x^m \times x^n = x^{\square}$

 d $\dfrac{x^7}{x^2} = x^{\square}$ **e** $\dfrac{x^9}{x^5} = x^{\square}$ **f** $\dfrac{x^m}{x^n} = x^{\square}$

2 **R**

 a **i** Work out the answers to these divisions: $\dfrac{5}{5}, \dfrac{9}{9}, \dfrac{12}{12}, \dfrac{350}{350}, \dfrac{x}{x}, \dfrac{x^5}{x^5}$

  ii What do you notice about your answers?

  iii Copy and complete: 'When you divide a number by itself the answer is always $\square$.'

 b **i** Copy and complete this pattern:

  $$\dfrac{x^5}{x^1} = x^4, \quad \dfrac{x^5}{x^2} = x^3, \quad \dfrac{x^5}{x^3} = x^{\square}, \quad \dfrac{x^5}{x^4} = x^{\square}, \quad \dfrac{x^5}{x^5} = x^{\square}$$

  ii What do you notice about your answers to $\dfrac{x^5}{x^5}$ in part **a i** and part **b i**?

  iii Copy and complete: 'Any number or letter to the power 0 = $\square$.'

Investigation

3 **a** Copy and complete the division patterns.

   i $\dfrac{3^2}{3^5} = 3^{2-5} = 3^{\square}$ and $\dfrac{3^2}{3^5} = \dfrac{3 \times 3}{3 \times 3 \times 3 \times 3 \times 3} = \dfrac{1}{3^{\square}}$, so $3^{\square} = \dfrac{1}{3^{\square}}$ and $\dfrac{1}{3^{\square}} < 1$

   ii $\dfrac{x^3}{x^4} = x^{3-4} = x^{\square}$ and $\dfrac{x^3}{x^4} = \dfrac{x \times x \times x}{x \times x \times x \times x} = \dfrac{1}{x^{\square}}$, so $x^{\square} = \dfrac{1}{x^{\square}}$

   iii $\dfrac{y^8}{y^{11}} = y^{8-11} = y^{\square}$ and $\dfrac{y^8}{y^{11}} = \dfrac{1}{y^{\square}}$, so $y^{\square} = \dfrac{1}{y^{\square}}$

 b Copy and complete:

   $x^{-n} = \dfrac{1}{\square}$ is true for all values of x and all values of n.

 c For at least five different positive integer values of x, work out:

   i x^{-1} **ii** x^{-2} **iii** x^{-3}

 d For at least five different fraction values of x between 0 and 1, work out:

   i x^{-1} **ii** x^{-2} **iii** x^{-3}

   Include unit and non-unit fractions.

 e Compare your answers to parts **c** and **d**. What do you notice about the value of x^{-n} when x is a positive integer, and when x is a fraction between 0 and 1?

 f For what values of x is x^{-n} an integer?

 g Investigate the values of x^{-n} when x is a negative integer, and when x is a negative fraction between −1 and 0.

4 Copy and complete:

a $(x^2)^3 = x^{\square}$
b $(x^5)^4 = x^{\square}$
c $(x^m)^n = x^{\square}$

5 **P-S**

a Match each lettered expression with its simplified numbered expression.

A $x^a \times x^b \times x^c$

B $\dfrac{x^a}{x^b \times x^c}$

C $\dfrac{(x^a)^b}{x^c}$

D $(x^a)^b \times x^c$

E $\dfrac{x^a}{(x^b)^c}$

F $\dfrac{x^a \times x^b}{x^c}$

G $x^a \times (x^b)^c$

1 x^{a+b-c}

2 x^{a+bc}

3 x^{ab+c}

4 x^{a-b-c}

5 x^{a-bc}

6 x^{ab-c}

7 x^{a+b+c}

8 x^{ac-b}

b There is one card left over. Write an expression card that goes with it.

6 Work out the value of each of these expressions.

a $7x^0 - 4y^0$
b $4m^0 \times 8n^0$
c $\dfrac{45}{5y^0}$

d $\dfrac{36 - 4a^0}{8b^0}$
e $18c^0 - \dfrac{10^2}{5d^0}$
f $8z^0 \left(12^0 - \dfrac{12y^0}{2}\right)$

7 Simplify these expressions. Write each one as a negative power and as a fraction. The first one has been started for you.

a $\dfrac{x^4}{x^7} = x^{4-7} = x^{\square} = \dfrac{1}{x^{\square}}$
b $\dfrac{y^2}{y^9}$
c $\dfrac{p^4}{p^5}$
d $\dfrac{z}{z^9}$

8 Simplify these expressions. Write each one as

i a negative power   ii a fraction.

a $\dfrac{6x^7}{2x^9}$
b $\dfrac{24y^3}{4y^7}$
c $\dfrac{56y}{7y^8}$
d $\dfrac{7p^8}{21p^{12}}$
e $\dfrac{8r^3}{72r^{10}}$
f $\dfrac{9q}{45q^{11}}$

9 Expand

a $x^2(x + y)$
b $x^2(x + cy)$
c $x^2(x + y + cy)$

10 Factorise

a $a^3 + ab$
b $ba^3 + ab^2$
c $a^3 + ab + bac$

11 **P-S** Copy and complete this grid. Write a power of x or a number in each square so that the answer to every row and column is $2x^2$.

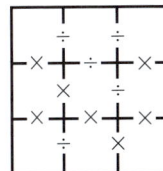

Reflect

12 When simplifying expressions with indices, when do you

a add the indices   b subtract the indices   c multiply the indices?

2.6 Expanding double brackets

- Multiply out double brackets and collect like terms

1 Expand and simplify

   a $x(x - 2)$ **b** $(x + 1)(x - 2)$

   c $(x - 2)(x + 2)$ **d** $(x + 2)^2 - 4x$

2 You can expand and simplify two sets of double brackets like this:

$$(x + 5)(x + 9) - (x + 1)(x + 7) = [x^2 + 9x + 5x + 45] - [x^2 + 7x + x + 7]$$
$$= [x^2 + 14x + 45] - [x^2 + 8x + 7]$$
$$= x^2 + 14x + 45 - x^2 - 8x - 7$$
$$= 6x + 38$$

Expand and simplify

   a $(x + 15)(x + 4) - (x + 11)(x + 2)$

   b $(x + 6)(x + 5) - (x + 8)(x + 3)$

   c $(x + 3)(x + 2) + (x + 13)(x + 1)$

   d $(x + 7)(x + 7) + (x + 3)(x + 3)$

   e $(x + 9)(x - 2) + (x - 4)(x - 1)$

   f $(x - 3)(x + 8) - (x + 7)(x - 6)$

3 **P-S / R** Show that $n(n + 4) - 2(n + 7) = (n + 2)(n - 6) + 2(3n - 1)$.

4 Multiply out the brackets in these expressions and simplify.

   a $\dfrac{(w + z)^2 - (w - z)^2}{6}$ **b** $\dfrac{(a + b)^2 - (a - b)(a + b)}{3}$

5 **P-S / R** Here is a square, a rectangle and two triangles.

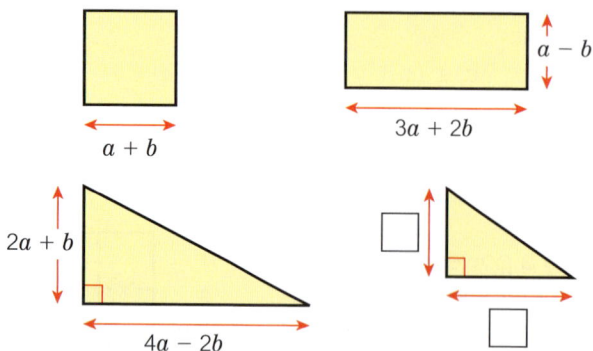

The total area of the square and the rectangle is the same as the total area of the two triangles.

   a Write an expression for the length and the height of the smaller triangle in terms of a and b.

   b Is your answer to part **a** the only answer? Explain why.

6 a Expand $x(x + 3)$.

  b Use your answer to part **a** to expand $x(x + 3)(x + 2)$.

  c Are your answers to parts a and b quadratic expressions?

7 You can expand three sets of brackets, $(x + 5)(x + 1)(x + 2)$, like this:
First expand and simplify two of the sets of brackets:

$(x + 5)(x + 1) = x^2 + x + 5x + 5 = x^2 + 6x + 5$

Then multiply the expression you get by the expression in the remaining set of brackets:

$(x + 2)(x^2 + 6x + 5) = x^3 + 6x^2 + 5x + 2x^2 + 12x + 10$

Q7 hint It doesn't matter which two sets of brackets you expand first. Be careful with the minus signs.

Then simplify to get the final expression:

  $= x^3 + 8x^2 + 17x + 10$

Expand and simplify

a $(x + 1)(x + 2)(x + 3)$ **b** $(x + 4)(x + 9)(x - 1)$ **c** $(x - 3)(x + 4)(x - 2)$

8 Expand

  a $(x + 1)^3$ **b** $(x + y)^3$

9 Make y the subject in each of these formulae.

  a $a = 2b + \sqrt{y}$

  b $T = 2x + \sqrt{y}$

  c $L = 2x + \dfrac{\sqrt{5y}}{k}$

10 Two formulae used in physics are $w^2 = \dfrac{k}{m}$ and $b = a\sqrt{1 - e^2}$

  a Make k the subject of the first formula.

  b Make e the subject of the second formula.

11 P-S Show that

  $\dfrac{1}{x} \times \dfrac{6}{x + 2} \times \dfrac{2}{x - 2} = \dfrac{12}{x} \div (x^2 - 4)$

Reflect

12 In several questions in this lesson you were asked to multiply more than two brackets together. What was the same and what was different about the process and your answers, compared with expanding double brackets?

2 Extend

1　**P-S**　The value of the perimeter of rectangle A is 5 more than the value of the area of rectangle B.
Solve an equation to find the value of a.

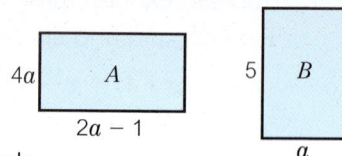

$4a$　　A　　　　5　　B

$2a - 1$

a

2　**P-S**　The area of the rectangle is equal to the area of the triangle.
What is the value of x?

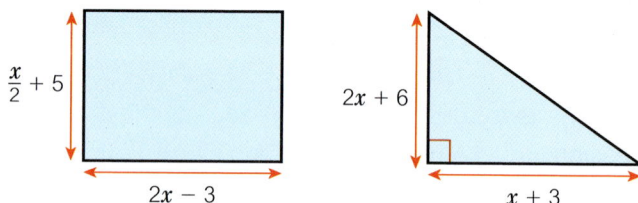

$\frac{x}{2} + 5$　　　　　　$2x + 6$

$2x - 3$　　　　　　$x + 3$

3　**P-S**　The volume of the sphere is one third of the volume of the cuboid.

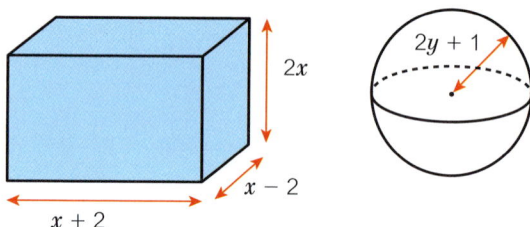

$2x$　　　　$2y + 1$

$x - 2$

$x + 2$

a　Write an equation linking the volume of the cuboid to the volume of the sphere.

b　Find the volume of the cuboid when $y = 2$. Your answer will include π.

c　Find the volume of the sphere when $x = 4$.

> **Q3 hint** The formula for the volume V of a sphere with radius r is $V = \frac{4}{3}\pi r^3$.

4　**R**　In Q2 of Lesson 2.2 you demonstrated that the expressions $\sqrt{m + n}$ and $\sqrt{m} + \sqrt{n}$ had different values for some values of m and n.
Follow these steps to prove this result more generally.

a　What is the square of $\sqrt{m + n}$?

b　Copy and complete to write and simplify an expression for the square of $\sqrt{m} + \sqrt{n}$.

$$(\sqrt{m} + \sqrt{n})^2 = (\sqrt{m} + \sqrt{n})(\sqrt{m} + \sqrt{n})$$
$$= \sqrt{m}\,\sqrt{m} + \ldots$$
$$= \ldots$$

> **Q4b hint** Expand the double brackets.

c　Are your expressions in parts **a** and **b** the same?
If not, what would need to be true for them to have the same value?

5　**R**　In Q3 of Lesson 2.2 you demonstrated that $\sqrt{mn} = \sqrt{m}\,\sqrt{n}$ was true for some values of m and n.
Square both sides of $\sqrt{mn} = \sqrt{m}\,\sqrt{n}$ separately and simplify to prove that this result is true for *any* non-negative values of m and n.

6 **R** Copy and complete:

    a $4^4 = 16^{\square}$ **b** $4^{2x} = 16^{\square}$ **c** $16^{6x} = 4^{\square}$

7 **P-S / R**

    a Given that $2^{x+3} = 2^{3x-7}$, state what must be the same.

    b Solve the equation in part **a** to find the value of x.

    c Will 2^{x+3} be an integer for all integer values of x? Explain.

8 **P-S / R** $(x-3)^{x+2} = 1$. Find the two possible values of x.

9 Expand

    a $a^3b(a - 2b)$ **b** $a^7b\left(\dfrac{1}{a} - \dfrac{2}{b}\right)$ **c** $\dfrac{a^3}{b}(3a + ab)$

10 Write each of these in its simplest form.

    a $(x+1)^2(x+1)^{-1}$ **b** $2x(3y+2)^{-2}$ **c** $(2x)^{-1}(3y+2)^{-2}$

11 Write each of these in its simplest form.

    a $3^{x+2} \div 3^{2x}$ **b** $12y^{x+2} \div 3y^{2x}$ **c** $12y^{x+2} \div 3y^{2x} + y$

Investigation

12 a Expand

      i $(x+1)^2$ **ii** $(x+1)^3$

   Here is Pascal's triangle.

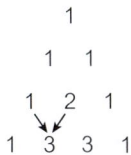

```
        1
      1   1
    1   2   1
  1   3   3   1
```

   b Compare the coefficients of the x terms in your two expressions from part **a** with the rows of Pascal's triangle.

   c Write the next few rows of Pascal's triangle.

   d Predict the expansions of

      i $(x+1)^4$ **ii** $(x+1)^5$

   e Expand the expressions to check your predictions.

   f What changes when the expressions are $(x+2)^2$, $(x+2)^3$, $(x+2)^4$, ...?

Investigation

13 For each equation, find numbers a and b that make the statement true.

    a $a^b = ab + a$ **b** $a^b = 10 + \dfrac{1}{b-a}$ **c** $a^a = 10a - a$

Reflect

14 In this unit you have solved equations and looked at how the index laws apply to algebra. What do you think is the most useful process you have learned about? Why?

3 Dealing with data

Master   Extend p35

3.1 Planning a survey

- Identify sources of primary and secondary data
- Choose a suitable sample size and what data to collect
- Identify factors that might affect data collection and plan to reduce bias

1 For the following data:

    i decide whether it is more likely to be **primary** or **secondary data**

    ii if it is primary data, give a suitable method for collecting it.

a The total time patients spent in A&E in every hospital in the UK from April 2010 to June 2011

b The numbers given by people who were asked to choose their favourite number

c The percentage of the UK population that used the internet in 2013

d The GCSE results of all pupils in England in 2014

e The percentage of people who write with their right hand

f The number of people in cars on a main road

> **Key point**   **Primary data** is data you collect yourself. **Secondary data** is collected by someone else.
> Different ways of collecting primary data include questionnaires, surveys and data logging.

2 R A school wants to investigate the type of food students eat at lunchtime.
There are 1500 students at the school.

a Suggest a sensible number of students to be sampled.

b Which of these surveying methods will give a biased result?
Explain your answers.

    i sending a questionnaire to all Year 10 email accounts

    ii sending a questionnaire to all students

    iii asking students in the lunch queue at the beginning of lunchtime

    iv asking students with a packed lunch

c Will the data be primary or secondary?

d R A student wants to do the same investigation for just their form group of 30 students. Is a 10% sample size appropriate?

> **Key point**   A question in a survey can be biased if it encourages people to give a particular answer.
> A good survey question should not be:
> - vague
> - leading
> - restrictive.

3 R A town council wants to know how the public library is being used. They give questionnaires to everyone in the library every Thursday afternoon for a month.
Why is this sample biased?

4 **R** The table shows some survey questions and the sampling method used for each one.
For each survey:
i write down the population
ii decide if the sample is random. Explain your answer.

	Survey	Sample
a	How long do patients spend in hospital A&E?	Every person leaving A&E on a Saturday night
b	What is the most common second language of people living in Denmark?	Students at a university in Denmark
c	What proportion of UK secondary school teachers are male?	Teachers at the local secondary school
d	What proportion of UK secondary school teachers are male?	Teachers in secondary schools in Leicester, Birmingham, Swansea and Aberdeen

5 A factory produces 1 kg bags of flour.
It randomly samples the bags of flour to check that they are the correct weight.
The factory produces 200 000 bags a week.
a Suggest how many bags they should sample each week.
b What level of accuracy should the bags be weighed to?
    A the nearest milligram   **B** the nearest gram   **C** the nearest 100 grams

6 **R** The owner of a business wants to find out if his employees are happy at work.
He considers two methods.
Method 1: Ask the questions to a random selection of people individually.
Method 2: Do an anonymous survey.
a Which method should he use? Explain your reasons.
b There are 1500 people in his company. What is a suitable sample size?

7 **R** Select the most appropriate sample size for each survey. Explain your choice.
a There are 50 000 trees in a forest.
    Researchers want to find out what proportion of trees are taller than 20 m.
    A 5000   **B** 1000   **C** 500   **D** 20
b The UK population is approximately 66 000 000.
    An organisation wants to find out how many people have had a flu vaccination.
    A 100   **B** 10 000   **C** 1 000 000   **D** 20 000 000
c The population of Manchester is 510 000.
    The council wants to find out how many people visit the doctor at least once a year.
    A 100 000   **B** 6000   **C** 100   **D** 5

8 **R** A fireworks factory wants to check if the fireworks it makes are exploding correctly.
Explain why a 10% sample would not be appropriate.

Reflect

9 Why is a 10% sample size sometimes inappropriate?
Think back to the questions you have answered in this lesson.

3.2 Collecting data

- Design and use data collection sheets and tables
- Design a good questionnaire

1 R Angie is carrying out a survey to find out how much people spend on clothes each month.

She plans to carry out the survey in a shopping centre.

a Explain why this sample could be biased.

b Suggest a way in which she could carry out the survey.

c Which question should she use in her survey?

Give a reason for your answer.

A How much do you spend on clothes each month?

B How much do you spend on clothing a month?

Tick the most appropriate box.

☐ £0–£20   ☐ £20–£40   ☐ £40–£60   ☐ £60–£80   ☐ £80–£100

C How much do you spend on clothing a month?

Tick the most appropriate box.

☐ £0–£39.99   ☐ £40–£79.99   ☐ £80–£119.99   ☐ £120+

D How much do you spend on clothing a month?

Tick the most appropriate box.

☐ £0–£20   ☐ £21–£40   ☐ £41–£60   ☐ £61–£80   ☐ £81–£100

d What is the problem with carrying out a survey on spending like this?

2 For the survey in Q1, Angie wants to compare spending on clothes for different age groups.

a Write a suitable question to find out people's age group.

b Design a two-way table for her to collect the data.

3 R Explain why each of these questions is unsuitable to use in a survey.

For each question write a more suitable question to replace it.

a What methods of travel have you used in the last 12 months?

☐ car   ☐ bus   ☐ train   ☐ taxi   ☐ none

b Petrol prices keep rising, so do you intend to use your car less during the next year?

c What do you do at weekends?

d Should the inadequate bus service in our town be improved?

e The main cause of bad behaviour in lessons is because the

☐ lesson is boring   ☐ teacher is not strict enough   ☐ lesson is too long

f Because killing animals is cruel, should more people become vegetarians?

g What kind of food do you eat most of?

4 **R** Sam wrote a questionnaire about bullying.

Questionnaire about bullying	
Question A	How often have you been bullied?
Question B	What do you do when you see someone being bullied?
Question C	Do you agree that bullies should be sent to prison?

a Explain why each of Sam's questions needs to be improved.

b Choose three questions from this list to replace questions A, B and C.

Question P	Why is bullying wrong?
Question Q	If you saw someone being bullied would you ☐ do nothing ☐ try to stop it ☐ tell someone in authority, such as a teacher?
Question R	When were you last bullied?
Question S	When do you think bullying usually happens? ☐ in lessons ☐ after school ☐ on the way home ☐ during lunch break ☐ on the school bus ☐ every day
Question T	Do you agree that bullies should be ignored?
Question U	Tick the option that best describes your experience. During the past year I have been bullied: ☐ never ☐ once ☐ between 2 and 12 times ☐ at least once per month ☐ at least once a week ☐ daily
Question V	Do you defend people who are being bullied?
Question W	Tick the option that is closest to your view. School bullies should be: ☐ sent to prison ☐ dealt with by a teacher who knows them well ☐ made to apologise to the person they bullied ☐ expelled from the school ☐ kept in after school for an hour for a whole term ☐ ignored ☐ banned from all sports

c Design a data collection sheet to collect people's answers to the questions you selected.

Investigation

5 **a** Design a survey that would allow you to collect enough data to describe the average student in your maths class.

b Design a data collection sheet for your survey.

c Try out your survey with a small group of students.
Record their responses in your data collection sheet.

d Do you need to make any changes to your questions or your data collection sheet?

Reflect

6 How does predicting the answers you may get from a survey question help you to design your data collection sheet?

3.3 Calculating averages

- Find the median from a frequency table
- Estimate the mean from a large set of grouped data
- Calculate the mean using an assumed mean

1 **P-S** Find a possible set of five negative whole numbers that have:
mean = −6, median = −6, mode = −6, range = 7

2 **P-S** A data set is
9 g, 12 g, 5 g, □, □, □, □
All the values are whole numbers of grams.
The mean is 8 g, the mode is 5 g and the median is 7 g.
Find as many possible data sets as you can.

3 Look at this set of numbers: 4, 5, 9, 10, 12
  a Calculate the mean.
  b Add 10 to each of the numbers. Recalculate the mean.
  c Subtract 10 from each of the original numbers. Recalculate the mean.
  d Multiply all of the original numbers by 10. Recalculate the mean.
  e Divide all of the original numbers by 10. Recalculate the mean.
  f **R** What impact does adding or subtracting a number from all of the data have
    on the mean? Why?

4 **a** Calculate the mean of
    30.2, 29.8, 30.04, 31, 30.5

> **Key point** An **assumed mean** is an estimated value for the mean, close to all the data values.

  b Now calculate the mean using this method.
    i Assume the mean is 30.
      Subtract this assumed mean from each of the values.
    ii Find the mean of your answers to part **i**.
    iii Add 30 to your value from part **ii**.
  c **R** Do you get the same answer in parts **a** and **b**? Which method did you find easier?
    Which method took less time?

5 Work out the mean of 102, 105, 95, 100, 92 using an assumed mean.

6 **R** Pip asks people how many songs they have on their phones. Here are her results:
  503, 495, 502, 501, 500, 490, 496, 504
  495, 492, 504, 502, 497, 496, 501, 502
  a What value could you use for an assumed mean?
  b Use this value to calculate the mean.
  c Find the mode.
  d Does the mean or the mode better represent the data?
    Explain your answer.

7 To set his pedometer, Jay needs to work out his stride length.
He walks eight steps across sand, and then measures each one.
Here are his results:

96 cm, 100 cm, 108 cm, 97 cm, 101 cm, 98 cm, 103 cm, 105 cm

Calculate his mean stride length.

8 Calculate the mean of each set of data.
  a 12, 8, −7, −2, 15, 22, 1, 19
  b 81, 76, 75, 83, 79, 81, 77, 82
  c −1, 0, 1, 2, −1, 3, 1, −2
  d 421, 458, 397, 406, 433, 421, 437, 395

9 R The ages of five students are:
10 years 3 months, 10 years 9 months, 10 years 1 month
9 years 11 months, 10 years 0 months
  a Work out the mean of their ages.
  b Which method did you use? Explain why.

10 The table shows the results of a survey into the lengths of rivers in North America.

Length of river, L (miles)	Frequency
$0 < L \leqslant 400$	21
$400 < L \leqslant 800$	18
$800 < L \leqslant 1200$	4
$1200 < L \leqslant 1600$	3
$1600 < L \leqslant 2000$	3
$2000 < L \leqslant 2400$	2
$2400 < L \leqslant 2800$	1
$2800 < L \leqslant 3200$	2

  a Find:
    i the modal class
    ii the class that contains the median.
  b Calculate an estimate for:
    i the mean
    ii the range.
  c Why can you only calculate an estimate for the range, and not an accurate range?

11 These frequency tables are for the same data grouped in two different ways.

Table 1

Class	Frequency
$0 \leqslant b < 20$	7
$20 \leqslant b < 40$	25
$40 \leqslant b < 60$	15
$60 \leqslant b < 80$	3

Table 2

Class	Frequency
$0 \leqslant b < 15$	3
$15 \leqslant b < 30$	11
$30 \leqslant b < 45$	21
$45 \leqslant b < 60$	12
$60 \leqslant b < 75$	3

Use each grouping to:
  a find the modal class
  b estimate the range
  c estimate the mean.
  d R Which grouping gives the more reliable statistics? Explain your answer.

Reflect

12 When is it more efficient to use an assumed mean to calculate a mean?
Use questions from this lesson to explain.

3.4 Displaying and analysing data

- Construct and use a line of best fit to estimate missing values
- Identify and suggest reasons for outliers in data
- Identify further lines of enquiry
- Draw line graphs to represent grouped data

1 **R** The table shows how many days of school some students missed, and those students' mean exam marks.

Number of days of school missed	1	12	21	15	8	7	6	10	11	22	16	19	4	9	5
Mean exam mark	79	65	45	60	68	71	70	65	67	46	56	56	73	66	74

Here are three students' scatter graphs for this data. Each student has predicted the mean exam mark for a student who missed 14 days of school.

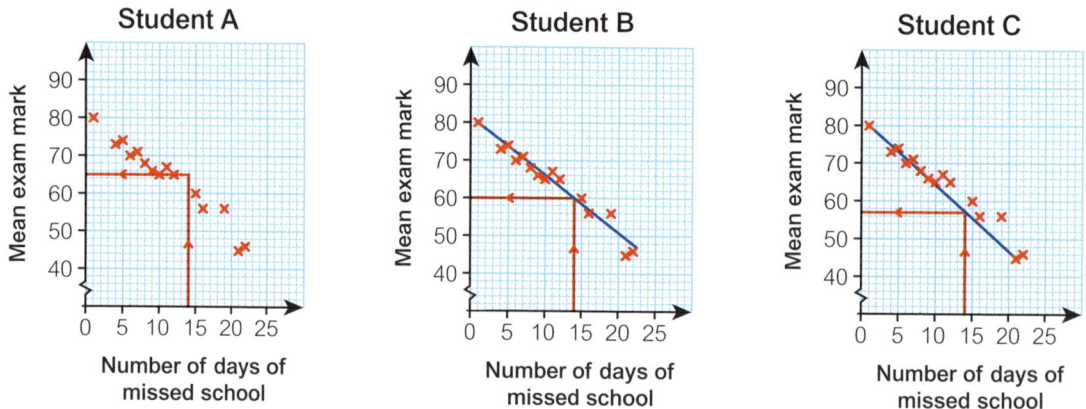

Student A

Student B

Student C

a Which student's prediction is the most accurate?

b Explain what each of the others could have done better.

2 **R** A nurse records the masses and heights of 18 patients at a clinic.

Mass (kg)	72	78	90	110	67	68	105	82	73
Height (cm)	171	175	188	145	168	167	190	180	174

Mass (kg)	101	76	89	91	90	82	76	79	91
Height (cm)	190	172	189	185	187	181	175	177	188

a Draw a suitable diagram to display the data.

b Identify any outliers in the data.

c Use your diagram to estimate:

　i the mass of a patient who is 175 cm tall

　ii the height of a patient who weighs 60 kg

　iii the height of a patient who weighs 130 kg.

d How reliable do you think each of your answers to part **c** is? Explain.

3 **P-S** Class 9Y carried out a survey to find out how many miles people drive each year.
The line graph shows their results.
Work out an estimate for

a the range   **b** the mean.

c What is the modal class?

> **Q3 hint** Make a table with these four columns: class; frequency; midpoint of class; midpoint × frequency.

Distance driven each year

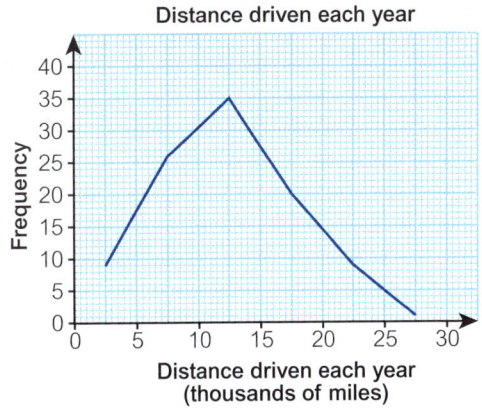

Distance driven each year
(thousands of miles)

4 The table show the ages of people visiting two doctors' surgeries in one week.

a Use the data to draw line graphs for the two surgeries on the same set of axes.

b Which age group made fewest visits to each surgery?

c **R** Jane says that the people at Surgery A make more visits than the people at Surgery B, so Surgery B patients must be healthier.
Explain why this is not necessarily true.

Age, a (years)	Surgery A frequency	Surgery B frequency
$0 < a \leqslant 10$	63	20
$10 < a \leqslant 20$	69	16
$20 < a \leqslant 30$	75	15
$30 < a \leqslant 40$	68	14
$40 < a \leqslant 50$	51	12
$50 < a \leqslant 60$	46	8
$60 < a \leqslant 70$	52	12
$70 < a \leqslant 80$	75	16
$80 < a \leqslant 90$	58	10
$90 < a \leqslant 100$	55	9

Investigation

5 The table shows the masses of some eggs and the length of time each takes to cook.

Mass (g)	53	55	58	59	61	63
Time (mins)	6	3.8	3.9	4.1	4.2	4.4

a Describe the correlation.

b Plot a scatter diagram, drawing a line of best fit.

c Calculate the mean mass of the eggs and the mean time spent cooking.

d Plot the mean point. Does it lie on your line of best fit?

e Check whether the 'mean' point lies on the line of best fit for the other scatter diagrams in this unit. What do you notice when it doesn't?

Reflect

6 **a** In which graph will predictions using the line of best fit be more reliable?

b Explain how the strength of the correlation affects the reliability of predicted values.

Graph A   **Graph B**

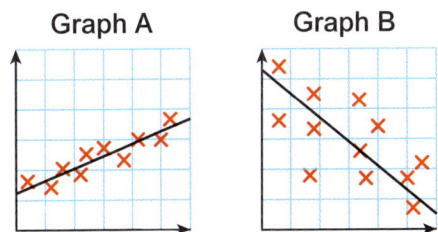

3.5 Presenting and comparing data

- Draw back-to-back stem and leaf diagrams
- Write a report to show survey results

1 P-S The tables show the population (in millions) of Asia and Europe by age and gender.

Asia

Age, a (years)	Male	Female
$0 \leqslant a < 20$	757	700
$20 \leqslant a < 40$	655	615
$40 \leqslant a < 60$	415	400
$60 \leqslant a < 80$	155	180
$80 \leqslant a < 100$	17	33

Europe

Age, a (years)	Male	Female
$0 \leqslant a < 20$	84	80
$20 \leqslant a < 40$	105	103
$40 \leqslant a < 60$	100	104
$60 \leqslant a < 80$	54	71
$80 \leqslant a < 100$	8	18

a Construct two pie charts to show the age distribution of the population in Asia and in Europe.

b Draw a graph or chart(s) to show the different proportions of men and women in each age group in Asia.

c Draw a graph to compare the numbers of males and females in each age group in Europe.

d Find the modal age group for each continent.

e Calculate an estimate of the mean age for each continent.

f Write a short report about the populations of Asia and Europe. Write at least one sentence about each graph you have drawn and each average you have found. You can draw more graphs if you wish.

> **Q1a hint** Find the total population in each age group for each continent.

2 R The line graphs show the ages of British adults who used the internet for social networking and for banking in one year.
The graph was plotted using grouped data with equal class widths.

a What is the same about the ages of adults who used the internet for social networking and banking?

b What is different?

> **Q2 hint** Find the modal class for each set of data. What is the trend in each set of data?

Age of British adults and internet use

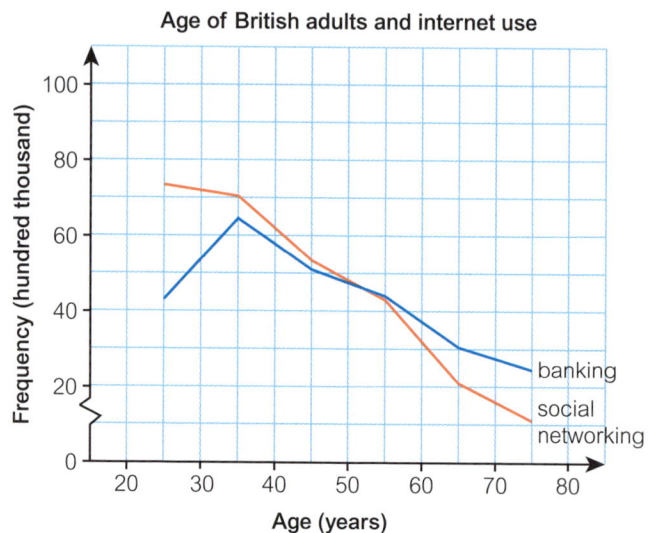

Source: ONS

3 R The frequency tables show how much employees earn in two companies.

Company A

Earnings per year, e (£ thousands)	Number of employees
$0 < e \leqslant 10$	2
$10 < e \leqslant 20$	26
$20 < e \leqslant 30$	49
$30 < e \leqslant 40$	16
$40 < e \leqslant 50$	11
$50 < e \leqslant 60$	3

Company B

Earnings per year, e (£ thousands)	Number of employees
$0 < e \leqslant 10$	5
$10 < e \leqslant 20$	9
$20 < e \leqslant 30$	26
$30 < e \leqslant 40$	62
$40 < e \leqslant 50$	5
$50 < e \leqslant 60$	2

a Draw a line graph for each set of data, using the same axes.

b Compare the two line graphs.

c Which company would you choose to work for and why?

4 R Students in a Year 9 class took a French test and a Spanish test.
The results for the French test were:

35	48	19	25	47	36	33	29	40	35
49	38	24	28	38	38	12	37	30	41

The results for the Spanish test were:

50	48	23	28	39	32	34	40	20	28
38	45	37	29	26	36	38	32	30	21

a Draw a back-to-back stem and leaf diagram for this data.

b The pass mark for both tests was 32.
What percentage of students passed

  i the French test   **ii** the Spanish test?

c Can you say how many students passed both tests?
Explain.

> **Q4a hint** In a back-to-back stem and leaf diagram, the lowest numbers are closest to the stem.

5 The table shows the times for the three-legged race at a village fair in 1967 and in 2005.

a Draw suitable diagrams to compare the two sets of data.

b Write two sentences comparing the two sets of data.

Time, T (seconds)	Frequency	
	1967	2005
$7 \leqslant T < 11$	1	6
$11 \leqslant T < 14$	9	9
$14 \leqslant T < 17$	9	6
$17 \leqslant T < 19$	4	0
$19 \leqslant T < 27$	5	0

Reflect

6 Think about the graphs, charts and tables you have used in this unit.
Which types of graph or chart or table could you use to

a compare the proportions of data in different groups

b compare frequencies for different groups

c find the modal class

d find the mode

e estimate the mean?

3 Extend

1 P-S The original mean of a set of data was 14.
A number was added to each of the data values and the new mean is now 11.
What number was added?

2 P-S The average age of the 15 members of a club in 2016 was 24.
In 2018, three new members joined and the average age was still 24.
What is the average age of the new members?

3 R A survey is given to 50 people.
The surveyor says that it is representative because the sample is more than 10% of
the population.
What is the largest the population can be?

4 R Martin would like to find out why people cheat in tests.
He finds out that someone he knows cheated and asks them to tell him who they know
that has cheated.
   a Why might this be biased?
   b Why might Martin have trouble finding enough people for his survey this way?
   c Martin decides to ask a teacher for a list of people who have been caught cheating to
   ask. What problems might this cause?

5 P-S / R The pie charts show the proportions of people who scored different amounts on
tests at a university in 2007 and 2017.

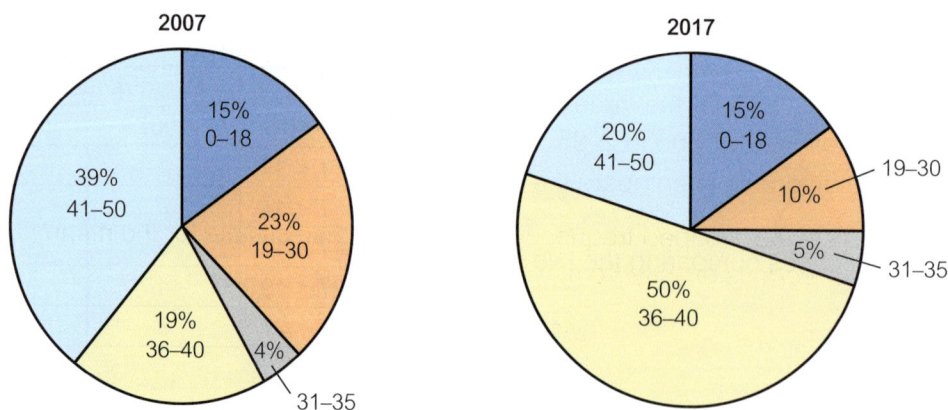

2007

15%
0–18

39%
41–50

23%
19–30

19%
36–40

4%

31–35

2017

15%
0–18

20%
41–50

10%
19–30

5%

31–35

50%
36–40

   a In 2007, 120 people scored between 0 and 18 marks.
   How many people sat the test in 2007?
   b The same number of people scored 31–35 marks in 2007 and 2017.
   How many people sat the test in 2017?
   c Estimate the mean scores in 2007 and 2017.
   d Compare how well people did in 2007 with 2017.

6 P-S / R The table shows the frequencies of different numbers of letters delivered to each house on Station Street in a week.

Number of letters	Frequency
$0 \leqslant L < 2$	3
$2 \leqslant L < 4$	7
$4 \leqslant L < 8$	2
$8 \leqslant L < \square$	8

a The estimated mean number of letters was 5.4. What is the missing number?

b Estimate the median.

c There are 28 houses on Park Crescent.
Using the same groupings as in the frequency table for Station Street, the estimated mean number of letters delivered to each house on Park Crescent is 5.4.
What could the frequencies for Park Crescent be?

d Draw two pie charts comparing the numbers of letters delivered in Station Street and Park Crescent.

e Write a sentence comparing the distributions.

7 R The table shows the percentages of the population who are living on less than $1.90 per day in different countries.

	2000	2002	2004	2006	2008	2010	2012	2014
Costa Rica	6.5	4.5	4.3	3.2	2.2	1.5	1.6	1.4
Indonesia	39.3	22.8	23.9	27.4	21.8	15.7	11.6	7.9
Moldova	35.7	16.3	8.6	2.4	1.3	0.5	0.3	0
Peru	16.3	15	13.5	13.3	9	5.5	4.7	3.7

a Explain why you cannot compare numbers of people from each country.

b Draw a suitable diagram to compare the data sets.

c Write a few sentences explaining the trends over time in the data and comparing the countries.

Investigation

8 Copy and complete the grouped frequency table so that the estimate for the mean length, L cm, of a worm is exactly 5 cm.

Length of worm	Frequency
$\square \leqslant L < \square$	$\square$
$\square \leqslant L < \square$	$\square$
$\square \leqslant L < \square$	$\square$
$\square \leqslant L < \square$	$\square$

Reflect

9 What do you think is more useful when comparing data sets – the mean, median, mode and range, or diagrams? Why?

4 Multiplicative reasoning

Master   **Extend p47**

4.1 Enlargement

- Enlarge 2D shapes using a positive whole number scale factor and centre of enlargement
- Find the centre of enlargement by drawing lines on a grid
- Understand that the scale factor is the ratio of corresponding lengths

1   **P-S**   The perimeter of the larger square is 20% greater than the perimeter of the smaller square.

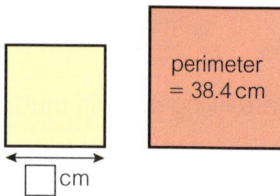

perimeter = 38.4 cm

☐ cm

Work out the side length of the smaller square.

2   **P-S / R**   The area of the larger square is 30% greater than the area of the smaller square.

a What is the side length of each square?

b What is the scale factor of enlargement from the smaller square to the larger square?

c Why do you think this is not the same as the scale factor for the areas?

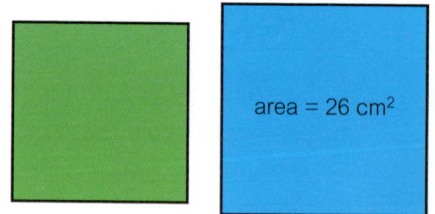

area = 26 cm²

3   **P-S / R**   Triangles B and C are enlargements of triangle A.

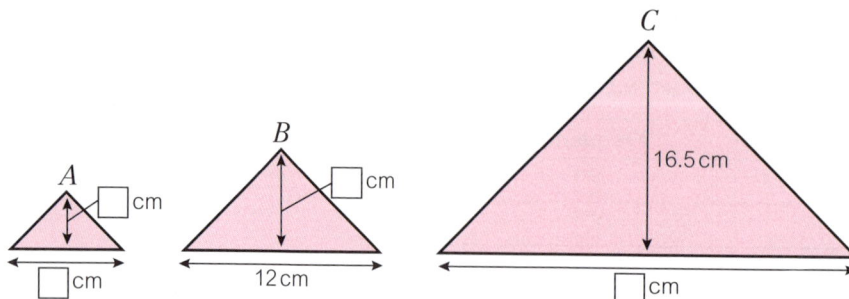

C

16.5 cm

A

☐ cm

☐ cm

B

☐ cm

12 cm

☐ cm

Triangle B has an area of 54 cm².
The scale factor of enlargement of the lengths of triangle A to triangle C is 2 : 11.
Work out the missing lengths.

Q3 hint Work out the height of triangle B first, from its area. Then use the ratio of the lengths.

4 Describe the enlargement that takes
  a ABC to $A'B'C'$
  b ABC to $A''B''C''$
  c $A'B'C'$ to $A''B''C''$.

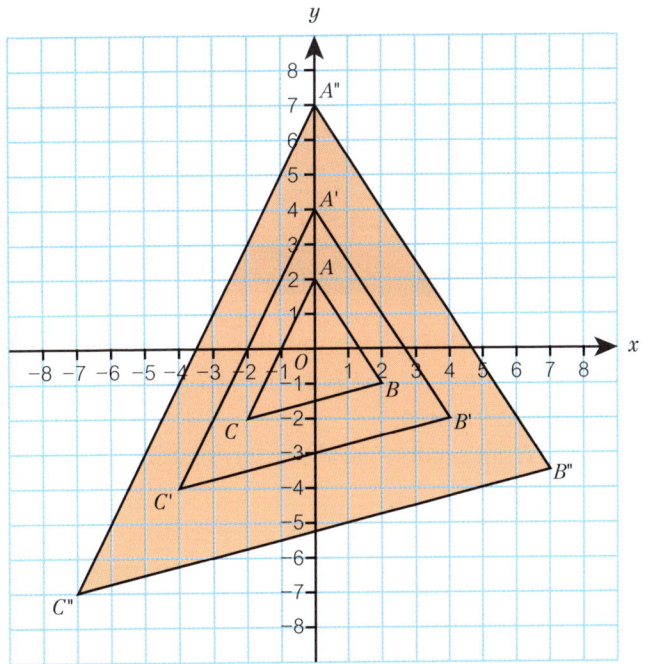

5 **P-S / R** The diagram shows an enlargement from triangle A to triangle B.
  a What are the coordinates of the centre of enlargement?
  b Triangle C is an enlargement of triangle A by the same scale factor. The centre of enlargement is (0.4, 0.4). What are the coordinates of the vertices of triangle C?
  c Triangle D is another enlargement of triangle A by the same scale factor and with one vertex at (0.4, 1). What are the possible coordinates of the centre of enlargement?
  d Why are there multiple possible answers to part **c**?

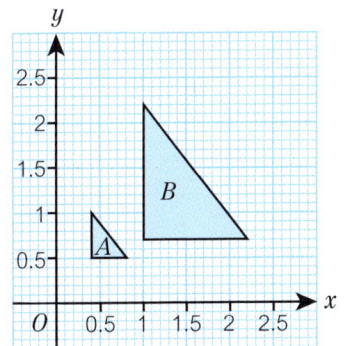

Investigation

6 A triangle is enlarged so that the enlargement touches the edge of a sheet of A4 paper and takes up the middle third of the long edge of the paper.

The centre of enlargement and the original triangle are both on the sheet of A4 paper.

Find the range of possible positive integer scale factors and the possible locations of the centre of enlargement.

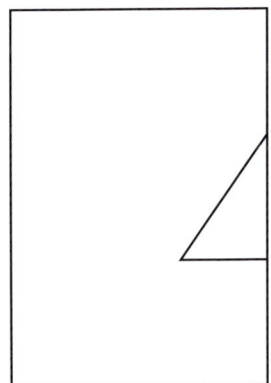

Reflect

7 Georgina calculates a scale factor and her answer is 1.3333...
Georgina says, 'My answer must be wrong, because scale factors can only be integers'.
Is Georgina's statement correct? Explain.

4.2 Negative and fractional scale factors

- Enlarge 2D shapes using a negative whole number scale factor
- Enlarge 2D shapes using a fractional scale factor

1 **P-S** The top triangle has an area of $3.6\,cm^2$.
The area of the bottom triangle is 40% of the area of the top triangle.
Work out the height of the bottom triangle.

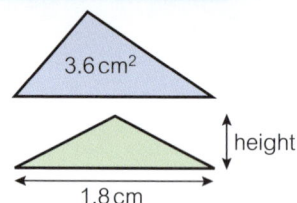

3.6 cm²

1.8 cm

height

2 **a** Describe the enlargement that takes shape A to shape B.
   b Describe the enlargement that takes shape B to shape A.

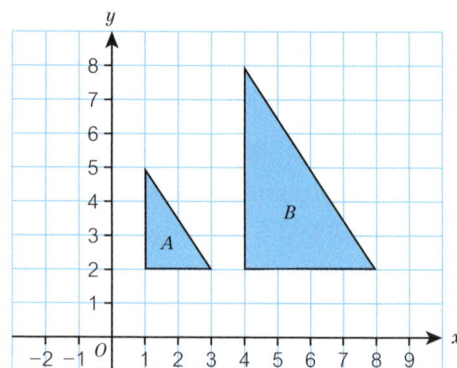

3 **a** Describe the enlargement that takes shape C to shape D.
   b Describe the enlargement that takes shape D to shape C.
   c **P-S** Antony says, 'I took shape D to shape C using a positive enlargement and then a rotation'.
   Describe fully the transformation that Antony may have used.

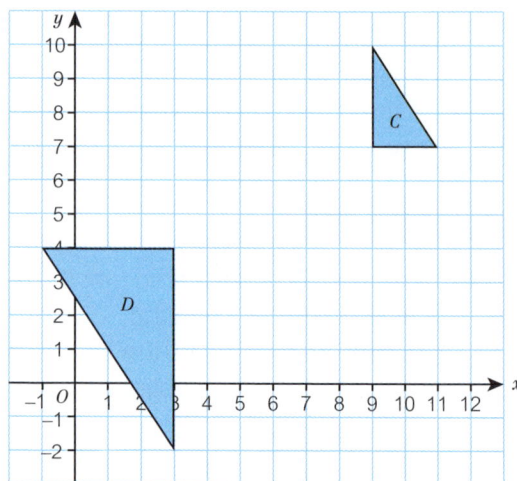

4 **R** Arif says,
'The inverse of an enlargement with scale factor 3 is an enlargement with scale factor −3'.
Why is Arif incorrect?

5 **a** Plot the points (1, 1), (1, 2), (3, 1), (3, 3) on a coordinate grid with axes from −10 to 10.
   Join the points to make a trapezium and label it E.
   b Enlarge shape E by scale factor −1, with centre of enlargement (0, 0).
   Label the new shape F.
   c Enlarge shape F by scale factor 3, with centre of enlargement (0, 0).
   Label the new shape G.
   d **P-S** What single transformation would map shape G back to shape E?

6 **P-S** Triangle A is enlarged by scale factor –0.5, with centre of enlargement (5, 5). The image is triangle B.
What are the coordinates of the vertices of triangle A?

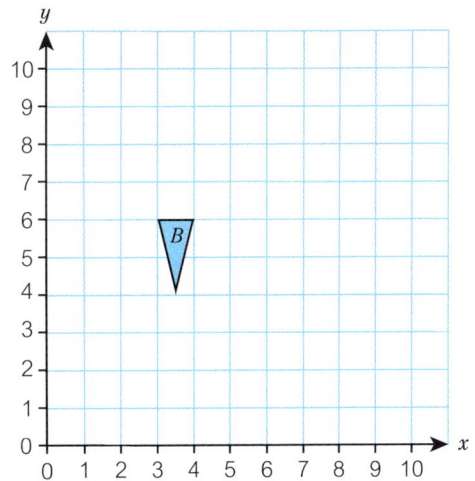

7 **P-S** Shape P is enlarged by scale factor $\frac{2}{3}$ from centre of enlargement (0, 1) to make shape Q.
Shape Q is enlarged by scale factor $\frac{1}{3}$ from centre of enlargement (1, 0) to make shape R.
What overall scale factor would enlarge shape R back to shape P?

8 **P-S / R** An ever-repeating pattern of triangles begins as shown in the diagram. Alice is writing instructions to map from one large triangle to the next, and complete the pattern.
She begins like this:

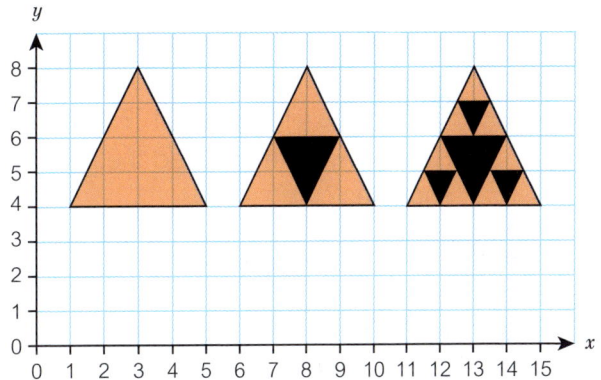

1   Draw a triangle with vertices at coordinates (1, 4), (3, 8) and (5, 4). Colour this triangle red.

2   Enlarge the triangle by scale factor $\frac{1}{2}$ using centre of enlargement (11, 4). Colour this triangle red.

a Copy and complete the instructions to draw all three large triangles in the pattern.

b Is there only one correct set of instructions? Explain.

c What are the instructions for the next large triangle in the pattern?

> **Q8a hint** You may use any transformations, or combinations of transformations.

Investigation

9 Look back at Q6 in Lesson 4.1. Find the range of *all* possible scale factors, including any negative and fractional values.

Reflect

10 In Q2 you described an enlargement from shape A to shape B, and then from shape B to shape A. In Q3 you described an enlargement from shape C to shape D, and then from shape D to shape C.
What is the same and what is different when the direction of enlargement changes?

4.3 Percentage change

- Find an original value using inverse operations
- Calculate percentage change

1 **P-S** Between 2011 and 2012, visitor numbers to a zoo increased by 15%.
   Between 2012 and 2013, visitor numbers to the zoo decreased by 20%.
   In 2013 there were 69 552 visitors. How many visitors were there in 2011?

2 **R** The bar chart shows the percentage of the people over the age of 65 in a village who
   use the internet for shopping.

   a In 2008 there were 200 people over the age of
     65 in the village.
     How many used the internet for shopping?

   b Between 2008 and 2012 the number of people
     over the age of 65 increased by 20%.

     i How many people over the age of 65 were
       living in the village in 2012?

     ii How many of these used the internet for
        shopping?

Percentage of over-65s using
the internet for shopping

   c Use your answers to parts **a** and **b ii** to work out:

     i the actual increase in the number of over-65s using the internet for shopping between
       2008 and 2012

     ii the percentage increase in the number of over-65s using the internet for shopping.

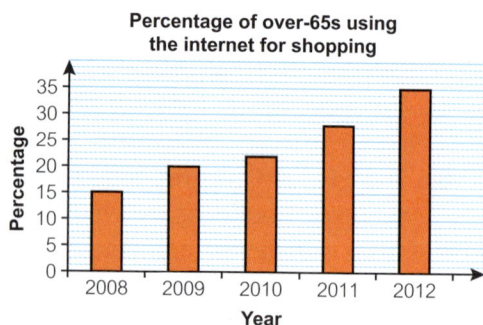

3 **R** 80% of a number is 300.

   a Calculate 10% of the number, then use this to find 100%.

   b What percentage decrease of the original number gives 300?

   c What would you need to divide 300 by to get the original number?

4 **R** The pie charts show the proportions of oil used for different energy needs in the UK
   in 1970 and 2012.
   In 1970 the total amount of oil used
   for energy in the UK was 146
   million tonnes.
   In 2012 the total amount of oil used
   for energy in the UK was 140
   million tonnes.

Oil used for energy
in UK in 1970

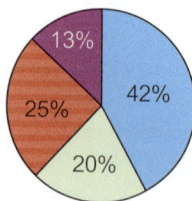

Oil used for energy
in UK in 2012

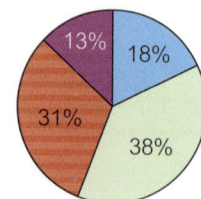

Key
- Industry
- Transport
- Domestic
- Other

   a 'Other' accounted for 13%
     in both 1970 and 2012.
     Does this mean that the same amount of oil was used for 'Other' purposes in
     1970 and 2012? Explain.

b Work out the percentage increase in the amount of oil used by transport from 1970 to 2012.

c Work out the percentage decrease in the amount of oil used by industry from 1970 to 2012.

5 **P-S** Sachin invests £840 into an investment that pays simple interest for 5 years. At the end of the 5 years his investment is worth £955.50. What is the yearly simple interest percentage?

6 The graph shows the percentage change in visitor numbers to Tintagel Castle.

It shows that in 2009 there were 18% more visitors than in 2008. It shows that in 2010 there were 4% fewer visitors than in 2009.

a In 2011, what was the percentage change in visitor numbers from 2010?

b In 2010 there were approximately 190 000 visitors.

Approximately how many visitors were there in 2011?

Give your answer to the nearest thousand.

c Approximately how many visitors were there in 2012? Give your answer to the nearest thousand.

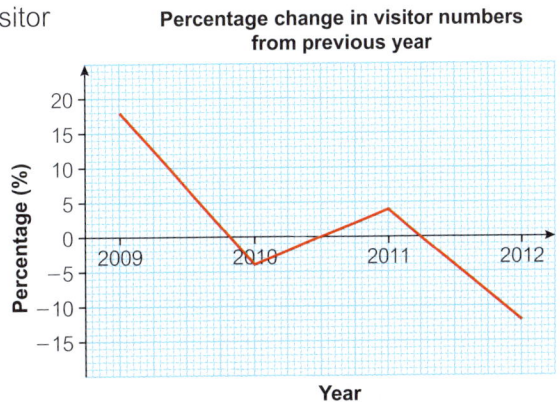

Percentage change in visitor numbers from previous year

Source: Visit England

7 **R** A researcher says that a decrease of more than 20% in the amount of bacteria is significant evidence that their antibacterial spray is having an impact.

Group C is the control group, where no antibacterial spray was administered. Is the researcher's claim valid? Explain.

Group	Before	After
A	127	91
B	143	113
C	136	94

Investigation

8 **a** Sketch a cuboid 6 cm by 4 cm by 2 cm.

b Sketch a second cuboid with one side length that is 50% bigger than the first cuboid.

c Work out the volume of each cuboid.

d Work out the percentage increase in the volume of the first cuboid. What do you notice?

e Test that this percentage increase is the same if you make one of the other side lengths of the first cuboid 50% bigger.

f What happens to the percentage increase in volume if you make two of the side lengths of the first cuboid 50% bigger? What about all three lengths?

Reflect

9 In Q3 you were asked to find the original number by finding 10% first. You were also asked to find a single division that would give the original number. Which method would you prefer to use to find the original number and why? Does the nature of the question change your answer? Explain.

4.4 Compound measures

- Solve problems using compound measures
- Solve problems using constant rates and related formulae

1 **P-S** Toby cycled 15 miles in $1\frac{1}{4}$ hours. He had a 30-minute rest, and then cycled a further 9 miles in 45 minutes. Work out his **average speed** for the whole journey.
Give your answer in

  a miles per hour

  b kilometres per hour

  c metres per second.

> **Key point**
>
> Average speed = $\dfrac{\text{total distance}}{\text{total time}}$

2 Work out the average speed for each journey.

  a A car travels 200 km in 5 hours.

  b An athlete runs 400 m in 64 seconds.

  c An aeroplane travels 2475 miles in $4\frac{1}{2}$ hours.

  d A swimmer completes a 50 m length in 40 seconds.

  e **R** Why are the speeds calculated in this question *average* speeds?

3 Three friends are comparing how fast they completed their weekend walks.
Alima says it took her 3.4 hours to travel 12 miles.
Hoda says it took her 3 hours and 30 minutes to travel 11 miles.
Jemma says it took her 205 minutes to travel 11.5 miles.
Assuming they each walk at a constant speed, who would finish a mile-long walk first?

4 **P-S** The diagram shows the dimensions of a piece of metal.
A force of 53.8 N is applied to the metal.
Work out the pressure in N/cm².

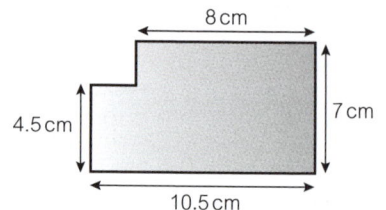

5 **P-R / R** Mrs Smith walks 500 m to the shops. This takes her 10 minutes.
She spends half an hour shopping, then walks home.
It takes her 20 minutes to walk home.

  a Minnie and Dan sketch graphs to show Mrs Smith's journey.

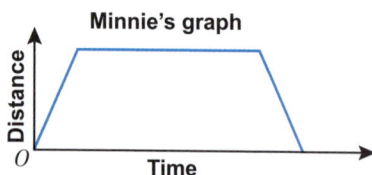

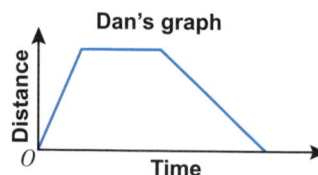

> **Q5a hint** Look at times for the different sections of the journey.

  They are both incorrect. Explain what is wrong with each graph.

  b Sketch a more accurate graph for Mrs Smith's journey.

  c How far does Mrs Smith walk in total? Give your answer in kilometres.

6 **P-S** Ellie left her house at 10 am. She walked 6 km in $1\frac{1}{2}$ hours.
Then she rested for half an hour before she walked back. She arrived home at 3 pm.
a Draw a graph to show this information.
b What speed was she walking on her walk back?

7 **P-S / R** Amir's remote-controlled car has a maximum speed of 32 km/h. A world-class athlete can run 200 m in 19.6 seconds. Amir says his car could beat the sprinter in a 200 m race. Is he correct? Show your working to explain.

8 **P-S / R** This distance–time graph shows trips taken by three different cyclists.
a Which cyclist travelled at the fastest speed?
b Which cyclist had the highest average speed for the entire journey?
A fourth cyclist completes the same trip as cyclist C, starting and finishing at the same time. She travels at a constant speed for the whole journey.
c Calculate her speed, giving your answer correct to 1 decimal place.

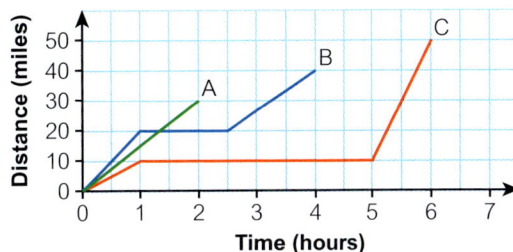

9 **P-S** 250 ml of cooking oil has a mass of 230 g.
Calculate the density of cooking oil in g/cm^3.

10 **P-S** The floor of this room is covered with rubber tiles with a density of 1200 kg/m^3.

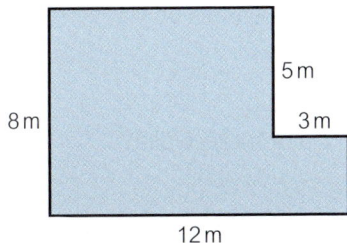

The tiles are 5 mm thick.
Estimate the total mass of the rubber tiles.

11 **P-S** An electrical solder is made by combining 15 g of tin with 85 g of lead.
Tin has a density of 7.3 g/cm^3 and lead has a density of 11.3 g/cm^3.
Calculate the density of the solder.

12 **P-S** At a depth of 10 m, water has a pressure of 9.8 N/cm^2.
Calculate the force applied to a diving mask with a surface area of 320 cm^2.

Reflect

13 In this lesson you have been calculating average speeds.
Is every speed you calculated an average?
When you calculate density and pressure, are these also average measures? Explain.

4.5 Direct and inverse proportion

- Solve best-buy problems
- Solve problems involving inverse proportion

1   **R**   When typing a given document, the number of mistakes made is inversely proportional to the time taken.

Rachel types a document in 24 minutes and makes 12 mistakes.

a Predict how many mistakes she would make if she spent 32 minutes typing the same document.

b Predict how long she should spend typing the document to make only 2 mistakes.

2   **P-S**   A printer company sells ink cartridges in three sizes: small, medium and large.

A small cartridge will print 300 pages and costs £3.50.

A medium cartridge will print 450 pages and costs £4.00.

A large cartridge will print 700 pages and costs £7.60.

Which cartridge is the best value for money?

3   **R**   For each situation, decide if it is a direct proportion or an inverse proportion situation or if no proportionality exists.

a Some people take a few hours to paint one wall.

How long would it take more people to paint the same wall?

b Some people take a few hours to paint one wall.

How long would it take the same number of people to paint more walls?

c Some people take a few hours to make a decision.

How long would it take fewer people to make the same decision?

d Some monkeys take a few hours to eat many bananas.

How long would it take more monkeys to eat the same number of bananas?

e Some monkeys take a few hours to eat many bananas.

In the same amount of time, how many monkeys would it take to eat more bananas?

4   **P-S**   A grant available from a charity is inversely proportional to the number of people awarded it. If 30 people are awarded the grant, they each receive £800.

One year, each person received £600. How many people were awarded the grant?

5   **P-S / R**   Gardener's Best compost is sold in 30-litre bags.

47 bags cost £293.75 + VAT (at 20%). Delivery is free.

Gardener's Gold compost is sold in 50-litre bags.

21 bags cost £200 (including VAT). Delivery is £60.

Assuming you have to pay VAT, which compost is better value for money?

Show your working.

6 **P-S / R**   Sally is writing a research report.
She fits 400 words to a page. The report is 28 pages long.
Sally is told the report must be no longer than 25 pages so she decreases the size of the text. Now she can fit 450 words to a page.
Will this reduce the report to the correct number of pages? Show your working.

7 **R**   Object A has a mass of 30 g and a volume of 15 cm3.
   a Three Object As are put together. What is the density of the three Objects together?
   b x Object As are put together. What is the density of the x Object As together?
   c Object B has a mass of 30 g but twice the volume of Object A.
      What do you need to multiply the density of Object A by to get the density of Object B?
   d Object C has a volume of 15 cm^3 but twice the mass of Object A.
      What do you need to multiply the density of Object A by to get the density of Object C?
   e Copy and complete the sentences:
      i Density is _____ proportional to mass.
      ii Density is _____ proportional to volume.
   f Object D has the same density as Object A but half the mass. What is the volume?

8 **R**   For each statement, say whether it is true or false.
   a Speed is directly proportional to distance if time is constant.
   b Speed is directly proportional to time if distance is constant.
   c The number of posters you make is directly proportional to your test score.
   d The amount of television you watch is inversely proportional to your test score.

9 **P-S / R**   A team of 6 people will take approximately 32.5 days to write a computer game.
   a Another person joins the team.
      This person works part time: half the hours of the others on the team.
      Estimate how long the team will take to write the computer game with this extra person.
   b After 14 days (with 6 people working full time, and 1 person working half time), the skill of the team increases so everyone works, on average, one and a half times as fast. How many more days do the team need to write the computer game?

Investigation

10 The gravitational force felt by an astronaut is inversely proportional to the square of their distance from the centre of the Earth.

Distance	Surface of Earth (6378 km)	Edge of atmosphere (7378 km)	Moon's orbit (390 778 km)
Gravitational force	9.8	7.3	0.0026

The table shows the gravitational force (rounded to 2 significant figures) at given distances from the centre of the Earth.

How far is an astronaut from the centre of the Earth if the gravitational force is half what it was when they were standing on the surface of Earth?

Reflect

11 Looking back at the questions you answered in this lesson, how did you decide whether the question used direct or inverse proportion? Give examples.

4 Extend

1 **P-S** Joanne drives 90 miles to visit friends. She plans to travel at an average speed of 55 mph and wants to arrive by 1 pm. Calculate the latest time Joanne should leave.

2 **P-S** The Channel Tunnel is 31.4 miles long. The speed limit for trains in the tunnel is 160 km/h. Work out the time taken for a train travelling at the speed limit to complete its journey through the tunnel.

3 **P-S** A roofer uses a board to reduce the pressure applied to a roof he is working on. The roofer has a weight of 880 N, and wants the maximum pressure applied to the roof to be 500 N/m². Calculate the minimum area of board he should use to distribute his weight.

4 **P-S** Objects that are less dense than their surroundings float.
The density of water at 4 °C is 1 g/cm³.

a Decide which of these objects will float in a bowl of water with a temperature of 4 °C.

	Object	Mass
A	Plutonium 1 cm × 1 cm × 1 cm	19.8 g
B	Polystyrene 20 cm × 5 cm × 2 cm	2 g
C	Iron 5 cm × 2 cm × 2 cm	160 g

b The density of mercury is 13.6 g/cm³. Which of the objects will float in mercury?

c Do your answers change when the volume of the objects is increased? Explain.

5 In 2012, the mean value of a residential property in the UK was £179 500. There were 23.4 million residential properties.

a Work out the total value of all the residential property in the UK in 2012.

b Write your answer as an ordinary number, correct to one significant figure.

c In 2013, the total value of residential property in the UK rose to £5 trillion. Work out the percentage increase in value since 2012.

6 **P-S / R** A triangle with base length 3 is enlarged so that the scale factor of enlargement from the original triangle to the new triangle is $\frac{7}{3}$. The bases of both triangles lie along the same horizontal line $y = \ldots$ and are 3 units apart in the x-direction. What is the distance of the centre of enlargement from the original triangle?

7 **P-S** Jimmy travelled for 2 hours from Barton to New Town.
He then travelled for 1.5 hours from New Town to Greene.
The distance from Barton to New Town is x miles and from New Town to Greene is y miles.
Write an expression for the average speed of Jimmy's total journey from Barton to Greene.

8 **P-S / R** The density of this prism is $6\,\text{g/cm}^3$.
The mass of the prism is $18\,\text{g}$.
A cube has sides that are the same length as the depth of the prism. It also has the same density as the prism.
What is the mass of the cube?

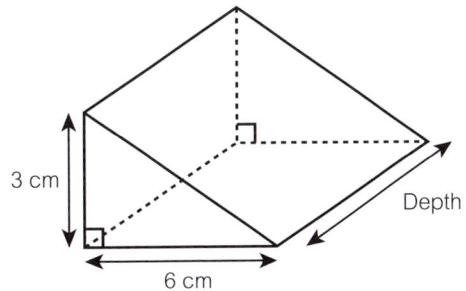

3 cm

6 cm

Depth

9 **P-S / R** The density of a cube is $1.7\,\text{g/m}^3$.
The mass of the cube is $6\,\text{kg}$.
The cube is pressing down with a force of $60\,\text{N}$.
What pressure is the cube exerting?

10 **P-S** The length of time a group of animals takes to eat an amount of food is inversely proportional to the number of animals in the group.
The number of animals increases by 15%.
What is the percentage change in the length of time taken?

Investigation

11 Each number in a set of numbers is increased by 10%, then decreased by 30%, then increased by 17.5%.

a By what percentage has the total of the numbers changed?

b By what percentage has the mean of the numbers changed?

c By what percentage has the range changed?

d Find a set of five percentage changes that result in the same mean, total and range as the original set of numbers.

Investigation

12 An ant travels from A to B to C to D
The distance x from A to B is three times more than the distance from B to C.
The time y taken to travel from A to B is twice the time taken to travel from B to C.

a Write an expression for the ant's average speed from A to C.
Give your answer in terms of x and y.

The distance from B to C is three times more than the distance from C to D.

The time taken to travel from B to C is twice the time taken to travel from C to D.

b Write an expression for the ant's average speed from A to D.
Give your answer in terms of x and y.

Reflect

13 In what ways is working with enlargement and proportion similar to working with ratio and to solving equations? What differences are there?

5 Constructions

Master   **Extend p59**

5.1 Using scales

- Use scales on maps and diagrams
- Draw diagrams to scale

1 Abigail is making scale drawings of a triangle.
The sides of triangle A are 30 cm, 40 cm and 50 cm.
The angle between the 30 cm side and the
40 cm side is 90°.

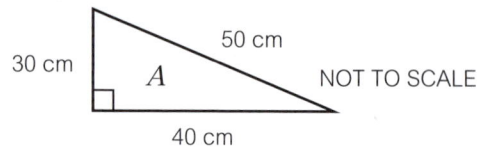

30 cm   50 cm A 40 cm   NOT TO SCALE

  a Triangle B is a scale drawing of triangle A at a
scale of 1 cm : 5 cm.
What is the area of triangle B?

  b How many times greater is the area of triangle A than the area of triangle B?

  c Triangle C is a larger scale drawing of triangle A using a scale of 1 m : 5 cm.
How many times greater is the area of triangle C than the area of triangle A?

  d What is the scale factor from triangle B to triangle C?
Write your answer as a ratio.

  e **R** Abigail says, 'The size of the angles will be bigger on triangle C because of the scale
factor.' Explain why Abigail is incorrect.

2 The diagram shows a man standing next to a house.

  a Use an estimation of the height of the
man to work out the scale factor of
the drawing.

  b How tall would the real house be?

3 **a** **R** A map has scale of 1 : 50 000.
Deb says, 'This means that 1 cm on
the map represents 50 000 cm in real life.'
Zac says, 'This means that 1 mm on the map represents 50 000 mm in real life.'
Show that they are both correct.

  b An estate agent has a 1 : 50 000 scale map covering a whole wall in his office.
What real-life distance does 1 metre on the map represent?

4   **P-S**   Here is a map of the walk along Hadrian's Wall in Northumberland. The walk from Bowness-on-Solway to Carlisle is 24 km in real life.

a Work out the scale of the map. Write it as a ratio.

b Estimate the total distance of the walk, from Bowness-on-Solway to Wallsend, in real life.

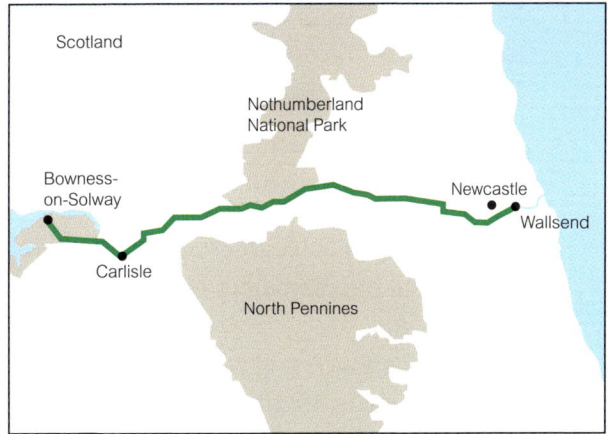

5   The Pyramid of Khafra is a square-based pyramid in Egypt.

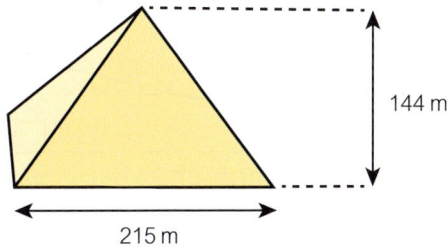

144 m

215 m

Make an accurate drawing of the plan and side elevation of the Pyramid of Khafra, using a suitable scale.

6   A biology book has this drawing of a cell.
Estimate the width of the cell.
Write your answer in millimetres, in standard form.

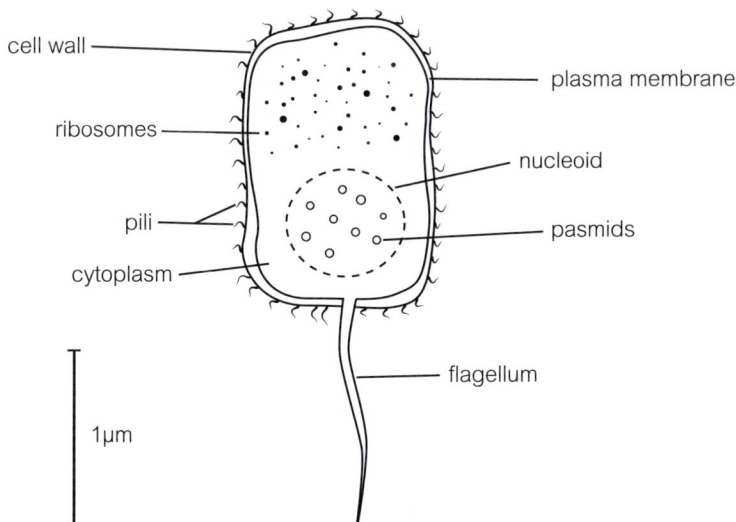

cell wall
plasma membrane
ribosomes
nucleoid
pili
pasmids
cytoplasm

flagellum

1μm

7 In a scale model of the planets in the Solar System, the Earth is represented by a table tennis ball with diameter 40 mm.

The table shows the real-life diameters of the planets in the Solar System.

Planet	Mercury	Venus	Earth	Mars	Jupiter	Saturn	Uranus	Neptune
Diameter (km)	4879	12104	12742	6779	139820	116460	50724	49244

a Work out the scale of the model for the Earth.

b Work out the diameters of the models of the other planets, using the scale you found in part **a**.

c When the Earth and Neptune are on the same side of the Sun, the distance from Earth to Neptune is 4.3 billion kilometres.
What would this distance be in the scale model?

d R Is this a practical scale for a model of the planets in the Solar System?

8 The regulations for building a wheelchair ramp state:

'Maximum slope for wheelchair ramps should be 10 cm of rise to every 120 cm of length.'

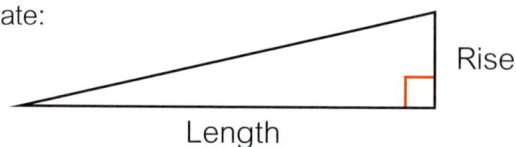

Rise

Length

Draw a scale diagram to work out the maximum angle between the ramp and the ground.

Investigation

9 **a** What scale would you need to use to fit a drawing of the Eiffel Tower (324 m) on to a piece of A3 paper?

b The Burj Khalifa is the tallest building in the world, at 830 m.
What scale would you need to use to draw the Burj Khalifa on a piece of A3 paper?

c The Empire State Building was once the tallest building in the world. It is 443 m tall.
It is drawn to the scale used for the Burj Khalifa in part **b**.
What is the difference in the heights of the drawings of the two buildings?

Reflect

10 Is it always necessary to have units in a map or diagram scale?
If there are no units, what should you do?

5.2 Basic constructions

- Make accurate constructions using drawing equipment

1 A 10 m rope is attached to a metal spike stuck into the ground.
   At the other end of the rope is a paintbrush.
   The rope is pulled tight and the end moved clockwise.
   a Sketch the shape the paintbrush draws on the ground.
   b Draw a scale diagram of this. Use a scale of 1 cm to 1 m.

brush

10 m rope

spike

2 On a netball court the goal circle is 8 feet from the goal post.

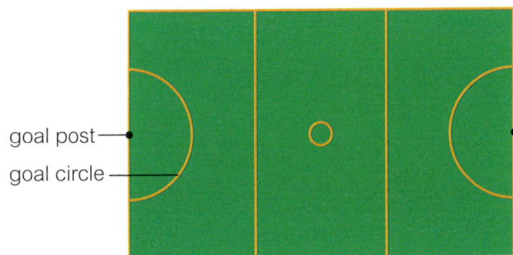

goal post —
goal circle —

Write instructions so the groundskeeper can mark the goal circles.

3 The diagram shows the first steps in constructing an angle bisector.
   a Construct an angle bisector for an acute angle like this.
   b On your construction, draw straight lines to join
      i B to C   ii A to C.
   c Explain why this construction method makes the lengths
      OB, OA, BC and AC equal.
   d What special type of quadrilateral is the shape OABC?
   e What property of the shape OABC do you use to draw the
      angle bisector?
   f When Sian constructs an angle bisector, she changes the radius to draw the arcs from B
      and A. What shape OABC will this give?
   g R   Will joining OC give Sian an angle bisector? Explain.

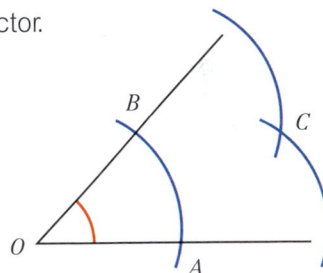

B

C

O

A

4 Draw a line AB that is 9 cm long and mark a point on AB that divides AB in the ratio 1 : 2.
   Construct a perpendicular to AB that goes through the marked point.

5 P-S
   a Construct two circles that intersect at one point only.
   b Construct two circles that intersect at one point only and where one of the circles
      is inside the other.

6 The diagram shows the first steps in constructing
a perpendicular bisector.

a Construct a perpendicular bisector for a line AB like this.

b On your construction, draw straight lines joining

  i A to C and A to D ii B to C and B to D.

c **R** Explain why this construction method makes the lengths AC,
BC, AD, BD equal.

d What special type of quadrilateral is the shape $ABCD$?

e What property of the shape $ABCD$ do you use to draw the perpendicular bisector?

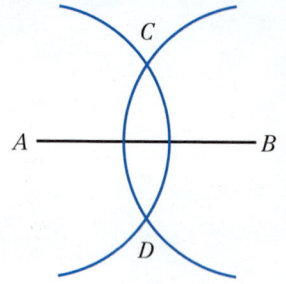

7 Draw a line AB that is 5 cm in length.

a Construct the perpendicular bisector of AB.

b The perpendicular bisector meets AB at point C. Label point C.
Label any other point on the perpendicular bisector as point D.

c Draw the angle bisector for angle ACD.

d Measure 3 cm along your angle bisector and label this point E.

e **R** Will everyone who follows these instructions have their point E in the same relative
position to the line AB? Explain.

f What is the shortest distance between the line AB and the point E?

8 **P-S / R** Draw three dots on your page that are not in a line.

a Use constructions to find a point that is equidistant from each of the three dots.

b Draw three dots on your page in a straight line. Is it still possible to find a point that is
equidistant from all three dots? Explain.

9 Follow these instructions:

a Draw a circle and mark a point on its circumference.

b Open your compasses to the same width as the radius of your circle and put the point at
the place you have marked on the circumference. Make a new arc on the circumference.

c Repeat this until you return to your original point.

d Join the points. What shape have you made?

e **R** Does this always work? Why?

10 a Construct two intersecting circles with the *same* radius.

  i Join the centres of the two circles with a line.

  ii Join the points where the circles cross each other with a line.

  iii What fact can you state about the two lines you have drawn?

b Repeat part **a** for two intersecting circles with *different* radii.

c **R** When you draw the perpendicular bisector of a line, you start by drawing arcs or
circles with the same radius. Explain why.

11 How does knowing how constructions use the properties of shapes help you to
remember how to do the constructions?

5.3 Constructing triangles

- Construct accurate triangles
- Construct accurate nets of solids involving triangles

1   Construct an equilateral triangle.
    a Construct a perpendicular bisector of the base of the triangle.
    b What angle sizes have you made?
    c Construct an angle bisector of one of the angles of the triangle.
    d What angle sizes have you made?

2   Construct an angle of exactly 60°.

3   Construct an angle of exactly 45°.

4   Construct an angle of exactly 105°.

Q4 hint Use your answers to Q2 and Q3.

5   The diagram shows an equilateral triangle with a circle that just fits inside it.
    Follow these instructions to construct an accurate copy.
    a Construct an equilateral triangle.
    b Construct the angle bisector of each angle.
    c Draw a circle using the point where the bisectors cross as its centre.

6   Repeat the instructions from Q5 but use a non-equilateral triangle.
    What is the same and what is different?

7   Follow these instructions:
    a Construct an equilateral triangle.
    b Construct the perpendicular bisector of each side.
    c Draw a circle using the point where the bisectors cross as its centre and the distance
       between the point and the vertices of the triangle as the radius.

8   Repeat the instructions from Q7 but use a non-equilateral triangle.
    What is the same and what is different?

9   a Construct a triangle with sides 5 cm, 12 cm and 13 cm.
    b What type of triangle is this?
    c R   Another triangle has sides 7.5 cm, 18 cm and 19.5 cm.
       Is this a right-angled triangle? Explain how you know.

10 P-S   Construct an isosceles right-angled triangle.
    What size are the angles in your triangle?

11 Follow these instructions to construct a square:

    a Draw a line 15 cm long.

    b Label the end points A and D.

    c Mark 5 cm intervals on the line, so that you have points A, B, C, D.

    d Construct perpendicular bisectors of AC and of BD.

    e Measure 5 cm along the new lines.
       Join them to make the square.

12 P-S A tetrahedron is a solid with four faces.

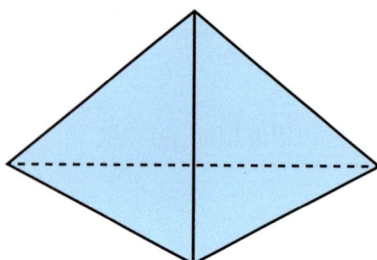

    In a regular tetrahedron, each face is an equilateral triangle.

    a Sketch a net of a regular tetrahedron.

    b Construct an accurate net of a regular tetrahedron
       with side length 6 cm.

13 P-S The cross-section of a triangular prism is an isosceles triangle.
This triangle has sides with lengths 5 cm, 8 cm and 8 cm.
The prism is 4 cm long.
Construct an accurate net for this prism.

14 a R Explain why a regular hexagon can be divided into six congruent
      equilateral triangles.

    b Construct a regular hexagon using equilateral triangles.

15 Construct a rhombus by following these instructions.

    a Draw an angle of any size.

    b Bisect the angle using arcs of circles of equal size.

    c Join your construction arcs to make a rhombus.

16 P-S

    a Construct a parallelogram with an area of 12 cm².

    b Construct a different parallelogram with an area of 12 cm².

Reflect

17 Look back at the questions in this lesson.
Describe two ways of constructing

    a a right angle   **b** a 45° angle.

5.4 Using accurate scale diagrams

- Construct and draw accurate scale diagrams
- Use scale diagrams to solve problems

1 **P-S** Copy the line AB. The point C lies on AB and is 4 cm from A.

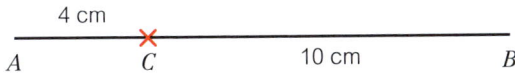

4 cm

A C 10 cm B

Construct a point P below the line so that the shortest possible distance from P to C is 5 cm.

2 Draw an angle of 80°. Construct the angle bisector.

a Measure a distance of 5 cm from the vertex along each arm of the angle and mark a new point.

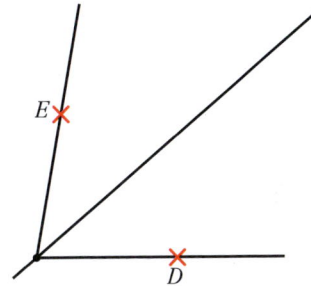

E

D

b Measure the shortest distance from each new point to the angle bisector.

c Repeat with two new points 7 cm from the vertex.

d What do you notice?
What could you say about any point on the bisector?

3 Riyad is planning the security for a bank.
He has a plan of the bank.
The blue dots show the movement detection sensors.
The red square is the safe Riyad is protecting.
The door to the room is on the left.

7 m

door

safe 5 m

a What scale is used here?

b **P-S** Draw an accurate scale drawing.
Choose your own scale.

c Each corner motion detector sees in a straight line across the room, at an equal distance from each wall it is attached to.
Add these lines onto your diagram.

d Each dot in the middle of the room shows a motion detector that can detect anything that comes within 0.5 metres of it. Show these areas on your diagram.

e **R** There have been budget cuts and Riyad is now only allowed to install two motion detectors. Which two do you think he should keep, to make it the most difficult to get to the safe undetected? Explain your reasoning.

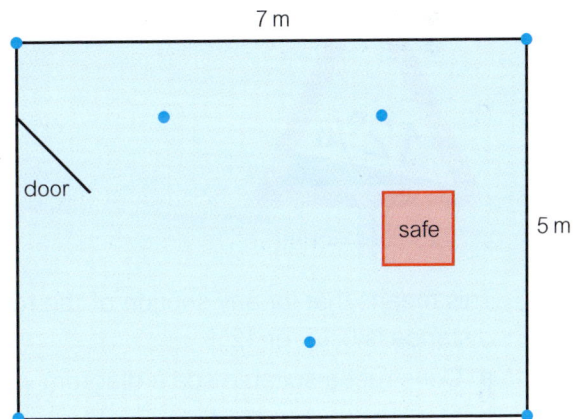

4 **P-S** A school has a set of six steps.
Each step is 15 cm tall.
The school needs to build a wheelchair ramp to reach the same height.
Wheelchair ramps must be at an angle of 5° to the ground.
Create and use a scale diagram to find the length of the slope of the ramp.

5 **P-S / R** Ashley is standing 8 metres away from a tree.
When she looks up at a 60° angle, she is looking directly at a bird's nest in the tree.
Ashley is 1.7 metres tall.

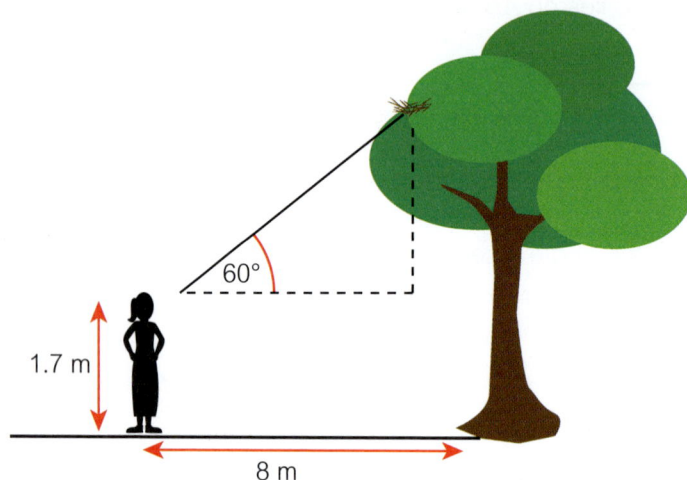

a By drawing a scale drawing, estimate the height of the nest.

b Explain why your answer to part **a** is an estimate and not an exact answer.

6 The gradient of a road is 12%.

This means that for any section of the road, the vertical height divided by the horizontal distance is 0.12, or 12%.

a Construct a suitable scale diagram with vertical height 1.5 cm.

b Measure the angle of the road to the horizontal.

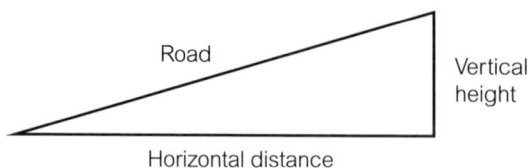

7 **P-S** Bryn wants to buy a tent.
He sees an advertisement for a tent like this.

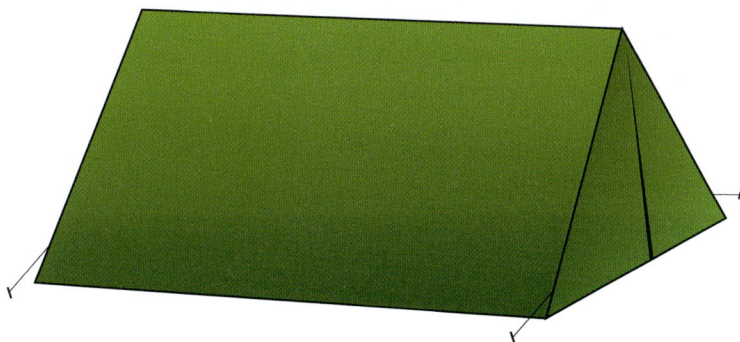

The advertisement shows the front of the tent is an isosceles triangle with sides 2.4 m and base 2 m.
Bryn is 1.73 m tall.
By drawing a scale diagram, decide whether Bryn would be able to stand up in the tent.

8 Gregory says that in a square, a line drawn from one vertex to $\frac{2}{3}$ of the way up the opposite side will cross the reflection of that line at 70°.

  a By drawing several different scale drawings of the diagram, investigate whether this is always, sometimes, or never true.
  b Repeat part **a** for a line drawn from one vertex to $\frac{1}{3}$ of the way up the opposite side.

9 In Q3 you solved a problem by using a scale drawing.
Would it have been possible to solve the problem without using a scale drawing?
Explain why, or why not.

5 Extend

1 **P-S** Asif is buying a new flat.
He wants to know if he can fit his sofa around a corner to get it into the flat's living room.
The sofa is 160 cm long and 80 cm deep.

a Make and cut out a scale drawing of the sofa to the same scale as this plan of the flat.

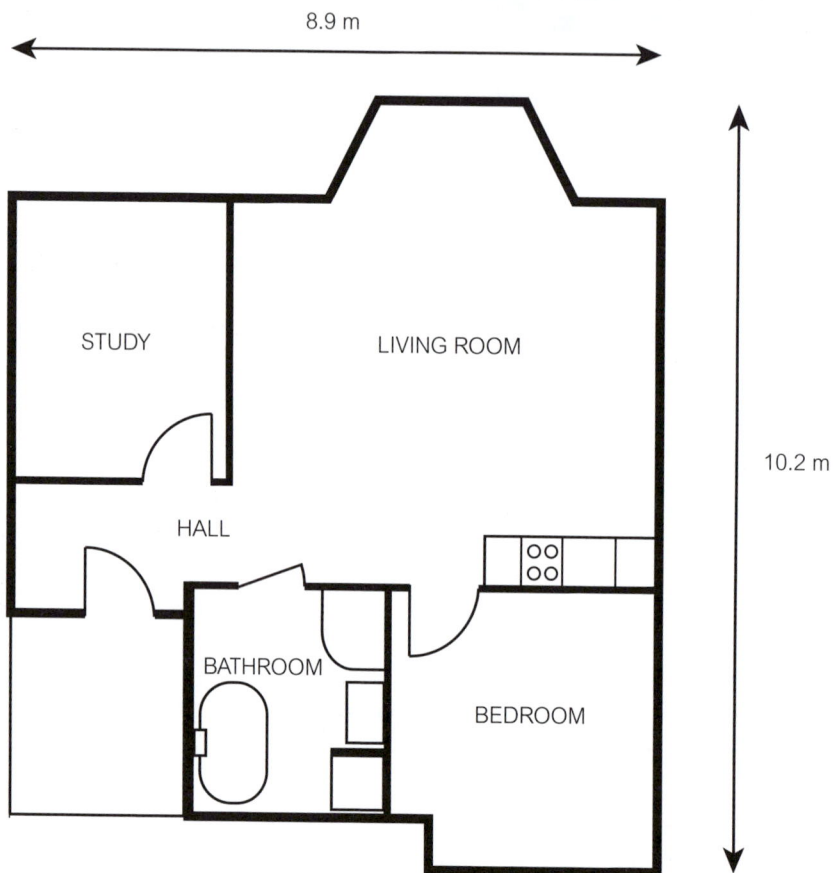

b Use your scale drawing to decide whether the sofa will fit through.

2 **R** Nazim is practising drawing triangles.
He wants to draw a triangle with side lengths of 3 cm, 3 cm and 7 cm.
Explain why Nazim will not be able to draw this triangle.

3 **P-S** For each set of sides, suggest the shortest possible integer length for a third side, to make a possible triangle.

a 3 cm, 3 cm, _____ **b** 3 cm, 7 cm, _____ **c** 3 cm, 5 cm, _____

4 On a map with scale 1 : 200 000, a road is 6 cm long.
How long will the same road be on a map with scale 1 : 150 000?

5 P-S Work out the surface area of this triangular prism.

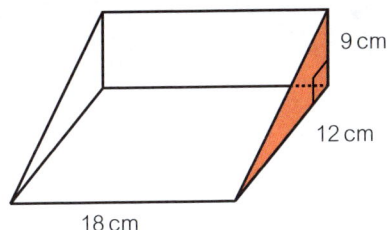

9 cm

12 cm

18 cm

6 P-S A field is in the shape of a triangle ABC, with measurements as shown.
By constructing a suitable diagram, find the shortest distance from A to BC.

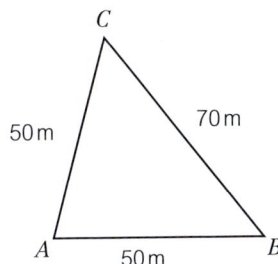

C

50 m

70 m

A 50 m B

7 P-S Use a ruler and compasses to construct a regular octagon inside a square.

> **Q7 hint** Start by dividing the angle at the centre of the square into eight equal parts.

8 P-S Use constructions to split a line segment AB into three equal parts.

> **Q8 hint** Start by drawing a line at an angle below the line segment AB and use compasses to mark three equal lengths along this line, starting at A. Then draw in the third side of triangle ABC.
>
> A B
>
> C

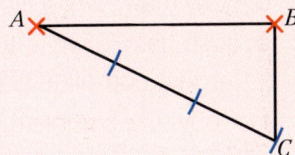

Investigation

9 In Lesson 5.3 you constructed these two diagrams using equilateral triangles.

  a What happens if you do the same constructions using a square instead of a triangle?

  b What happens if you use a rectangle?

  c Try this for other shapes and see what happens. Do you notice any patterns?

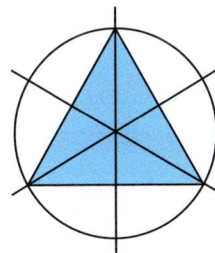

Reflect

10 Throughout this unit you have used constructions to create shapes.
In what ways has this improved your understanding of the properties of these shapes?

6 Sequences, inequalities, equations and proportion

Master   Extend p71

6.1 nth term of arithmetic sequences

- Use the nth term to generate a sequence
- Find and use the nth term of a sequence

1 **P-S** Look at the pattern of black and white tiles.

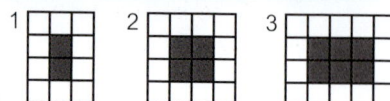

  a Copy and complete the table.

Pattern number	1	2	3	4	5
Number of white tiles	10	12			
Number of black tiles	2	4			

  b Write down the nth term for the sequence of:

    i black tiles   ii white tiles.

  c How many black tiles will there be in the 15th pattern?

> **Q1c hint** Use the nth term.

  d How many white tiles will there be in the 20th pattern?

  e Josh has 75 white tiles and 67 black tiles. Which is the largest complete pattern he can make?

  f Copy and complete the table for the sequence of the total number of tiles (black and white).

Pattern number	1	2	3	4	5
Total number of tiles	12				

  g Find the nth term for the sequence of the total number of tiles.

  h **R** Add together the nth term for the sequence of black tiles and the nth term for the sequence of white tiles. What do you notice?

2 a Copy the table and write in the first five square numbers.

Term	1st	2nd	3rd	4th	5th
Square numbers	1	4			
Triangle numbers	1	3			

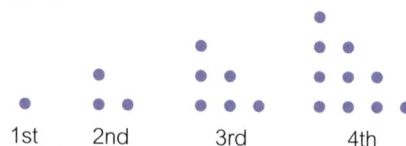

  b Write the first five triangle numbers in your table. Use the diagrams to help you.

  c Add together the 1st and 2nd triangle numbers. Is your answer a square number?

  d Find other pairs of triangle numbers that add to make a square number.

  e Split these square numbers into two triangle numbers: i 36   ii 49   iii 81

3 Here is a sequence of fractions: $\frac{2}{7}, \frac{3}{10}, \frac{4}{13}, \frac{5}{16}, \frac{6}{19}, \ldots$

  a Work out the nth term of the sequence of numerators.

  b Work out the nth term of the sequence of denominators.

  c Write the nth term of the sequence of fractions.

4 Here is a sequence of fractions: $\frac{5}{8}, \frac{7}{10}, \frac{9}{12}, \frac{11}{14}, \frac{13}{16}, \ldots$

    a Find the nth term of the sequence.

    b R Convert the fractions to decimals. Is this a linear sequence? Explain.

5 **a** Write the first five terms of the sequence with nth term: **i** $3n - 2$ **ii** $5n + 2$

    b Divide each term of the sequence with nth term $3n - 2$ by the corresponding term in the sequence with nth term $5n + 2$. Write the terms as fractions.
Write the nth term of this new sequence.

    c Add the corresponding terms of the sequences with nth terms $3n - 2$ and $5n + 2$.
Write the nth term of this new sequence.

    d Subtract each term of the sequence with nth term $3n - 2$ from the corresponding term in the sequence with nth term $5n + 2$. Write the nth term of this new sequence.

    e R Write the nth term of the sequence formed by finding the product of the corresponding terms in the sequences with nth term $3n - 2$ and $5n + 2$.

6 **a** Copy and complete the table for the sequence with nth term $2n - 3$.

Term	1	2	3	4	5
$2n - 3$	−1				

    b Copy and complete the table of values for $y = 2x - 3$.

x	−2	−1	0	1	2
$y = 2x - 3$	−7				

    c What is the same and what is different about the tables in parts **a** and **b**?

    d R Do the values of y form a linear sequence? Explain.

    e R Is the graph of $y = 2x - 3$ a straight line? Explain.

7 **R** Decide whether each statement is true or false.

    a The sequence with nth term $6n - 8$ has only one negative term.

    b The sequence with nth term $8 - 6n$ has only one negative term.

    c The sequence with nth term $8 - 6n$ is an increasing sequence.

    d The sequence with nth term $8 - 6n$ has a first term of 8.

    e The first term of the sequence with nth term $6n - 8$ is less than the first term of the sequence with nth term $8 - 6n$.

8 **R** Show that the sequence with nth term $-5n + 12$ has only two positive terms.

Investigation

9 A linear sequence has common difference -3.

    a What is the first negative term when the first term is: **i** 1   **ii** 2   **iii** 3

    b Continue this pattern up to the sequence with first term 20. What do you notice?

    c Predict the pattern for a linear sequence with common difference -4.
Check your prediction.

Reflect

10 In Q1–Q5 you found the nth terms of sequences by finding two separate nth terms and combining them. Do two linear nth terms always combine to give a linear nth term? Use examples from this lesson to explain.

6.2 Non-linear sequences

- Recognise and continue geometric sequences
- Recognise and continue quadratic sequences

1 State whether each sequence is arithmetic, geometric, quadratic or 'other'.

  a 2, 5, 8, 11, 14

  b 2, 5, 12.5, 31.25

  c 2, 5, 7, 12, 19, 31

  d 2, 5, 10, 17, 26

2 **R** Brooke says,
'If you know the first two terms of a sequence, you can continue the sequence'.
Explain why Brooke is wrong.

3 The first two terms of a sequence are 4, 7.

  a Continue it as an arithmetic sequence for three more terms.

  b Continue it as a geometric sequence for three more terms.

  c Continue it as a quadratic sequence for three more terms.

  d R Was there only one possible answer for each part? Explain.

4 Copy and complete the tables for these sequences:

a

Position (n)	1	2	3	4
Term ($n + 2$)				

c

Position (n)	1	2	3	4
Term ($n^3 + 2$)				

b

Position (n)	1	2	3	4
Term ($n^2 + 2$)				

d

Position (n)	1	2	3	4
Term ($n^4 + 2$)				

5 **R** Work out the 1st, 2nd and 3rd differences for each sequence in Q4.
What do you notice?

6 **R** Look at this sequence:
   2, 2$\sqrt{5}$, 10, 10$\sqrt{5}$, ...

  a Find the next three terms in the sequence.

  b What type of sequence is it?

7 The nth term of a sequence is 3^n.

  a Work out the first three terms of the sequence.

  b What type of sequence is it?

  c What is the term-to-term rule of the sequence?

  d Work out the first three terms of the sequence 2^n.

  e Work out the first three terms of the sequence 4^n.

  f R What can you conclude about these types of sequences?

8 R The number of radioactive atoms in a material decreases every 6 hours.
Here are the recordings for the first 30 hours:
   1024, 512, 256, 128, 64
   a What type of sequence is it forming?
   b What is each term multiplied by?

9 A sequence is made of squares.
The side lengths of the squares increase by 1.2 cm each time.
The side length of the first square is 6 cm.
   a What is the nth term of the sequence of the side lengths of the squares?
   b What are the areas of the first five squares?
   c What type of sequence do the areas form?
   d A different sequence of squares is made, where the side lengths are multiplied by 1.2 each time.
      i What type of sequence is formed by the side lengths?
      ii What type of sequence is formed by the areas?

10 P-S Here are the first four terms of some sequences.

n^2	1, 4, 9, 16
$n^2 + 1$	2, 5, 10, 17
$n^2 - 3$	−2, 1, 6, 13
$2n^2$	2, 8, 18, 32
$2n^2 - 1$	1, 7, 17, 31
$2n^2 + 2$	4, 10, 20, 34

   a What are the 2nd differences of the sequences with n^2 in the nth term?

> **Q10a hint** Find the 2nd differences of all the sequences.

   b What are the 2nd differences of the sequences with $2n^2$ in the nth term?
   c Work out the 2nd differences of this sequence:
      7, 13, 23, 37, …
   d Write the term involving n^2 for the sequence in part **c**.
   e Work out the nth term for the sequence 7, 13, 23, 37, …

> **Q10d hint** Use your answers to parts **a** and **b**. Is it n^2 or $2n^2$?

11 Find the nth term of each sequence.
   a 9, 15, 25, 39, 57
   b −5, 1, 11, 25, 43
   c −4, 5, 20, 41, 68
   d 4, 13, 28, 49, 76
   e 1.5, 3, 5.5, 9, 13.5

12 a Work out the first five terms of the sequence with nth term $\dfrac{n^2 - 1}{n + 1}$.
   b Expand $(n + 1)(n - 1)$.
   c R Use your answer to part **b** to explain your answer to part **a**.

13 P-S The second term of a quadratic sequence is 8.
The third term is 12. The fourth term is 18. What is the first term?

Reflect

14 In Q4 and Q5 you compared the differences in various sequences.
What is the relationship between the highest power in the nth term and the differences?

6.3 Inequalities

- Represent inequalities on a number line
- Find integer values that satisfy an inequality

1 In a science experiment, Greg mixes vinegar and calcium carbonate to make a 'volcano'. He uses 150 ml of vinegar. In order to get the volcano to erupt Greg must use x grams of calcium carbonate, where $3x \leqslant 150$.

    a Solve the inequality.

    b Greg has 35 g of calcium carbonate. Does this satisfy the inequality?

> **Key point** You can solve inequalities in a similar way to solving equations.

2 Solve these inequalities. Show each solution on a number line.

    a $x + 3 > 5$

    b $x - 6 > 14$

    c $2x < 10$

    d $\frac{x}{3} > 9$

    e $2x + 1 > 13$

    f $3x - 2 < 7$

> **Q2 hint** You can solve an inequality in a similar way to solving an equation.

3 **R** Muhammed and Arthur both solve the inequality $7 - 2x > 11$.

Muhammed's method:

$$7 - 2x > 11$$
$$7 > 11 + 2x$$
$$-4 > 2x$$
$$-2 > x$$

Arthur's method:

$$7 - 2x > 11$$
$$-2x > 4$$
$$x < -2$$

    a Show that the two solutions $-2 > x$ and $x < -2$ are equivalent.

    b What did Arthur do between line 2 and line 3?

    c Which method do you prefer and why?

4 Solve these inequalities.

    a $8 - x < 11$ **b** $-2x > 7$

    c $-4x < 12$ **d** $5 - x > -7$

    e $-\frac{x}{2} > 6$

> **Q4 hint** Check that your answers make sense by substituting your solution into the original inequality

5 Solve these inequalities. Show each solution on a number line.

    a $2(x + 3) < 18$ **b** $5(x - 3) > 17$

    c $6(x + 7) < -3$ **d** $8 > 8(x - 2)$

6 Copy and complete the solution to the inequality $1 < x + 3 < 7$.

$1 < x + 3$ $x + 3 < 7$

$\square < x$ $x < \square$

$\square < x < \square$

7 Solve these inequalities. Show each solution on a number line.

a $-2 < x + 4 < 5$ **b** $0 \leqslant y - 5 \leqslant 3$

c $8 \geqslant 2y > 2$ **d** $2 > \dfrac{x}{4} \geqslant -1$

> **Q7 hint** Do the same operation to all three parts of the inequality so that the variable is on its own in the middle.

8 **P-S** Kyle says, 'I think of an integer and double it. The answer is greater than 2 but smaller than 14'.

a Write an inequality to represent this information.

b Solve the inequality and show the solution on a number line.

c Write down all the numbers Kyle could have chosen.

> **Q8a hint** $\square < 2x < \square$

9 Solve these inequalities. Show each solution on a number line.

a $2n + 1 \leqslant 5$ **b** $3n - 8 > 1$

c $\dfrac{x}{2} + 7 < 11$ **d** $\dfrac{x}{3} - 2 \geqslant -4$

10 Solve these inequalities. Show each solution on a number line. The first one has been started for you.

a $-1 \leqslant 2y + 3 < 9$

$-1 - 3 \leqslant 2y < 9 - 3$

$-4 \leqslant 2y < 6$

$-\dfrac{4}{2} \leqslant y < \dfrac{6}{2}$

$\square \leqslant y < \square$

b $1 < 3x - 2 < 10$

c $19 > 5n - 1 > 4$

d $29 > 4p + 1 > -7$

11 **P-S** Lucy says,
'I think of an integer, multiply it by 3 and then subtract 5. The answer is greater than 7 but smaller than 12'.

a Write an inequality to represent this information.

b Solve the inequality and show the solution on a number line.

c Write down all of the numbers Lucy could have chosen.

Reflect

12 You have solved many different inequalities in this lesson.
What is the same and what is different about solving inequalities and solving equations?
Look at your answers to Q4 and Q7 to help you think about the differences.

6.4 Solving equations

- Construct and solve equations including fractions or powers

1 Use inverse operations to solve these equations.
Write your solutions to 1 decimal place.

 a $x^3 = 75$ **b** $x^3 = 95$ **c** $x^3 + 2 = 49$

 d $x^3 - 7 = 87$ **e** $2x^3 = 145$ **f** $3x^3 - 1 = 59$

2 R

 a Work out x^3 when $x = 3$.

 b Work out x^3 when $x = 4$.

 c Hester says that the solution to $x^3 = 39$ must be between 3 and 4.
  Show that Hester is correct.

 d Copy and complete Hester's table:

x	x^3	Comment
3		Too small
4		Too big
3.5		
3.4		
3.3		

 e Explain why the value of x must be between 3.3 and 3.4.

 f What value is halfway between 3.3 and 3.4? Write this in your table.

 g Use the values in your table to show that the solution to $x^3 = 39$ is between 3.35 and 3.4.
  Explain why $x = 3.4$ to 1 decimal place.

 h Solve $x^3 = 39$ using a calculator.

 i This method is called 'trial and improvement' because you estimate the solution, try it out
  and then improve your estimate.
  What are the advantages and disadvantages of using trial and improvement to find the
  solution to $x^3 = 39$?

3 Use trial and improvement to find the value of y (to 1 decimal
place) in these equations.

 a $y^2 + y = 46$ **b** $y^3 + y = 425$ **c** $y^3 + 2y = 75$

 d $y^3 - y = 94$ **e** $y^3 - y^2 = 431$ **f** $y^3 - 4y = 167$

> **Q3a hint**
>
> | y^2 | $y^2 + y$ | Comment |
> |---|---|---|
> | | | |

4 **P-S** A packaging company uses the formula $T = x^2 + x$ to calculate how much tape (T), in
cm, is needed to wrap a cube-shaped package of side length x cm.
What is the side length of a package that needs

 a 45 cm of tape   **b** 65 cm of tape?

Give your answers correct to 1 decimal place.

5 **P-S** The diagram shows a box made from a cube with an additional cuboid attached.
The area of the cuboid's end face is $7\,\text{cm}^2$.
The entire box has a volume of $140\,\text{cm}^3$.
How long is each side of the cube?
Give your answer to 1 decimal place.

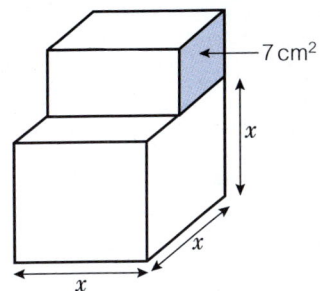

6 Solve:

a $\dfrac{x-2}{3} = \dfrac{x+3}{6}$ **b** $\dfrac{11x+6}{5} = \dfrac{3x+8}{2}$

c $\dfrac{4x-9}{3} = \dfrac{3x+2}{4}$ **d** $\dfrac{4x+23}{9} = \dfrac{2x+14}{6}$

7 **P-S** The diagram shows an isosceles triangle ABC.

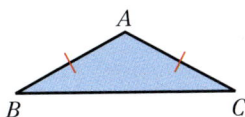

In triangle ABC, $\angle ABC = \dfrac{11x-10}{10}$ and $\angle ACB = \dfrac{7x+46}{8}$.

a Write an equation using the fact that $\angle ABC = \angle ACB$.

b Solve your equation to find the value of x.

c Work out the size of $\angle ABC$ and $\angle ACB$.

d Work out the size of $\angle BAC$.

Investigation

8 **a** Copy and complete the table to find a solution to $x^3 - 6x + 3 = 0$.
Give your solution correct to 1 decimal place.

x	$x^3 - 6x + 3$	Comment
1		
3		

b Repeat part **a**, starting with $x = 1$ and $x = 0$.

c Repeat part **a**, starting with $x = 0$ and $x = -3$.

d What do you notice?

e Is it the same if you are solving $x^3 - 6x + 3 = 1$?

Reflect

9 In Q1 and Q2 you solved equations $x^3 = \ldots$ using a calculator and using trial and improvement. Which way did you prefer? Why?

6.5 Proportion

- Write formulae connecting variables in direct or inverse proportion
- Use algebra to solve problems involving direct or inverse proportion

1 The table shows the cost of hiring a car.

Number of days	2	5	9
Cost (£)	27	67.50	121.50

   a R Show that the cost of hiring a car is in direct proportion to the number of days.

   b Write a formula connecting cost and number of days.

2 The table shows the distances
(in metres and yards) that a golfer hits
a ball with different clubs.

   a Calculate the missing distances x, y and z.
   Give your answers to the nearest integer.

Club	Distance (yards)	Distance (metres)
9-iron	140	128
7-iron	162	x
4-iron	y	194
Driver	z	306

   b R How did you work out the missing distances?

3 The circumference of Sian's head is 48 cm. Her height is 162 cm.

   a Write Sian's head circumference to height as a ratio.

   b Sian assumes that head circumference and height are in direct proportion.
   Use this model to predict:

   i the height of a person with head circumference 35 cm

   ii the head circumference of a person 185 cm tall.

4 P-S The South African rand, R, varies in direct proportion with the UK pound, P.
One day 801 South African rand are worth £45.

   a Write a formula for converting pounds to rand.

   b How many South African rand could you buy with £250?

   c How many UK pounds could you buy with 650 South African rand?

5 P-S x and y are in direct proportion.

   a Write a formula for y.

   b Work out the missing value t.

x	0.7	t	3.5
y	4.2	14.4	21

6 The table shows data from a science experiment.

   a Work out the value of xy for each pair of values.

   b R Is y **inversely proportional** to x? Explain.

x	0.9	2.5	7.5	20
y	40	14.4	4.8	1.8

   c Check whether these sets of data are inversely proportional.

i

P	1	3	9	20
Q	540	440	230	73

ii

r	2.5	8	20	40
s	20	6.25	2.5	1.25

7   The weight, W, of an object is in direct proportion to the mass, m, of the object.
    On Earth, a 14 kg object weighs 137.2 N.

    a Work out the weight of an 18 kg object on Earth.

    b The formula connecting mass and weight is
       $W = m \times$ acceleration due to gravity.
       What is the value of the acceleration due to gravity on Earth?

    c On the Moon, the acceleration due to gravity is 1.6 m/s^2.

       i   What is the formula connecting the weight and mass of objects on the Moon?

       ii Work out the weight of the 14 kg object on the Moon.

> **Q7 hint** Mass is measured in kg. Weight is a force and is measured in N (newtons).

> **Q7b hint** The units for the acceleration due to gravity are m/s^2.

8   The pressure, P, exerted by an object is inversely proportional to the area, A.
    When an object is placed on an area of 8 cm^2, the pressure is 180 N/cm^2.

    a Write a formula linking P and A.

    b Work out the pressure when the same object is placed on an area of 30 cm^2.

    c Work out the area when the pressure exerted by the object is 576 N/cm^2.

9   Variable x is proportional to the square of y. You can write this as $x = ky^2$.
    When x is 20, y is 2.

    a Work out the value of k.

    b Work out the value of x when y is 5.

    c Work out the value of y when x is 80.

10 **P-S** A stone is dropped from a tall building.
    The distance it falls is proportional to the square of the time it takes to fall.
    The stone falls 19.6 metres in 2 seconds. How far will it fall in 4 seconds?

11 a Match each statement with the correct equation.

    A y is proportional to the square of x

    B y is inversely proportional to the cube of x

    C y is inversely proportional to x

    D y is proportional to x

    i $y = kx$

    ii $y = \dfrac{k}{x^3}$

    iii $y = kx^2$

    iv $y = \dfrac{k}{x^2}$

    v $y = \dfrac{k}{x}$

    b **P-S** Write a statement for the extra card.

12 What is the same about all the equations where y is proportional to x^n?
    Think about the equations when n = 1, 2 or 3.
    What is the same about all the equations where y is inversely proportional to x^n?

6 Extend

1　P-S

　　a　For which values of x are these statements true?

　　　　i　$\dfrac{2x}{3} = \dfrac{4x}{6}$

　　　　ii　$\dfrac{3x + 1}{2} = \dfrac{2x + 1}{3}$

　　　　iii　$\dfrac{3x^2 + 3}{9} = \dfrac{x^2 + 1}{3}$

　　　　iv　$\dfrac{3x}{8} = \dfrac{8x}{3}$

　　b　An identity is true for all values of x.
　　　　Write whether each statement from part **a** is an equation or an identity.

　　c　R　Why do you think equations like the one in part **iv** are sometime called 'trivial cases'?

2　P-S　An aeroplane travels 720 miles in 90 minutes.
　　The distance travelled, d, is in direct proportion to the time, t.

　　a　Work out how far the aeroplane travels at this speed
　　　　i　in 140 minutes
　　　　ii　in 1 hour 15 minutes.

　　The formula connecting distance and time is $d = s \times t$.

　　b　What is the speed of the plane in miles per hour?

　　c　The distance from London to New York is 3450 miles.
　　　　Use your formula to work out the journey time flying from London to New York.

> **Q2b hint**
> 90 minutes = $\square.\square$ hours.

3　R　The first five terms of a sequence are 10, 21, 38, 61, 90.

　　a　What type of sequence is it?
　　b　Find the first five terms of the sequence with nth term $2n + 5$.
　　c　Subtract your sequence in part **b** from the original sequence.
　　d　What type of sequence did you create in part **c**?
　　e　What is the nth term of the sequence?
　　f　What do you think the nth term of the original sequence is?

4　P-S　Two arithmetic sequences have the same third term.
　　One sequence has nth term $8n + a$ and the other has nth term $b - 2n$.

　　a　The first term of the first sequence is 19.5. What is the value of b?
　　b　The fifth term of the second sequence is 0. What is the value of a?
　　c　R　How many possible values of a and b are there if you don't know any of the terms
　　　　in either sequence?

5　a　P-S　How many terms in the sequence with nth term $3n^2 + 2n + 1$ are less than 100?

　　b　Write the nth term of a linear sequence that will have exactly three terms which are
　　　　greater than the third term of the sequence with nth term $3n^2 + 2n + 1$.

6　P-S　Write the nth term of a sequence whose 1st differences follow the linear sequence $6n$.

7 **P-S** The 11th term of the sequence with nth term $\dfrac{3n + a}{a - 2n^2}$ is 1000. What is the value of a?

8 **P-S** The sum of the first three terms of the sequence with nth term $2n^2 + b$, where b is a constant, is 40. What is the value of b?

9 **P-S / R** The diagram shows a square, a rectangle and two triangles.

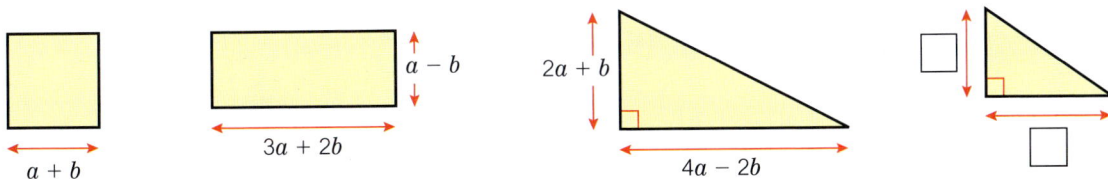

The total area of the square and the rectangle is the same as the total area of the two triangles.

a Write an expression for the length and the height of the small triangle in terms of **a** and **b**.

b Is your answer to part **a** the only answer? Explain why.

10 **P-S** Copy and complete the inequality so that the smallest possible value of x is 12.

$$\dfrac{\square x + \square}{\square} \geqslant \square$$

11 **P-S** Copy and complete the inequality so that the only possible integer value of x is 3.

$$\square + \square x < \square x + \square < \square + \square x$$

Investigation

12 The nth term of a sequence is $2n + 1$.

a What is the sum of the first:

i three terms   **ii** four terms   **iii** five terms?

b What pattern do you see?

c Repeat part **a** with $3n + 1$.
What is the same and what is different?

d Predict what will happen with $4n + 1$. Check your answers.

Investigation

13 **P-S** The diagram shows the first 3 hexagons in a pattern.

How many dots will there be in H_{15}?

Reflect

14 In this unit you have worked with algebraic representations. How has the algebra helped you to see underlying patterns and relationships in the mathematics?

7 Circles, Pythagoras and prisms

Master   **Extend p83**

7.1 Circumference of a circle

- Calculate the circumference of a circle
- Estimate calculations involving pi (π)
- Solve problems involving the circumference of a circle

1 The circumference of a circle is 25 cm.
   a What is the radius? Write the entire number shown by your calculator.
   b How many times greater than the diameter is the circumference?
      Give your full calculator value.
   c **R** Why is your answer to part **b** not exactly π?

2 **P-S** A cylindrical electromagnet core is rotated 165 times to wind 17.5 m of copper wire onto it.

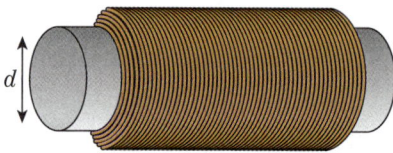

   a Work out the diameter d of the core.
   b **R** Explain why you cannot give an exact measure for the diameter.

3 **P-S** A quarter-circle has a perimeter of 50 cm.
   Work out its radius, r cm.

   > **Q3 hint** Write an equation involving π and r.

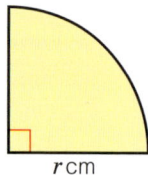

   r cm

4 **P-S** The diagram shows a car wheel.
   On a journey to work and back, the wheel rotates 50 000 times.
   What is the total length of the journey?
   Give your answer in kilometres to 1 decimal place.

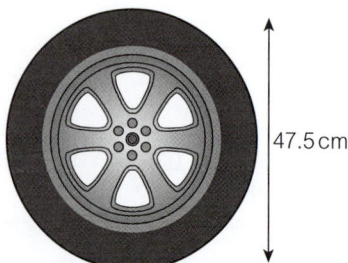

   47.5 cm

5 **R** **a** What fraction of the circle is shaded?

b What fraction of the circumference is **arc** AB?

c Calculate

    i the circumference of the circle

    ii the length of the arc AB.

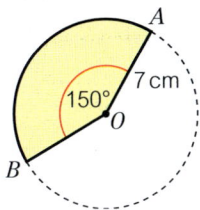

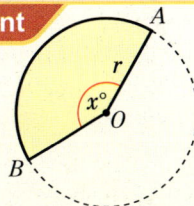
6 **P-S** Work out the radius of each **sector**.

a

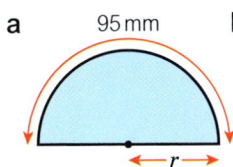

95 mm

b

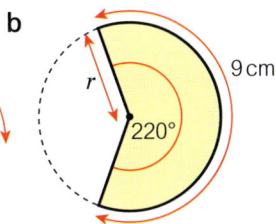

c

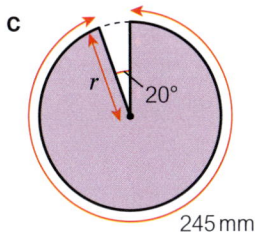

245 mm

7 **P-S / R** The length of an arc of a circle is 18 cm.
The radius of the circle is 3 cm.

a What is the angle of the arc?

b Why can you not give an exact answer to part **a**?

8 **P-S** The perimeter of $\frac{3}{8}$ of a circle is 24 cm. What is the radius?

9 **P-S** The diagram shows five **concentric** circles.

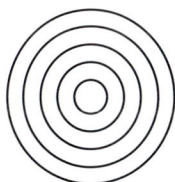

The smallest circle has a circumference of 2π cm.
The largest circle has a circumference of 6π cm.
There is an equal space between every circle and the next.
What is the space between each pair of circles?

10 **P-S** The diagram shows four concentric circles.
Circle 1 has a radius of 3 cm.
There is a space of 1 cm between each circle and the next.

a Write the circumference of each circle, 1 to 4, in terms of π.

b What is the circumference of circle n, in terms of π?

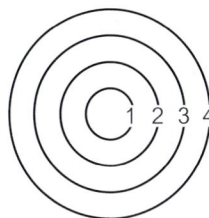

Reflect

11 In every question in this lesson, you have used π.
When has this affected the accuracy of your answers? Explain.

7.2 Area of a circle

- Calculate the area of a circle
- Solve problems involving the area of a circle

1   **P-S**   The diagram shows a donkey tethered to a rail using a 5 m rope.

   Q1 hint Draw a diagram to show the area it can graze.

   a   Work out the area that the donkey can graze.

   b   The donkey walks around the edge of the grazing area five times. How far has it walked?

     30 m

2   The radius of a circle is 10 cm.

   a   Use the π button on your calculator to calculate the area of the circle.

   b   Use an estimate of π to 1 decimal place to calculate the area.

   c   Use an estimate of π to the nearest integer to calculate the area.

   d   Use the fraction $\frac{22}{7}$, an approximation of π, to calculate the area.

   e   **R**   Which method do you think is the best to use if you don't have a calculator? Why?

3   **P-S**   The diagram uses area to represent the values of two football clubs in 2019.

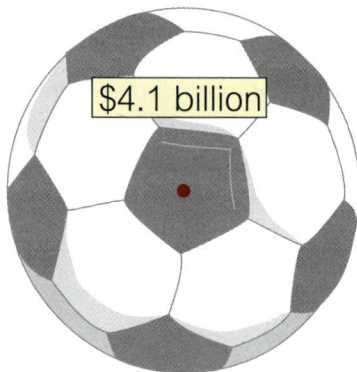

$4.1 billion

$? billion

Manchester United   Arsenal

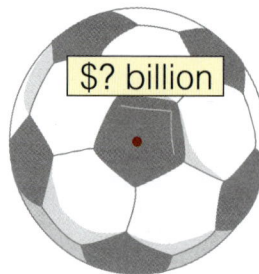

   a   Measure the radius of each circle.

   b   Estimate the value of Arsenal.

Investigation

4   The diameter of a circular patio is 3.6 m.

   a   Work out its circumference and area.

   b   The diameter is doubled. What happens to: **i** the circumference   **ii** the area?

   c   Work out a rule to describe how the circumference and area change for different diameters of patio.

5 The diagram shows a children's sandpit.
Work out the area of the sandpit.

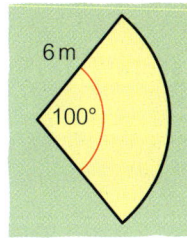

6 m
100°

Key point

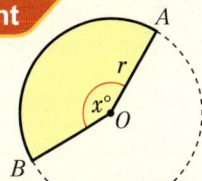

Area of sector = $\frac{x}{360} \times \pi r^2$

6 **P-S** The diagram shows a company logo.

On their advertisement, the diameter of the logo is 15 m. The white and pink sectors are all equal in size. Work out the area of pink used.

7 **P-S** The area of each sector is given. Find the missing angle or length.

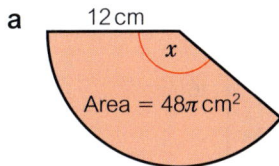

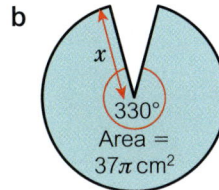

a
12 cm
x
Area = 48π cm²

b
x
330°
Area = 37π cm²

8 **P-S** Work out the area of the shaded region.

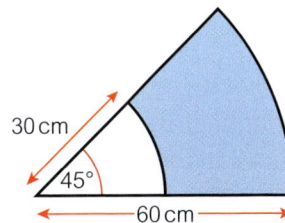

30 cm
45°
60 cm

9 **P-S** This circular company logo has a diameter of 4 m.
Each yellow sector has a central angle of 20°.
Work out the area of the logo painted yellow.

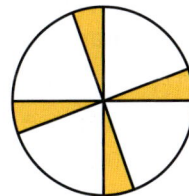

10 **P-S** Here is the net of a cone. Calculate the surface area.

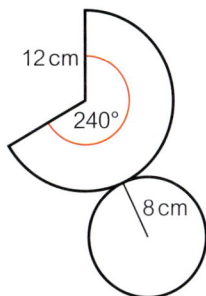

12 cm
240°
8 cm

7.3 Pythagoras' theorem

- Find the length of an unknown side of a right-angled triangle
- Solve problems involving right-angled triangles

1   Use a ruler to accurately draw a right-angled triangle with base 5 cm and height 4 cm.
   a Measure the length of the hypotenuse.
   b Use Pythagoras' theorem to calculate the length of the hypotenuse.
   c **R**   Is your answer to part **a** or part **b** more accurate? Explain.

2   **R**   a Work out the length of the hypotenuse of each of these triangles.

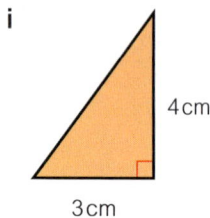

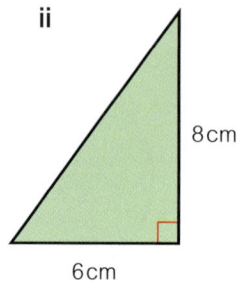

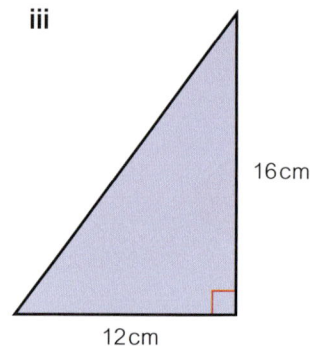

   i   ii   iii

   4 cm   8 cm   16 cm

   3 cm   6 cm   12 cm

   b What do you notice?
   c Predict the length of the hypotenuse of a triangle with base 27 cm, height 36 cm.
      Use Pythagoras' theorem to check your prediction.

3   **R**   When the base, height and hypotenuse of a right-angled triangle are all integers, this is
   called a **Pythagorean triple**. For example, (3, 4, 5) is a Pythagorean triple.
   a Show that (7, 24, 25) is also a Pythagorean triple.
   b Without calculating, use the Pythagorean triple (7, 24, 25) to write the base, height and
      hypotenuse of three other right-angled triangles.

4   **R**   Use Pythagoras' theorem to show whether a triangle with these sides is
   right-angled or not.
   a 5 cm, 12 cm, 13 cm   b 8 m, 15 m, 17 m   c 10 cm, 40 cm, 41 cm
   d 5 cm, 11 cm, 13 cm   e 9 m, 15 m, 17 m   f 9 cm, 40 cm, 41 cm

5   Use your answer to Q4 to write three more Pythagorean triples.

6   a **P-S**   Work out an approximate value for the missing
      side length of this triangle.
   b **R**   Would an answer worked out using Pythagoras' theorem
      be an overestimate or an underestimate for this triangle?

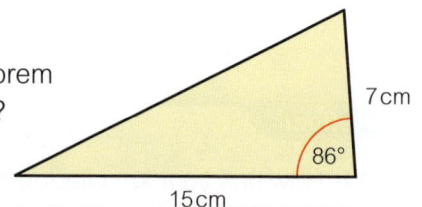

7 cm

86°

15 cm

7 Work out the distance between each pair of points, correct to 1 decimal place.

a (2, 3) and (7, 5)   **b** (0, 6) and (8, 4)
c (−2. 3) and (4, 6)   **d** (5, 2) and (3, −1)
e (−3, −2) and (1, 6)   **f** (−4, 3) and (2, −5)

> **Q7 hint** Draw a diagram.

> **Q8 hint** Assume that the string does not stretch.

8 **P-S** The diagram shows a bow being stretched to release an arrow.
  a Write down length CD.
  b Work out the length AB before the bow was stretched.

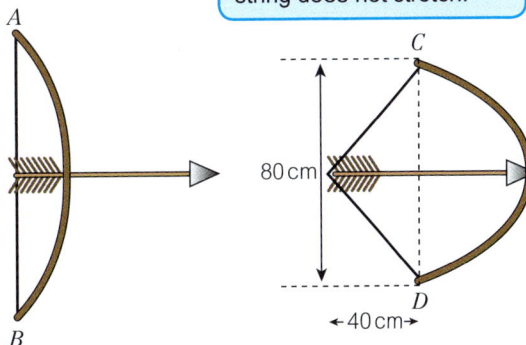

9 The diagram shows a regular hexagon.
  a Copy and complete:
    $6x = \square$, so $x = \square$
  b Copy and complete:
    $x + 2y = \square$, so $y = \square$
  c What type of triangle is each of the six triangles?
  d Use Pythagoras' theorem to calculate h, the perpendicular height of one triangle.
  e Calculate the area of one triangle.
  f Calculate the area of the hexagon.

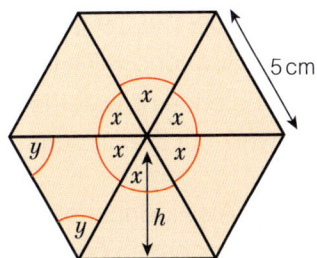

10 **P-S** The diagram shows a swing in two different positions.
  Work out the height h (in metres) of the swing seat at point B.

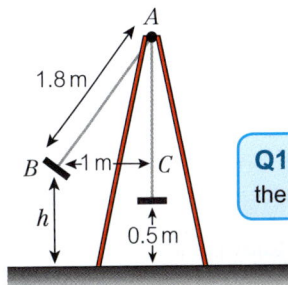

> **Q10 hint** Work out the length AC first.

11 The diagram shows a square-based pyramid.
  a Write the length of the distance x.
  b Use Pythagoras' theorem to calculate e, the slant height of the pyramid.
  c Calculate the area of one triangular face of the pyramid.
  d Calculate the area of the base of the pyramid.
  e Calculate the surface area of the pyramid.
  f Calculate the volume of the pyramid.

> **Key point**
>
> Volume of a pyramid =
> $\frac{1}{3} \times$ area of base $\times$ height

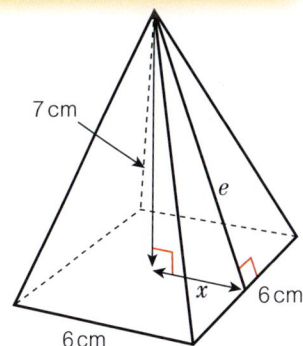

Reflect

12 In Q1 and Q2 you used graphical methods and Pythagoras' theorem to calculate missing lengths in right-angled triangles. Which method did you prefer? Why?

7.4 Prisms and cylinders

- Calculate the volume and surface area of a right prism
- Calculate the volume and surface area of a cylinder
- Convert between m³, cm³ and mm³

1 **P-S** The interior of a toilet cistern measures 15 cm by 30 cm by 15 cm.

  a The cistern takes 1 minute to completely refill after flushing.
   Work out the rate of flow in ml/s.

  b A cuboid brick measuring 215 mm by 102.5 mm by 65 mm is placed in the bottom of
   the cistern to save water.

   i Work out the new volume of water in the cistern.

   ii How long will it take to fill the cistern now?

  c The price of water is 0.34375 p per litre. If the cistern is flushed 2000 times in a year,
   work out the amount of money saved by using the brick.

2 **P-S** A cylindrical paint roller has a diameter of 10 cm and length of 30 cm.
   The roller has to be refilled with paint every 20 complete revolutions.

  a Work out the number of times a painter will need to refill the roller when painting a ceiling
   measuring 1 m by 5 m.

  b **R** Explain why your answer will not be exact.

3 **P-S / R** A cylinder has a height of 10 cm and a radius of 5 cm.

  a Calculate the area of the end face of the cylinder.

  b What is the area of the end face of:

   i a triangular prism   ii a cuboid   iii a hexagonal prism

   with the same height and volume as the cylinder?

  c Compare the area of the end face of each shape with the area of the end face of the
   cylinder. What do you notice?

4 a A triangular prism has length 10 cm, and its triangular faces have base 6 cm and height
   6 cm. Calculate its volume.

  b **P-S** Calculate the volume of

   i a cuboid with length 10 cm, base 6 cm and height 6 cm

   ii a regular hexagonal prism with length 10 cm and side lengths of 6 cm

   iii a regular octagonal prism with length 10 cm and side lengths of 6 cm

   iv a cylinder with radius 6 cm and length 10 cm

  c **R** Which prism's volume was closest to the volume of the cylinder? Why?

5 **P-S** The diagram shows an army hut. The hut has a
   semicircular cross-section and is 12 m long.
   The area of the metal roof is 175 m².
   Make a scale drawing of the front end. Use a scale of
   1 cm to 1 m.

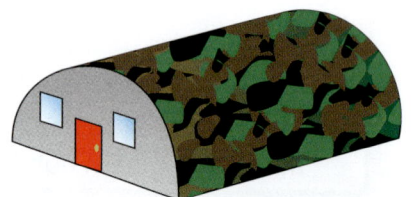

6 **P-S** A hospital patient receives drops of saline solution at a rate of 2 ml/min from a cylindrical container with diameter 5 cm and height 20 cm.

    a How long does it take to empty a full container?

    b There are 15 drops per ml. How many drops are in a full container?

    c Draw a graph to show the height of the saline solution in the container during the first hour.

7 **P-S** Which of these prisms has the larger surface area and volume?

a

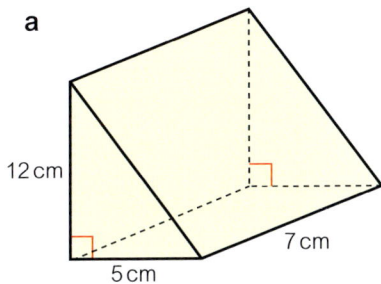
12 cm   7 cm   5 cm

b

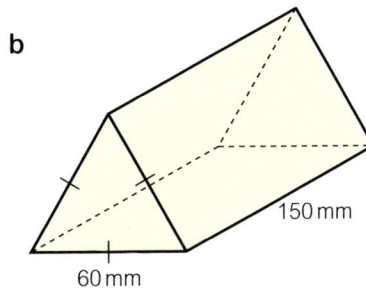
150 mm   60 mm

8 **P-S** The capacity of this cylindrical glass is 320 cm³.

    a Work out the internal radius of the glass.

    b 4 of these glasses fit exactly in this box.

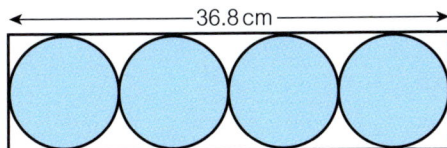
36.8 cm

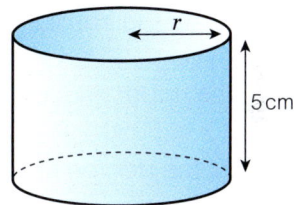
r 5 cm

    How thick is the glass? Round your answer to 2 decimal places.

9 **R** A cake recipe asks for a 15 cm by 15 cm by 10 cm cuboid cake tin.
Will a circular tin, with diameter 16 cm and height 10 cm be suitable for the volume of cake mix?
Show your working to explain.

10 Each cylinder has a volume of 2000 cm³. **a**
Work out the missing length for each.
Round your answers to 2 decimal places.

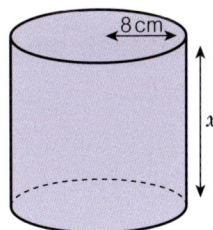
8 cm x

b

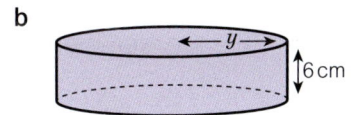
y 6 cm

11 The density of gold is 19.3 g/cm³.

    a Work out the mass of a cuboid bar of gold with volume: **i** 15 cm³   **ii** 0.1 cm³   **iii** 1 mm³

    b Convert 19.3 g/cm³ to mg/mm³.

Reflect

12 What is the same and what is different about working out the surface area of a cylinder and working out the surface area of a prism?

7.5 Errors and bounds

- Find the lower and upper bounds for a measurement
- Calculate percentage error intervals

1 **P-S** A recipe makes 800 g of cake mix, correct to the nearest 10 g. The mixture is divided equally between 4 cake tins.
Calculate the maximum **absolute error** for the amount of cake mix in each tin.

Key point

The **absolute error** is the maximum difference between the measured value and the actual value.

2 A bag of sugar has a mass of 500 g, to the nearest 10 g.
   a Calculate the absolute error for the mass of 8 bags of sugar.
   One bag of sugar is divided equally between 8 bowls.
   b Calculate the absolute error for the mass of sugar in each bowl.

3 **P-S** The upper and lower bounds for the weight, x kg, of an elephant are given as $4950 \leqslant x < 5050$.
Work out the degree of accuracy that the elephant was weighed to.

4 **R** A toy shop is checking its stock.
It has 400 packs of cards to the nearest 50.
Trent says that the error interval is $375 \leqslant n < 425$.
Ivy says that the error interval is $375 \leqslant n \leqslant 424$.
Lucy says they are both right. Explain why.

5 **P-S** A rabbit runs 250 m, to the nearest 10 m, in 55 seconds, to the nearest second.
Find the upper bound for its average speed.
Give your answer correct to 2 decimal places.

6 The measurements on the triangle are correct to the nearest 10 cm.

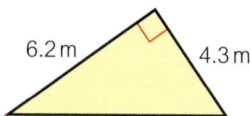
6.2 m   4.3 m

Find the upper and lower bounds for:
a the perimeter of the triangle
b the area of the triangle
c the volume of the triangular prism, with this triangle as its cross-section and a length of 15.2 m, to the nearest 10 cm.

7 **P-S** Blackpool Tower is 158 m tall to the nearest metre.
Baked bean tins are 11 cm tall to the nearest cm.
If you stacked 1500 baked bean tins on top of each other, would they definitely reach the top of the tower?

8 **P-S** A natural mineral stone has a mass of 120 g with an error interval of ±5%.
A shipment contains 10 000 stones to the nearest 50.
Work out the range of possible values for shipment mass, M.
Write your answer as an inequality.

9 **P-S** A tub of paint will cover an area of $1.5 \text{m}^2 \pm 10\%$.
The fence is 3 metres long, correct to the nearest metre, and 1.3 metres tall, correct to 1 decimal place.
a How many tubs of paint need to be bought to have enough to paint the fence?
b Give the error interval for the number of tubs of paint needed.

10 **P-S** The diagram shows a dartboard.
Its dimensions are in the table.

Bull diameter	12.7 mm ± 0.2 mm
Dartboard diameter	451 mm ± 3 mm

a Work out the lower and upper bounds for the area of the whole dartboard.
b Work out the lower and upper bounds for the area of the bull.
c A dart thrown at random hits the dartboard.
Work out the lower and upper bounds for the percentage probability P that the dart hits the bull.

Investigation

11 A room is 3.15 metres by 7.87 metres (both to the nearest cm).
a What is the error interval for the area, A?
b Round both original measurements to 1 decimal place and repeat part **a**.
c Round both original measurements to the nearest integer and repeat part **a**.
d Give the area of the room to an appropriate degree of accuracy.
e Choose two different numbers for the original measurements and repeat parts **a** to **d**.
What happens to the error interval as the accuracy of measurement changes?

Reflect

12 In Q4 you considered two different correct ways of stating an error interval.
When is there more than one way of correctly stating an error interval?

7 Extend

1 P-S The diagram shows a chain on a bike.
The radius of the smaller cog is 7 cm and the
radius of the larger cog is 13 cm.
The angle where the chain is against each cog
is shown. Work out the length of the chain.

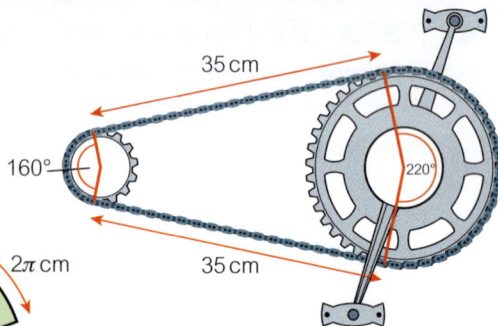

35 cm

160°   220°

35 cm

2 P-S Work out the size of angle x.

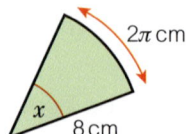

2π cm

x
8 cm

3 P-S The diagram shows a **chord** AB
and a shaded **segment**.

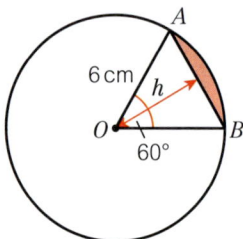

A
6 cm h
O
60° B

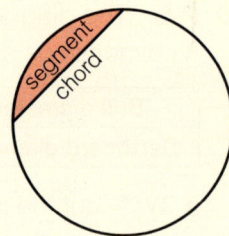

a What is the area of the sector shown?
The height, h, of triangle AOB is 5.2 cm.
b What is the area of triangle AOB?
c Work out the area of the segment.

Q3b hint What type of triangle
is triangle AOB?

4 P-S The diagram shows the start of a pattern
called the spiral of Theodorus.
It is made of right-angled triangles placed
edge to edge.

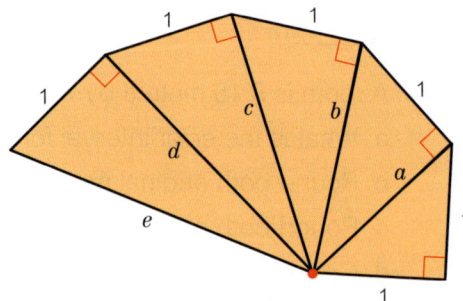

1   1
1   c b 1
d
e a
1
1

a Work out length a, giving your answer as a **surd**.
b Work out these lengths, giving each answer as a
surd: **i** b **ii** c **iii** d **iv** e
c What is the length of the hypotenuse of the nth triangle
in the spiral?
d R Why was it necessary to leave the answers to part **b**
as surds to answer part **c**?

Q4a hint A **surd** is a square
root $\sqrt{\square}$ that cannot be
simplified any further.

5 P-S / R What is the total area of the unshaded parts of this circle?

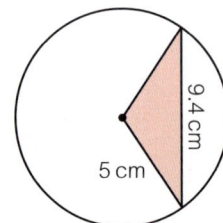

9.4 cm
5 cm

6 **P-S / R** The surface area of a cylinder is 600 cm².
One of the circular faces is shaded.
The ratio of the shaded to unshaded areas is 2 : 10.
What is the volume of the cylinder?

7 **P-S / R** The triangular prism has the same volume as the cylinder.

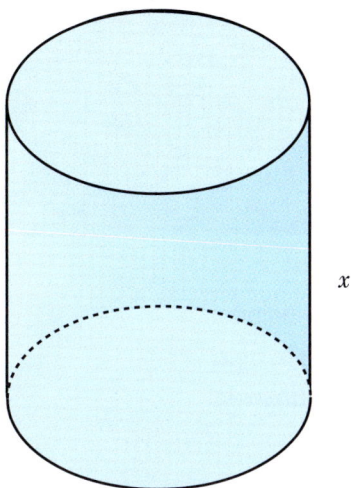

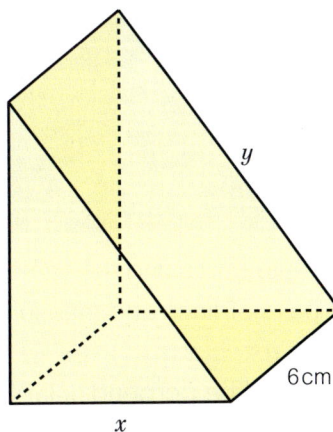

The cylinder has a surface area of 264 cm² and a radius of 5 cm.
What is the length of side y?

Investigation

8 A prism is a cuboid with no lengths less than 1 cm and a volume of 180 cm³.
What is the greatest possible surface area of the prism?

Investigation

9 **a** The radius of a circle is 6 cm.
The arc length of the circle is 6 cm.
What is the angle of the sector?

b What is the area of the sector?

c The radius of a circle is 5 cm.
The arc length is the same as the radius.
What is the angle of the sector? What is the area?

d The radius of a circle is r cm.
The arc length is the same as the radius.
What is the angle of the sector?

e How many of these angles are in a full turn?

Reflect

10 In this unit you worked with a variety of shapes.
What tips would you give to help someone who is struggling with a shapes question?
Compare your tips with others in your class.

8   Graphs

Master   Extend p95

8.1   Using $y = mx + c$

- Draw a graph from its equation, without working out points
- Write the equation of a line parallel to another line
- Write the equation of a line perpendicular to another line
- Compare graph lines using their equations

1   Draw a coordinate grid using the same scale on both axes.

   a   Plot these pairs of lines and measure the angle between the lines:

      i $y = 3x$ and $y = -\frac{1}{3}x$　　　　　　　　**ii** $y = 4x$ and $y = -\frac{1}{4}x$

   b   Which line would be perpendicular to $y = 5x$? Check your answer.

2   **R**   Line AB is perpendicular to line CD.

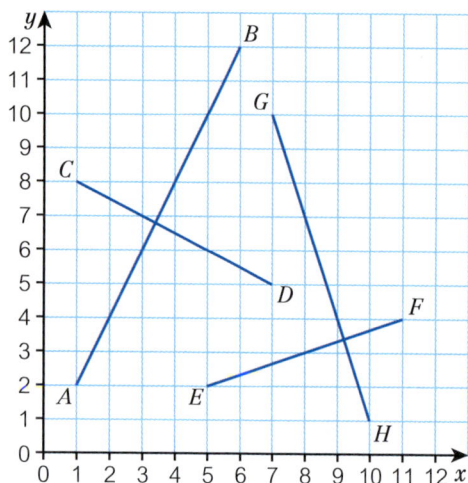

   a   Work out the gradient of line AB.

   b   Work out the gradient of line CD.

   c   Multiply the gradients of the two lines together.

   Line EF is perpendicular to line GH.

   d   Repeat parts **a** to **c** for this pair of lines.

   e   Copy and complete:

      When two lines are perpendicular, their gradients multiply to ☐.

3   **R**   For each pair of lines, decide whether they are parallel, perpendicular or neither.
Show or explain how you know.

   a $y = 2x - 1$ and $y = 2x + 3$　　　　　　　**b** $y = -\frac{1}{2}x + 5$ and $y = -\frac{1}{2}x - 7$

   c $y = -2x + 3$ and $y = \frac{1}{2}x + 5$　　　　　　**d** $y = -\frac{1}{2}x - 7$ and $y = 2x + 9$

4 **P-S** Each line has a partner which is perpendicular except one. Which one?

A $y = \frac{1}{6}x - 3$ B $y = -\frac{1}{2}x + 3$ C $y = -3x + 1$ D $y = -\frac{1}{5}x + 4$

E $y = 4x - 7$ F $y = -6x + 1$ G $y = 2x - 3$ H $y = -x + 2$

I $y = x + 4$ J $y = \frac{1}{3}x - 4$ K $y = 5x + 2$

5 Write the equation of a line perpendicular to:

a $y = 2x - 1$ **b** $y = -3x + 12$

c $y = \frac{1}{2}x$ **d** $y = -\frac{1}{2}x - 4$

Q5a hint $2 \times \square = -1$

6 **P-S** Find the equation of a straight line perpendicular to $y = 3x + 2$, which goes through the point $(6, 0)$.

7 **P-S / R** Find the equation of the line perpendicular to:

a $y = -2x + 1$, which goes through the point $(3, 2)$

b $y = \frac{1}{5}x + 2$, which crosses the y-axis at -4.

8 **R** Decide whether each statement about the line $y = \frac{1}{2}x - 7$ is true or false.

a It goes through the point $(-1, -7.5)$.

b It is parallel to $2y = x + 12$.

c It is perpendicular to $y = -2x$.

d It crosses the y-axis at $(0, 7)$.

9 **P-S** For the line $y = 3x + 2$, write four true statements like those in Q8.

10 **P-S** A rectangle has side AB that is part of the line with equation $y = 0.1x - 3$.
Side BC is part of a line that goes through the point $(0, -15)$.
The other two sides, CD and AD, meet at the point $(0, 5)$.
Write the equations of the lines that make the sides BC, CD and AD of the rectangle.

11 **R** Is it easier to identify perpendicular lines if the coefficient of x is written as a decimal or a fraction? Explain your reasoning.

Reflect

12 What is the same and what is different about finding the equations of parallel lines and the equations of perpendicular lines?

8.2 More straight-line graphs

- Draw graphs with equations in the form $ax + by = c$
- Rearrange equations of graphs into the form $y = mx + c$

1 Which of these equations are equivalent?

    A $y = 3 - 2x$ **B** $y - 2x = 3$ **C** $y + 2x = 3$

    D $y = 3x - 2$ **E** $y = 2x + 3$ **F** $y - 3x = 2$

> **Q1 hint** Rearrange the equation to make y the subject.

2 **R** Oscar says that $3y = 2x + 5$ and $y = -\frac{1}{2}x + 5$ are perpendicular. Explain why he is wrong.

3 Decide whether each pair of lines are parallel, perpendicular or neither.

    a $y = 3x + 7$ and $3y = 9x - 4$ **b** $2y = 3x + 8$ and $3y = 2x + 9$

    c $x = y - 7$ and $5x - 5y = 7$ **d** $-x = 4 + y$ and $3x - 4y = 1$

4 A line has the equation $8y + 2x = 16$.

    a By substituting in $y = 0$, find the coordinates where the line crosses the x-axis.

    b By substituting in $x = 0$, find the coordinates where the line crosses the y-axis.

    c Draw the graph.

    d Rearrange the equation to the form $y = mx + c$.

    e Write the gradient of a line perpendicular to it.

Investigation

5 **a** Work out the gradients of $3x + 2y = 10$ and $2x - 3y = 6$.

    b Show that the two lines are perpendicular.

    c Repeat steps **a** and **b** for $8x - 10y = 20$ and $10x + 8y = 12$.

    d Write the equation of a line perpendicular to:

        i $5x - 4y = 12$ **ii** $2y - 8x = 14$

6 **P-S** An arrow pointing south-east is drawn on a coordinate grid. The arrow starts at $(1, -2)$.

    a What is the equation of the line that the arrow pointing south-east lies on? Give the equation in the form $ax + by = c$.

    b What other point of the compass lies on this line?

7 **P-S** A line has the equation $0.025x - y = -100$.

    a Write the equation of the parallel line that passes through $(0, 1000)$.

    b Write the equation of the perpendicular line that passes through $(0, 0)$.

8 **P-S** Lily says, 'I have drawn a line. A line perpendicular to it has equation $0.4x - y = -1$. My line passes through the point $(10, 5)$.' What is the equation of Lily's line?

9 **a** Points (1, 4), (3, 2) and (−2, 7) all lie on the same line. Write the equation of the line in the form $ax + by = c$.

   b Points (1, 2), (3, 4) and (−2, −1) all lie on the same line. Write the equation of the line in the form $ax + by = c$.

   c R Explain how you can tell these lines are perpendicular.

Q9a hint What do you notice about the sum of the x- and y-coordinates for each point?

Q9b hint What do you notice about the difference between the x- and y-coordinates for each point?

10 Find the equation of the line that passes through points $A(8, 3)$ and $B(1, −4)$.

11 P-S

   a Points (1, 2), (2, 4) and (5, 10) all lie on the same line. Write the equation of the line.

   b Points (1, 3), (2, 5) and (5, 11) all lie on the same line. Write the equation of the line.

   c Find the equation of the line that passes through (2, 7) and (5, 13).

   d R Kamal says these three lines are parallel. Explain how he knows.

12 Find the equation of the line that passes through points $C(3, 2)$ and $D(6, 8)$.

13 a Find the equation of the line that passes through (3, 8) and (0, 2).

   b Find the equation of the line that passes through (1, 4) and (4, 10).

   c R Without doing any additional calculations, write the equation of the line that passes through (5, 12) and (−1, 0). Explain how you arrived at your answer.

   d R Explain why (6, 14) is a point on both $y = 2x + 2$ and $y = x + 8$.

14 R How many points do you need to know, to be able to work out the equation of a straight line?

15 R Noel says, 'The coordinates of a point on my graph are (5, 5), so the equation of the line must be $y = x$.' Explain why he is wrong.

16 P-S A line passes through points (2, −2) and (4, −6).

   a Find the equation of a line perpendicular to it that passes through the midpoint of the two points.

   b R Why is it not possible to find the equation of a new line that is parallel to the original line that passes through the midpoint of the two points?

17 P-S A line segment starts at the point (4, 5) and ends at the point (−3, −2). Write the equation of the line that is its perpendicular bisector.

18 P-S / R A kite has a diagonal that is the line $3x + y = −2$. One of the vertices of the kite is the point (3, 2). Write the equation of the line that is the other diagonal of the kite.

19 P-S / R Two lines that form part of a parallelogram are $\frac{4}{3}x − y = −4$ and $\frac{4}{3}x − y = 21$. The vertices of the parallelogram are at (0, 4), (12, 20), (24, 11) and (12, −5). What are the equations of the other two lines that form the parallelogram?

Reflect

20 In Q4, you were asked to substitute certain values in order to find two points to draw a straight line. Would *any* values work? Are some values easier to use? Why?

8.3 Simultaneous equations

- Solve simultaneous equations by drawing graphs
- Solve problems using simultaneous equations

1 P-S 20-second advert slots on television cost £x and 30-second slots cost £y.
During a commercial break, five 20-second adverts and one 30-second advert cost
£16 500. Two 20-second adverts and three 30-second adverts cost £17 000.
  a Draw a graph to model these situations.
  b Work out the cost of one 20-second advert and the cost of one 30-second advert.

2 P-S At a barbecue, in the afternoon 15 burgers and 12 drinks are sold for a total of £84.
In the evening 56 burgers and 48 drinks are sold for a total of £320.
  a Draw a graph to model this situation.
  b Estimate the cost of 1 burger and the cost of 1 drink.

3 P-S / R Look at this pair of equations:
  $$2x + 2y = 20 \quad (1)$$
  $$5x + 3y = 44 \quad (2)$$
  a Explain why $x + y = 10$.
  b What is the value of $3x + 3y$?
  c Rearrange your equation from part **b** so that $3y = \ldots$
  d Rearrange equation (2) so that $3y = \ldots$
  e Equate your equations from parts **c** and **d**. Work out the value of x.
  f Substitute your value of x from part **c** into equation (1) to work out the value of y.
  g Check your values of x and y by substituting into equation (2).
  h Use a similar method to solve this pair of equations:
  $$3x + 3y = 36$$
  $$2x + 5y = 27$$

4 P-S A camp site charges for entrance and then for each night of camping.
The Walter family paid £343 for 9 nights of camping.
The Ali family paid £235 for 6 nights of camping.
Let x represent the entrance fee and y represent the cost per night.
  a Write an equation to model the Walter family's charge.
  b Write an equation to model the Ali family's charge.
  c Work out the cost of one night.
  d Work out the entrance fee.

5 **P-S / R** At a school fair, bottles of water cost 60p and cans of fizzy drink cost 80p. Sally sells 45 drinks altogether and makes a total of £31.80.

    a Write an equation to model the number of drinks sold.

    b Write an equation to model the total money taken.

    c Draw the graphs on suitable axes.

    d How many bottles of water and how many cans of fizzy drink did Sally sell?

    e Rearrange each equation so that $x = \ldots$

    f Equate your equations from part **e**. Work out the value of y.

    g Substitute your value of y into your equation from part **a** to work out the value of x.

    h Did you prefer the graphical or the algebraic way of working out the solutions? Why?

6 On the same axes draw the graphs of:

    a $2y + 3x = 12$ and $4y + 6x = 24$

    b $2x + 5y = 10$ and $2x + 5y = 20$

    c What do you notice about these lines?

    d How many solutions are there to each pair of simultaneous equations?

7 **R** Do these pairs of equations have:

no solution, one solution or **infinitely many solutions**?

If possible, find the values of x and y that satisfy each pair of equations.

    a $x - y = 3$ **b** $3x + y = 9$ **c** $5x + y = 13$

       $3x - y = -5$ $6x + 2y = 12$ $5x - y = 7$

    d $4x + 5y = 20$ **e** $2x - 6y = 4$ **f** $5x + 3y = -9$

       $8x + 10y = 40$ $3x - 9y = 2$ $2x - 4y = 12$

8 **P-S / R** Write your own pair of equations that have:

    a no solution

    b one solution of $x = -8$, $y = \frac{1}{2}$

    c infinitely many solutions.

Reflect

9 In Q7, you were asked to state how many solutions there were to a pair of equations. Why were there only three options for the number of solutions?

8.4 Graphs of quadratic functions

- Draw graphs with quadratic equations in the form $y = x^2$
- Interpret graphs of quadratic functions

1 **P-S** The length, s ft, of a car skid mark can be estimated using the formula $s = 0.05v^2$, where v mph is the speed of the car when the brakes are applied.

  a Make a table of values for $v = 0$ to 60.

  b Use graph paper to plot the graph of $s = 0.05v^2$.

  c A car driver saw a deer in the road and skidded to a stop. The skid mark was 95 ft long. Estimate the speed of the car when the brakes were applied.

  d It takes approximately 1.4 seconds for a driver to react before braking.

     i Estimate the distance the car travelled before the driver applied the brakes in part **c**.

     ii Estimate the distance the car travelled from the time the driver saw the deer until the car stopped.

  > **Q1d i hint** Convert the speed in miles per hour to feet per second.

2 **P-S** Tara launched a toy paratrooper from the top of a cliff. The height, h m, of the toy above sea level after t seconds is given by the formula $h = 25t - 5t^2 + 50$.

  a Make a table of values for $t = 0$ to 8.

  b Plot the graph of h against t.

  c Use your graph to estimate:

     i the maximum height of the toy

     ii the time it took to reach the ground.

  50 m

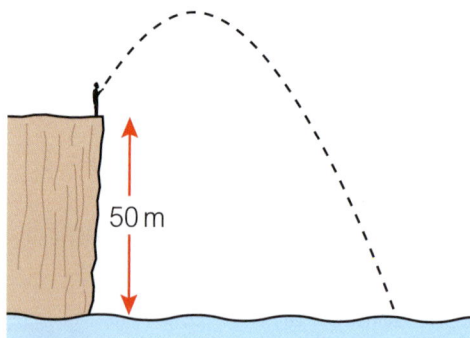

3 **P-S** The perimeter of this rectangle is 20 cm.

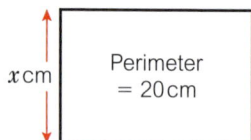

  > **Q3 hint** Write an expression for the length of the rectangle.

  x cm — Perimeter = 20 cm

  a Write a formula for the area A cm^2 of the rectangle in terms of x.

  b Plot the graph of A for $x = 0$ to 10.

  c Use your graph to estimate:

     i the maximum possible area of the rectangle

     ii the dimensions of the rectangle when the area is 15 cm^2.

4 **P-S** Here are the graphs of two equations.

a Write the equation of each graph.

b Use the graphs to solve the simultaneous equations.

c Substitute your x- and y-values from part **b** into your equations from part **a** to check your solutions are correct.

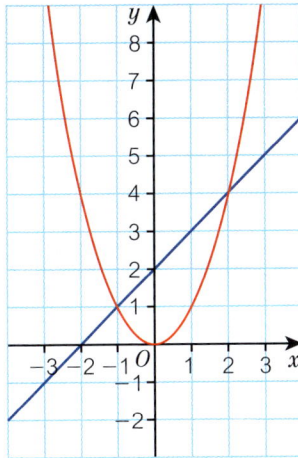

Key point A pair of simultaneous equations may have one linear equation and one quadratic equation.

5 Here are the graphs of the equations $y = -2x + 1$ and $y = x^2 + 1$.

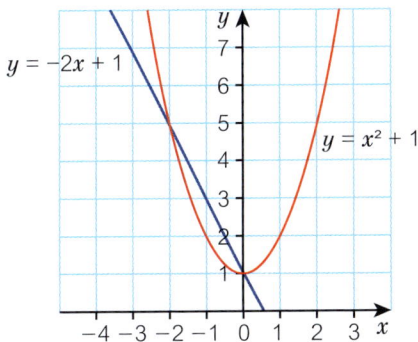

Use the graphs to solve the simultaneous equations.

6 For each pair of equations:

    i $y = -3x + 5$ and $y = x^2 + 7$

    ii $y = 2x + 3$ and $y = x^2 - 1$

a plot their graphs

b write down the coordinates of the point of intersection.

Q6 hint First make a table of values from $x = -5$ to $x = 5$.

Investigation

7 Plot the graph of $y = x^2 + 2$.

a Draw a line that touches the graph where the x-coordinate is 1. Find the gradient of the line.

b Repeat part **a** for x-coordinates 2, 3 and 4.

c What do you notice?

d Does the same happen for other quadratic graphs? Show your working.

Reflect

8 What is the same and what is different about the solutions to simultaneous equations where one is linear and one is quadratic compared to when they are both linear?

8.5 More non-linear graphs

- Draw and interpret non-linear graphs

1 a Copy and complete the table of values for $y = x^3$.
   b Plot the points in your table on a coordinate grid.
      Join the points with a smooth curve and label your
      graph with its equation.
   c What type of symmetry does the graph of $y = x^3$ have?

x	−3	−2	−1	0	1	2	3
y							

2 a Use your graph from Q1 to estimate: **i** 1.8^3 **ii** $\sqrt[3]{7}$
   b Use a calculator to work out parts **a i** and **ii**.
   c **R** Which of your answers are more accurate? Explain.

3 a Draw a table of values for: **i** $y = 2x^3$ **ii** $y = 5x^3$.
   b Plot the graphs of $y = 2x^3$ and $y = 5x^3$ on the same axes.
   c What is the same about your two graphs, and your graph of $y = x^3$? What is different?
   d **R** What do you think the graphs of $y = 3x^3$ and $y = \frac{1}{2}x^3$ would look like?

> **Q3a hint** Use a copy of the table from Q1.

4 a Draw a table of values for $y = -x^3$.
   b Plot the graph of $y = -x^3$.
   c Describe the transformation that takes the graph of
      $y = x^3$ on to $y = -x^3$.
   d **i** What do you think the graph of $y = -2x^3$ will look like?
      ii Plot the graph of $y = -2x^3$ to test your prediction.

> **Q4c hint** Look at the graph of $y = x^3$ you drew in Q1.

> **Key point** A **cubic graph** contains a term in x^3 but no higher power of x.
> $y = x^3$, $y = 2x^3$, $y = -x^3$ and $y = x^3 + 5x$ are all cubic.

5 **R** Two of these graphs are not cubic. Which two?
   Explain how you know.

> **Q5 hint** Look at the shapes of the graphs. What shape are quadratic graphs? What shape are cubic graphs?

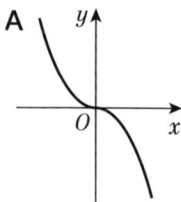

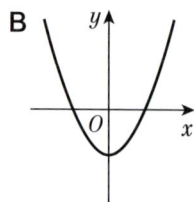

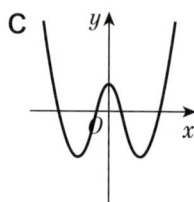

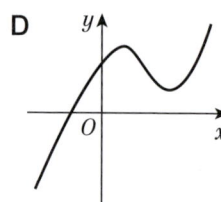

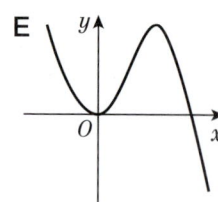

6 **P-S** The diagram shows a packing box for cube soaps with sides x cm.

    a Write a formula for the volume, y cm^3, of the box.

    b Draw an x-axis from 0 to 5 and y-axis from 0 to 800. Plot the graph of your formula.

    c The volume of a box is 500 cm^3. Estimate the side length of a block of soap.

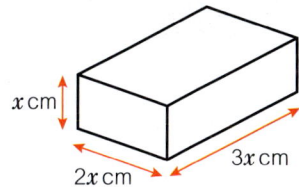

x cm $2x$ cm $3x$ cm

> **Q6c hint** Draw the line $y = 500$.

7 **P-S** The mass of air, A grams, in a ball of radius x cm is given by the formula $A = 0.1x^3$.

    a Copy and complete the table of values:

x	0	2	4	6	8	10
x^3				216		
$A = 0.1x^3$				21.6		

> **Q7a hint**
>
> | x | 6 |
> |---|---|
> | x^3 | $6 \times 6 \times 6 = 216$ |
> | $A = 0.1x^3$ | $0.1 \times 216 = 21.6$ |

    b Plot the graph of the function $A = 0.1x^3$.

    c Use your graph to estimate the mass of air in a similar ball with radius 9.2 cm.

    d Another ball contains 30 g of air. Estimate its radius.

8 **a** **P-S** Plot the graph of $y = x^2$.

Draw axes with x from 0 to 4 and y from 0 to 80.

    b Explain how you can use your graph to find the two square roots of 4.

    c Use your graph to estimate the square root of 7.

    d **i** On the same axes, plot the graph of $y = x^3$.

       ii Use your graph to estimate the cube root of 50.

    e The two graphs intersect at two points. What are the points of intersection?

    f Copy and complete the statements using $<$, $>$ or $=$

       $x^2 \square x^3$ for $x = 0$

       $x^2 \square x^3$ for $0 < x < 1$

       $x^2 \square x^3$ for $x = 1$

       $x^2 \square x^3$ for $x > 1$

> **Q8e hint** Look at the points for which one graph is greater than the other

Reflect

9 Decide whether each of these descriptions could be true for a cubic, a quadratic or a linear graph. (Some of them could be true for more than one type of graph.)

    a Has rotational symmetry but not reflective symmetry.

    b Has reflective symmetry.

    c Must cut the x-axis at least once.

    d Cuts the x-axis exactly twice.

    e Cuts the x-axis three times.

8 Extend

1 **P-S** Use the numbers 1, 2, 3, 4 and 6 to fill in the boxes to complete these equations of two perpendicular lines.

$$y = \square x + \square \qquad \square y + \square x = \square$$

2 **R** Afrah says, 'A set of two linear equations that are perpendicular to each other will always have exactly one solution.'
Explain whether Afrah is correct.

3 **P-S / R** A line passes through $A(-4, 8)$ and $B(2, 6)$. The line is called L_1.

a Find the equation of a line perpendicular to L_1 that passes through the midpoint of the line segment AB.

b Find the equations of two more lines that can be drawn to make a rectangle.

c Using L_1 and the line from part **a**, a third line is drawn that makes a triangle with area 30. How many possible equations of this line are there?

d L_1 meets the line L_2.
The equation of L_2 is $2y + x = 6$.
At what point do L_1 and L_2 meet?

4 **P-S / R** Write the equation of a linear graph that does not have any points of intersection with the curve with equation $y = x^2 + 2x$.

5 **P-S / R** Write three equations of lines that will have infinitely many points of intersection with the line $2y + 5x = -4$.

6 **P-S / R** The three lines L_1, L_2 and L_3 are drawn.
L_1 is the line with equation $y = 3 + x$.
L_2 is perpendicular to L_1 and passes through the point (1, 8).
L_3 has the same y-intercept as L_1 and the same x-intercept as L_2.
X is the mean of the x-coordinates of the points of intersection of the three lines.
Y is the mean of the y-coordinates of the points of intersection of the three lines.
Work out the coordinates of the point (X, Y).

7 **P-S / R** Work out all of the possible solutions to the simultaneous equations
$y = x^2 - 16$ and $y = -x^2 + 16$.

8 A rope bridge forms an arc that can be modelled by the equation $y = 0.1x^2 - 2x + 5$.

a Plot the graph of the equation, using an x-axis that goes from 0 to 20.

b **R** What could the values of x and y represent in this model?

9 **P-S / R** Find the equation of a line that has no points of intersection with $y = 3x + 2$, and which passes through the point (8, 11).

10 You can write the equation $y = 3x + 2$ as a function machine. $x \rightarrow \boxed{\times 3} \rightarrow \boxed{+2} \rightarrow y$

The function gives an output value y for every input value x.

You can reverse the function machines to find the **inverse function**.

$$y = \frac{x-2}{3} = \frac{x}{3} - \frac{2}{3}$$

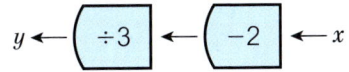

$y \leftarrow \boxed{\div 3} \leftarrow \boxed{-2} \leftarrow x$

a Find the inverse function of: **i** $y = 2x$ **ii** $y = 3x$ **iii** $y = x$

b Plot the graphs of $y = 2x$ and its inverse function on the same axes.

> **Q10b hint** You could use a graph plotting package.

c **i** Do the same for $y = 3x$ and its inverse function, and $y = x$ and its inverse function.

   ii What do you notice about the graph of a function and its inverse function?

   iii Write a rule connecting the graph of a function and its inverse function.

> **Q10c iii hint** What transformation takes the graph on to the graph of its inverse function?

d Test your rule for a more complex function.
Plot the graph of $y = 3x + 2$ and its inverse function on the same axes.
Does this graph obey your rule?

e **i** Draw the graph of $y = 4x - 1$.

   ii Use your rule to draw the graph of the inverse function.

   iii Work out the equation of this line.

   iv Check your graph is correct by finding the inverse function of $y = 4x - 1$.

11 **P-S / R**   Here are the graphs of the equations $y = x^2 + 2x - 5$ and $y = 3x - 3$.

a Explain how the graphs can be used to find solutions to $3x - 3 = x^2 + 2x - 5$.

b Explain why the graphs can be used to find solutions to $-3 = x^2 - x - 5$.

c Explain why the graphs can be used to find solutions to $0 = x^2 - x - 2$.

d The graph of $y = x^2 + 2x + 5$ is drawn on a new set of axes.
What additional line would you draw to solve $0 = x^2 + x + 2$?

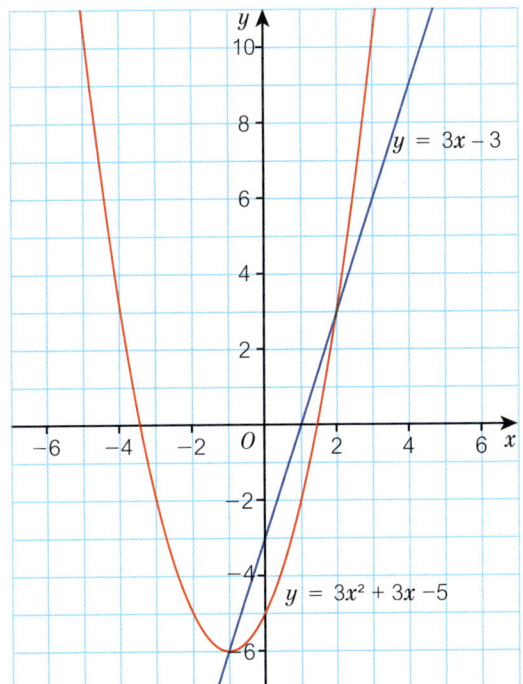

$y = 3x - 3$

$y = 3x^2 + 3x - 5$

12 What did you find most challenging in this unit? Why was it the most challenging?

9 Probability

Master   Extend p107

9.1 Mutually exclusive events

- Identify mutually exclusive outcomes and events
- Work out the probabilities of mutually exclusive outcomes and events

1   **P-S / R**   A coin is taken at random from a moneybox containing 5p coins from different years.

P(year is 2012) = 0.2   P(year is 2000) = 0.1   P(year is 1999) = 0.05

   a Explain why these events are mutually exclusive.

   b What is the probability that the coin is from:

     i 2000 or 2012   **ii** 1999 or 2000   **iii** 1999, 2000 or 2012?

2   **R**   The computer sound cards made on a production line are either scrapped, repaired or passed. 4% are scrapped and 8% are repaired.

Show that the probability a sound card is passed is 88%.

3   **P-S**   Blue, white and red balls are put into a bag.

The table shows the probability of picking a ball of each colour.

Colour	blue	white	red
Probability	0.25	x	x

Work out the value of x.

4   **P-S**   In a 'lucky dip' at a fete, there are three different prizes: teddy, yoyo and bubbles.

The table shows the probability of picking each prize.

Prize	teddy	yoyo	bubbles
Probability	0.3	$2x$	$3x$

Find the ratio of teddies to yoyos to bubbles. Write your ratio with integers.

5   **P-S / R**   A bag contains red, white, green and purple counters.

The table shows the probability for each colour.

Colour	red	white	green	purple
Probability	0.05	0.4	0.35	0.2

   a Explain why there must be more than 10 counters in the bag.

   b What is the smallest possible number of counters in the bag?

6 **P-S / R** A spinner has five equal sections numbered 1, 2, 3, 4, 5.

    a What is the probability of getting an even number?

    b What is the probability of getting a prime number?

    c What is the probability of getting an even number or a prime number?

    d Why do your answers to parts **a** and **b** not sum to your answer to part **c**?

    e How could one number on the spinner be changed so that your answers to parts **a** and **b** *do* sum to your answer to part **c**?

7 **R** Lucy has some raffle tickets numbered from 1 to 50.
She says that the events 'picking a square number greater than 10' and 'picking a multiple of 3' are mutually exclusive. Is Lucy correct? Explain.

8 **R** 'The two outcomes are mutually exclusive.' Write *true* or *false* for each pair:

    a Being late to class and being early   **b** Passing Maths and passing English

    c Doing your homework and having a shower at home

    d It raining and the sun shining   **e** Rolling a 6 and rolling a prime number

    f Dancing and sleeping.

9 **R** There are 300 people at a conference.
The probability that a person picked at random is wearing red is 18%.
The probability that a person picked at random is wearing high heels is 16%.
Explain why you cannot calculate the probability of a randomly selected person at the conference *not* wearing red or high heels from this information.

10 **P-S**

    a Design a 6-sided spinner so that getting a prime number and getting an even number are mutually exclusive outcomes.

    b Design a 6-sided spinner so that getting a prime number and getting an even number are *not* mutually exclusive outcomes.

    c Design a 6-sided spinner so that getting a green side and getting a prime number are mutually exclusive.

    d On your spinner from part **c**, what is the probability that you get a green side that has a prime number?

11 **P-S / R** For a 5-sided spinner, $P(\text{prime}) = \frac{2}{5}$ and $P(\text{square number}) = \frac{1}{5}$

    a Design two different spinners with these probabilities.

    b From the probabilities given, is it possible to work out $P(\text{even number})$? Explain.

12 **P-S / R** The word MATHEMATICS is written with each letter on a separate piece of paper.
A piece of paper is picked at random.

    a State two outcomes that would be mutually exclusive.

    b State two outcomes that would *not* be mutually exclusive.

Reflect

13 Why is it important to know whether events are mutually exclusive when calculating combinations of probabilities?

9.2 Experimental and theoretical probability

- Calculate estimates of probability from experiments
- Decide whether a dice or spinner is unbiased

1 From a normal pack of playing cards, what is the theoretical probability of picking:
   a a jack   **b** a heart?

2 **R** For which of these events can you work out the theoretical probability?
   a A scheduled aeroplane will be delayed.
   b A letter pushed through a letter box will fall stamp side up.
   c The next domino turned over will have an even number of dots.

3 **R** In a fantasy game, players use a spinner to see which creature they have to be.
   a What is the theoretical probability of landing on vampire if the spinner is fair?
   b How many times would you expect the spinner to land on each creature in 100 spins?
   These are the results for 100 spins.

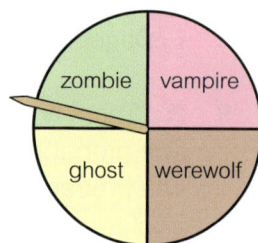

Creature	vampire	werewolf	ghost	zombie
Frequency	22	27	25	26

   c Kuni says that the spinner is fair. Do you agree?
      What could she do to be more confident that the spinner is fair?

4 **R** All students who complete a work experience placement with a travel agency are entered into a prize draw. They always give four prizes – one to a boy and another to a girl from each of the two local schools.
   Explain why this might not give everybody a fair chance of winning.

5 The frequency table shows the weights of organic savoy cabbages grown without pesticide or artificial fertiliser.
   a Estimate the probability that an organic savoy cabbage weighs 1.3 kg or more.
   b A supermarket only buys savoy cabbages that weigh between 0.9 kg and 1.3 kg. A farmer produces 20 000 organic savoy cabbages each year. How many of these can the farmer expect to sell to the supermarket?
   c R A savoy cabbage on a market stall weighs 1450 g. The stallholder says it is organic. Do you believe him? Explain.

Weight, w (kg)	Frequency
$0.6 \leqslant w < 0.7$	20
$0.7 \leqslant w < 0.8$	60
$0.8 \leqslant w < 0.9$	90
$0.9 \leqslant w < 1.0$	130
$1.0 \leqslant w < 1.1$	220
$1.1 \leqslant w < 1.2$	150
$1.2 \leqslant w < 1.3$	80
$1.3 \leqslant w < 1.4$	40
$1.4 \leqslant w < 1.5$	10

6 **R** Some students build a game to raise money for charity.
A ball falls at random into one of the holes.
Red wins a prize of 50p, blue wins 20p, yellow wins nothing.

a Copy the table and complete the first three columns:

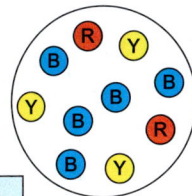

Colour	Probability	Prize	Expected number of wins in 200 games	Expected prizes in 200 games

b In 200 games:

   i how many times would you expect the ball to fall into each colour?
Fill in the fourth column.

   ii how much money would be won on each colour? Fill in the last column.

   iii how much are the expected prizes in total?

c How much should the students charge to play the game to make a profit?
Explain your answer.

7 **R** Two people are playing a dice rolling game with dice numbered from 1 to 6.
Monwara claims that Graham's dice is not fair, and that it lands on 6 too often.
Graham rolls his dice five times and gets three 6s and two 5s.
Monwara says that is proof.
Giving reasons, explain whether you think Graham's dice is fair.

Investigation

8 **a** What is the theoretical probability of flipping heads with a fair coin?
Write your answer as a decimal.

  b **i** Flip a coin 20 times and record the results in a frequency table.

    ii Calculate the experimental probability of heads.
Write your answer as a decimal.

  c **i** Combine your data with a classmate.

    ii Calculate the experimental probability of heads based on the total 40 flips.

Flipping heads with a coin

  d Combine the data of more classmates, one at a time.
Calculate the experimental probability of heads based on 60, 80, 120 ... flips.

  e Plot the results on a graph like the one shown on the right.

  f What do you notice about the experimental probabilities as the number of trials increases?

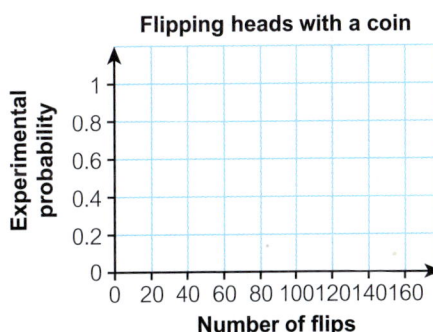

Reflect

9 For a fair coin, why could the experimental probability of heads be close to but not exactly $\frac{1}{2}$?

9.3 Sample space diagrams

- List all the possible outcomes of one or two events in a sample space diagram
- Decide if a game is fair

1 P-S Katya divides two spinners into three equal parts.
She writes a number on each part.
Katya spins both spinners.
She works out 'silver number – gold number'.

 a Copy and complete this sample space diagram
 to show all possible results, and the values
 of a, b, c, p and q.

 b Is each score equally likely?

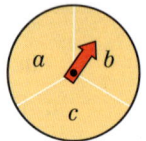

Gold spinner		p	7	q
	a	1		
	b	2	4	
	c	3	5	7

Silver spinner

2 P-S / R Katya uses the same spinners as in Q1.
She writes different numbers on them and works out 'silver number – gold number'.

The probability of getting a difference of 5 is $\frac{2}{9}$.

The probability of getting a difference of 7 is $\frac{1}{9}$.

 a Copy and complete this sample space diagram
 for each outcome.

 b What is the probability of getting a difference
 that is less than 9?

Gold spinner			
4	1	2	
3			
			8

Silver spinner

3 P-S / R In a probability experiment, Khalid spins this
fair spinner twice and adds the results together.

 a Copy and complete the sample space diagram:

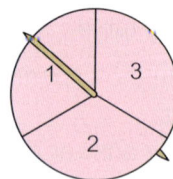

		First spin		
		1	2	3
Second	1	2		
spin	2			
	3			

 b Khalid does 45 trials. How many times would he expect a total of 4?

 c Khalid repeats the experiment 100 times.
 He gets an even number 70 times.
 Do you think the spinner is fair? Explain.

4 P-S Julia always hits 5, 20 or 1 with a dart.
She throws two darts and adds their scores.
What is the probability that her total score will be

 a 40   **b** 6

 c less than 20   **d** at least 20?

5 R

    a Alfie and Kim each flip a coin.
       Alfie wins if the two coins show the same face.
       Kim wins if the two coins show different faces.
       Is this game fair? Explain.

    b Alfie and Kim each spin a spinner like this.
       Alfie says, 'Using the same rules as our coin game will be fair.
       I win if the two spinners land on the same number.'
       Is Alfie correct? Explain.

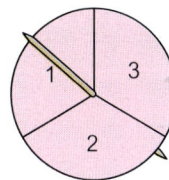

6 R   Julie rolls a 4-sided dice (numbered 1 to 4) and a
6-sided dice (numbered 1 to 6) and adds the scores together.
Is she more likely to get a score less than 6, or of 6 or more?
Explain how you found your answer.

7 P-S / R   Two 4-sided dice (numbered 1 to 4) are rolled and the numbers are multiplied to
give the score. Jay challenges Mitra to a game. If the score is even, Jay gets a point. If the
score is odd, Mitra gets two points.

    a Explain why the game is not fair.
    b Who is more likely to win?
    c How could the rules be changed to make the game fair?

8 P-S   Two 5-sided spinners are spun.

    The probability of getting two even numbers is $\frac{3}{5}$.

    The probability of one of the numbers being prime is $\frac{1}{5}$.

    Create a possible sample space diagram for the two spinners.

9 P-S / R   Two ordinary 6-sided dice are rolled and the numbers are multiplied together.

    a Show that there are only two ways of scoring 8.

    b Show that P(8) = $\frac{1}{18}$

10 P-S / R   A 7-sided spinner and an 8-sided spinner are spun.
The numbers on the spinners are multiplied together.

    The probability of a number greater than 16 is $\frac{47}{56}$.
    a Give possible values of a, b and c.
    b Ollie spins the 7-sided spinner and gets a.
       What is the probability that he will get c on the second spinner?
    c If Ollie had got a different score on the 7-sided spinner, would the answer
       to part **b** change?

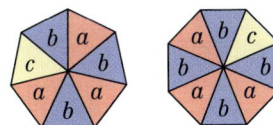

Reflect

11 In Q6, Q7 and Q9 you thought about the outcomes of rolling two dice.
To answer the question, did you need to fill out the sample space diagram completely?
Explain your reasoning.

9.4 Two-way tables

- Show all the possible outcomes of two events in a two-way table
- Calculate probabilities from two-way tables

1 **P-S** A school recorded photocopier use over the autumn term.

	Black and white	Colour	Total
A3	981	1724	2705
A4	13776	2379	16155
Total	14757	4103	18860

a Giving your answers to 2 decimal places, estimate the probability of the next copy being:

   i black and white, A4   **ii** colour.

The autumn term was 16 weeks. The spring term is 12 weeks.

b The school needs to order photocopy paper for the spring term.
Paper comes in packs of 500 sheets. How many packs does the school need to order of:

   i A3 paper   **ii** A4 paper?

2 **P-S / R** The table shows the numbers of recorded burglaries and bicycle thefts in different areas in 2018.

Area	Population (thousands)	Burglaries	Bicycle thefts
Cumbria	498.4	2103	296
Dyfed-Powys	516.8	1515	159
Essex	1820.4	12276	2254
Gwent	587.7	3634	369
Humberside	929.9	8341	2246
Leicestershire	1083.2	8415	2124
Merseyside	1416.8	11083	1890
Norfolk	898.4	3528	1242
Staffordshire	1126.2	6032	1233
Wiltshire	716.4	3222	826

a Which area had:

   i the lowest risk of burglary   **ii** the highest risk of bicycle theft?

b A newspaper headline says, 'Dyfed-Powys, the safest place in the UK!'

   i Does the data support this claim?

   ii Explain why the statement might not be true.

c Sam lives in Humberside. In 2018, her house was burgled and her bike was stolen.
She said, 'The chances of that were 1 in a million.'
Was she right? Explain your answer.

3 Zak flips a coin and picks one of these letter cards.

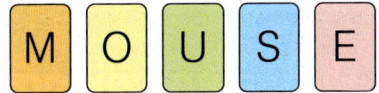

| M | O | U | S | E |

a Draw a two-way table to record his results.

b R Jo wants to find out if the experimental probability of 'heads and a vowel' is equal to the theoretical probability.

Heads and a vowel	Not (heads and a vowel)

She records her results in this table.

Is Jo's table or the one you drew for part **a** better for recording the results? Explain.

c Calculate the theoretical probability of 'heads and a vowel'.

d R Which table is better for completing part **c**? Explain.

4 **P-S / R** 32 people were interviewed and asked whether they preferred tea or coffee.

a Copy and complete the two-way table.

b Gary says that women like coffee more than men do. Using the two-way table, explain whether Gary is correct.

	Tea	Coffee
Men	6	
Women	14	11

c What is the probability that a person picked at random is a woman who prefers coffee?

d Given that a woman is selected, what is the probability that she prefers coffee?

e Why are your answers to parts **c** and **d** not the same?

f A second set of people were interviewed. From that sample, 18 men preferred tea. Estimate how many people were interviewed.

5 **P-S / R** 80 students were asked if they preferred veggie burgers or hotdogs.

a The probability of a Year 7 student being asked was $\frac{3}{20}$. How many students who were not Year 7 were asked?

b 40% of those asked liked hotdogs. $\frac{1}{8}$ more students liked veggie burgers. The rest did not have a preference. What was the probability that a randomly selected student liked veggie burgers?

c Only students in Years 7, 8 and 9 were asked. Only three students in Year 9 were asked. All three Year 9 students liked hotdogs. $\frac{1}{3}$ of the Year 7 students liked hot dogs. Twice as many Year 7 students had no preference compared with Year 8 students. Draw and complete a two-way table showing the information.

d A student's favourite food is veggie burgers. Which year group are they most likely to be in?

e Another student's favourite food is hotdogs. Explain why you cannot say which year group they are most likely to be in.

6 **R** Shay draws this table to record the results when he rolls two dice. Consider the possible 'even' or 'prime' results from rolling a dice. Explain why this table is not suitable.

		Dice 2		
		Even	Prime	Neither
Dice 1	Even			
	Prime			
	Neither			

Reflect

7 What is the same and what is different about sample space diagrams and two-way tables?

9.5 Venn diagrams

- Draw Venn diagrams
- Calculate probabilities from Venn diagrams

1　**R**　The Venn diagram shows two events when a 10-sided dice is rolled: square numbers and numbers less than 7.

  a Explain why the two events are *not* mutually exclusive.
  b What is the probability of rolling a square number?
  c What is the probability of rolling a number less than 7?
  d What is the probability of rolling a square number or a number less than 7?

square numbers　　less than 7

9　　4　3　5
　　1　　2　6
7　8　10

  e True or false: P(rolling a square number or a number less than 7)
  　　　　　= P(rolling a square number) + P(rolling a number less than 7)?

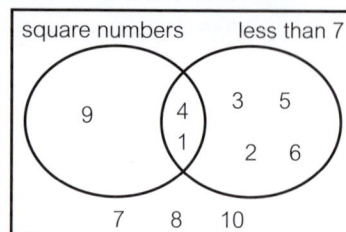

Explain.

2　The two-way table shows 10 people's choice of courses at a meal.

	Abi	Bea	Carl	Dean	Erin	Farouk	Gary	Hal	Izzy	Jack
Starter	✓			✓	✓		✓		✓	✓
Main		✓	✓		✓	✓	✓	✓	✓	✓
Dessert	✓		✓	✓			✓	✓	✓	✓

  a Copy and complete the Venn diagram for this information.
  b Calculate the probability that a person picked at random:
  　i had exactly two courses
  　ii did not have dessert.

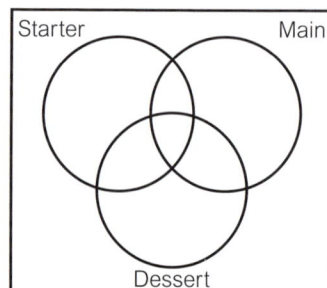

Starter　　　　　　Main

Dessert

3　This spinner is spun once.

  a What is the probability it will land on:
  　i 2
  　ii not 2?
  b Add the probabilities together. What do you notice?
  c Draw a Venn diagram to help explain your answer to part **b**.
  d Copy and complete this rule:
  　Probability of an event happening + Probability of the event *not* happening = ___
  e When you know the probability of an event happening, how can you work out the probability of it not happening?

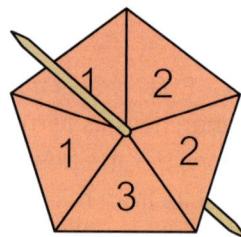

1　2
1　2
3

4 **P-S / R** The Venn diagram shows people's choice of pepperoni (*P*), ham (*H*) and mushrooms (*M*) as pizza toppings in a restaurant.

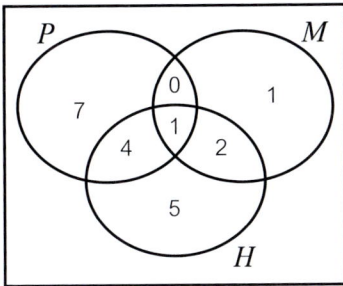

a How many people had:
  i three toppings
  ii only one topping?
b How many people had pizza?
c What is the probability that one of these people, picked at random, had two toppings?
d 20 more customers' pizza choices are added to the Venn diagram.
   The probability of all three toppings being chosen is now $\frac{1}{10}$.
   How many of the new people chose all three toppings?
e The probability of a customer having a topping on their pizza is 75%.
   How many people did not have a topping on their pizza?
f A total of 7 people had both mushrooms and pepperoni on their pizza.
   What is the probability of having mushrooms and pepperoni but not ham on a pizza?
g A total of 14 of the customers had mushrooms on their pizza.
   In a week, the restaurant expects to serve 300 people.
   Each time pepperoni is added to a pizza, 30 g of pepperoni is used.
   How much pepperoni should the restaurant order for the week?

5 The Venn diagram shows the numbers of people wearing a hat or coat at a festival.

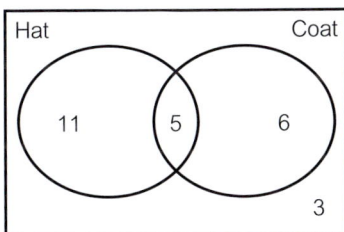

a How many people attended the festival?
b What is the probability that a person picked at random was wearing a hat?
c Work out the probability that a person picked at random was wearing a hat or a coat but not both.
d **R** Explain why you cannot add the probability of wearing a coat to the probability of wearing a hat to get the probability of a person wearing either or both.

Reflect

6 What would a Venn diagram showing two mutually exclusive events look like?

9 Extend

1 **P-S** Milly has a set of 10 consecutive numbers.
She picks a number at random from this set.

P(multiple of 3) = $\frac{3}{10}$

P(square number) = $\frac{1}{10}$

P(square number greater than 45) = $\frac{1}{10}$

In this set of numbers, the events 'square number' and 'multiple of 3' are mutually exclusive.
What could the numbers be?

2 **R** Show that for any set of three consecutive numbers, P(multiple of 3) = $\frac{1}{3}$.

3 **P-S** There are 80 students in a year group.
54 of them passed Maths. 63 of them passed English. 6 of them passed neither.
   a Draw a Venn diagram to show this information.
   b What is the probability that one of these students, picked at random, passed both
   maths and English?

4 **P-S** Three Halloween parties were organised.
One was witch themed, one was vampire themed and one was elf themed.
160 people were asked which parties they attended.

   10 people didn't attend any of the three parties.

   Of the people who attended at least one party, there were twice as many who went to
   only the vampire party as missed only the vampire party.

   81 people attended all three parties.

   19 people attended all except the witch party.

   $\frac{1}{5}$ of the number who didn't attend any of the parties attended only the elf party.

   A total of 109 people attended the elf party.
A person who attended the elf party is selected at random.
Given that they did not attend all three parties, is this person more likely to have attended or
not attended the vampire party?

5 **R** Explain why the data in Q4 cannot be displayed in a two-way table.

6 **P-S / R** Geri is creating a game.
She will charge 50p to play the game. She will give a prize of £2 if you win.
A player will roll two 4-sided dice and multiply the numbers to get a score.
Geri estimates that 160 people will play the game. She wants to make a profit of £40.
Suggest what Geri should count as a 'win'.

7 **P-S** The two-way table shows the results of a survey of a class of 28 students. The probability of a girl who is wearing her blazer being selected is 0.25.

	Wearing blazer	Not wearing blazer
Girl	a	b
Boy	c	d

A girl who is wearing a blazer has to go home early.
Now, the probability of a student being selected who is not wearing their blazer is $\frac{2}{3}$.
There are twice as many girls not wearing blazers as boys not wearing blazers.
What is the probability of a boy who is not wearing his blazer being selected?

8 **a** Draw a 5-sided spinner and label it with any five numbers so that P(odd) = $\frac{2}{5}$.

b Draw a sample space diagram for the spinner and calculate P(odd, odd), when the spinner is spun twice.

c **R** Nat says, 'Odd and even are mutually exclusive, so P(even, even) must be equal to P(odd, odd).' Explain why Nat is wrong.

9 **P-S** A point with integer coordinates between −5 and 5 is plotted at random on this grid.
Find the probability that this point:

a lies on the line $y = x$

b has its y-coordinate greater than its x-coordinate.

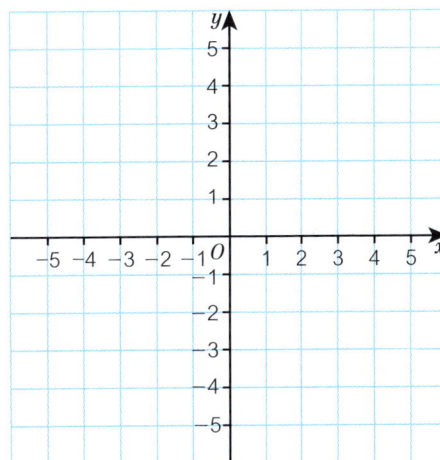

10 There are four blood groups: O, A, B and AB.
In the UK:
42% of people have blood group A
10% of people have blood group B
4% of people have blood group AB.

a What is the probability that a person in the UK picked at random has blood group O?

b Work out the probability that a person in the UK picked at random has blood group B or AB.

c A person with blood group B can receive blood from group O or group B.
What is the probability that a person picked at random could give blood to a person with blood group B?

Investigation

11 A Venn diagram shows the probability of three events A, B and C.

What is the least amount of information that could be given that would let someone fill in the entire Venn diagram?

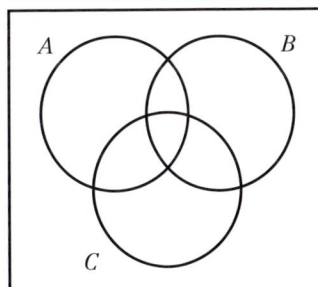

Reflect

12 John has two coins that he suspects are biased.
He flips the two coins together 100 times. They both land on heads 40 times.
Are the coins biased? Use what you have learned in this unit to explain.

10 Comparing shapes

Master   **Extend p121**

10.1 Congruent and similar shapes

- Use congruent shapes to solve problems about triangles and other polygons
- Work out whether shapes are similar, congruent or neither

1 R **a** Construct a triangle with an angle of 35°, a length of 6 cm, and an angle of 45°.
   b Are triangles constructed using these instructions always congruent? Explain.
   c What can change in part a to construct mathematically similar triangles?

2 R AC is a diagonal of the rectangle $ABCD$.
Explain why triangle ABC is congruent to triangle ADC.

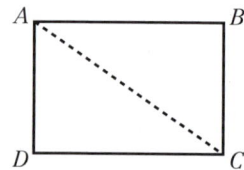

3 R The centre of this circle is O.
Prove that triangle OBC and triangle OAC are congruent.

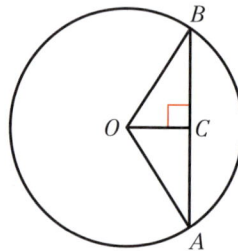

4 R Eight congruent isosceles right-angled triangles are arranged to make an octagon.
   a Is the octagon a regular octagon?
   b Is the hole in the centre a regular octagon? Explain how you know.

> **Q4 hint** Think about its exterior angles.

5 R By splitting the red parallelogram into congruent triangles, work out the fraction of the hexagon that is red.

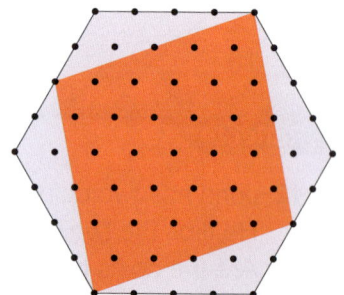

6 **R** In triangles PQR and STU, $QR = UT$ and $UP = RS$.
Which of the reasons for congruency (AAS, ASA, SAS or SSS) cannot be used to show that PQR and STU are congruent? Explain.

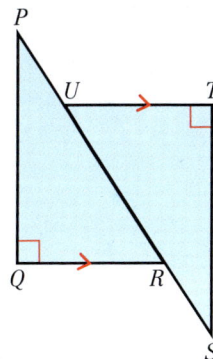

7 **R** A rectangle $ABCD$ is split into two triangles ABC and ACD.
Are these two triangles congruent? Give reasons.

8 **R** Draw a triangle with any side lengths and angles.
Bisect one of the angles.
Will the two new triangles always, sometimes or never be congruent?

9 **R** An isosceles triangle EFG is split into two triangles with a line that touches the midpoint M of one of the three sides. $EF = FG$.
  a Which side would the line touch if the two newly created triangles are congruent?
  b Give the conditions of congruency for these two new triangles.
  c Explain why the triangles would not be congruent if the new line touched either of the other two sides.

10 **R** In triangles HIJ and KLM, $HI = KL$, $HI = IJ$, $KL = LM$ and angle HIJ = angle LKM.
State whether triangles HIJ and KLM are congruent. Give reasons.

11 **P-S / R** In triangles NOP and QRS, $NO = RS$ and $OP = 2QS$.
Given that the two triangles NOP and QRS are congruent, state the corresponding angle pairs.

12 **R** Triangles ABC and BCD are formed by three lines crossing a pair of parallel lines.
Is there enough information in the diagram to determine whether ABC and BCD are congruent?
If there is, give the corresponding vertices with reasons.
If not, state what additional information would be needed.

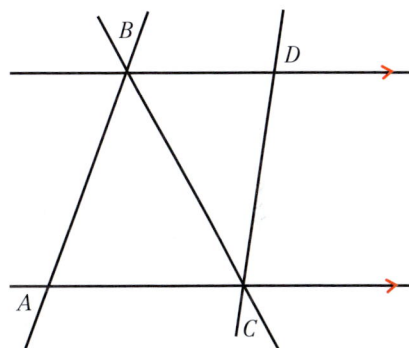

13 **R**
  a Cherise says, 'Two triangles have the same angles. The two triangles must be similar.'
    True or false?
  b Cherise says,'Two quadrilaterals have the same angles. The two quadrilaterals must be similar.'
    True or false?

Reflect

14 Is it possible for two shapes to be both similar and congruent? Explain your reasoning.

10.2 Ratios in triangles

- Solve problems involving similar triangles

1 R a Show that kites *ABCD* and *EFGH* are similar.

  b Find the value of *x*.

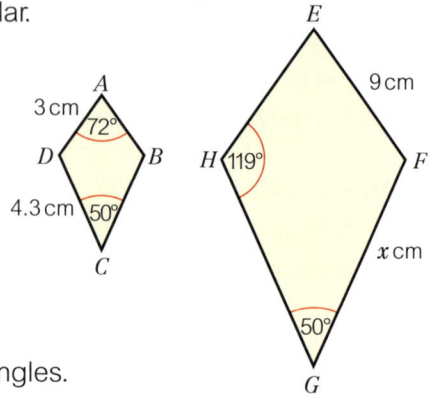

2 R Fatima is solving a problem about similar triangles.

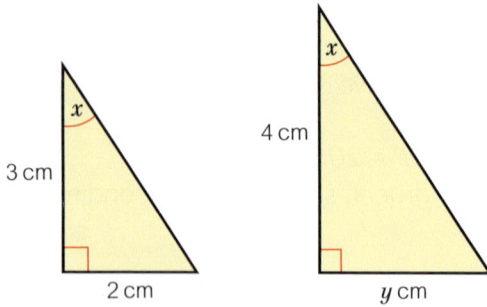

Fatima says that she knows that *y* is $2\frac{2}{3}$ because of the ratio between the two adjacent sides on the first triangle.

Is Fatima correct? Give reasons.

3 P-S / R All three triangles in this diagram are mathematically similar.

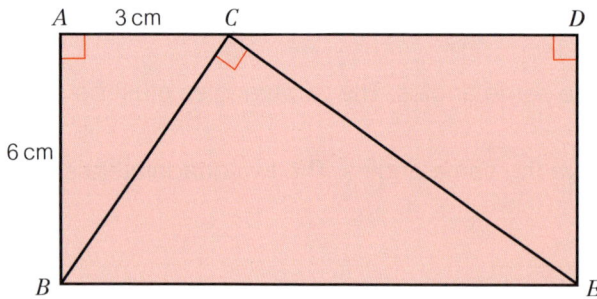

  a Work out the perimeter of the rectangle *ABED*.

  b Find the proportion of the area of the rectangle taken by triangle *CDE*.

4 **P-S / R** The length AG is 54 cm.
The length CE is 6 cm. $AD = DG$.
CE, BF and AG are parallel.
$DC = 3$ cm.
BF is 12 cm less than AC.
What is the perimeter of the trapezium $BCEF$?

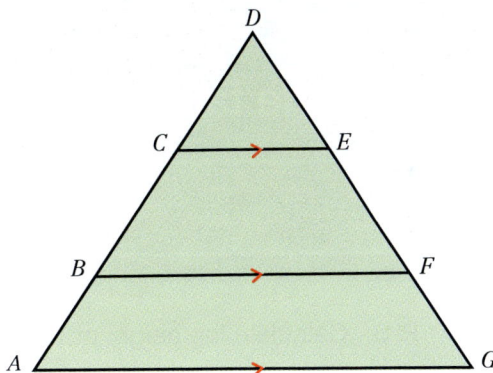

5 **R** The length of FG is 3 times the length of BC.
$AB = CD$ and $EF = GH$.
BC is parallel to AD.
FG is parallel to EH.
Angle ABC is 110° and angle FGH is 110°.
Show that the two trapezia are similar.

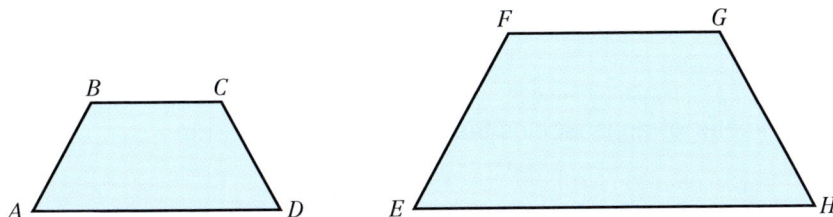

Investigation

6 **a** On a coordinate grid, plot a rectangle with corners at (0, 0), (0, 2), (1, 0) and (1, 2).

  b Plot a second rectangle with corners at (0, 0), (0, 4), (2, 0) and (2, 4).

  c Give reasons why these two rectangles are similar.

  d Draw a line from (0, 0) through the diagonals of both rectangles. What do you notice?

  e Test if the same thing happens with other similar rectangles with a common vertex.

  f What happens if the two rectangles are not similar?

  g Does the same thing happen with other quadrilaterals?

Reflect

7 In Q2, a problem about similar triangles was solved by looking at the ratio of corresponding side lengths within each triangle rather than the ratios of corresponding side lengths between the two triangles.
Which method do you prefer and why?

10.3 The tangent ratio

- Use the tangent ratio to work out an unknown side of a right-angled triangle

1 **P-S** Calculate the height of the isosceles triangle.

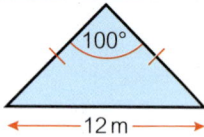

2 **P-S** Calculate the perimeter of the triangle.

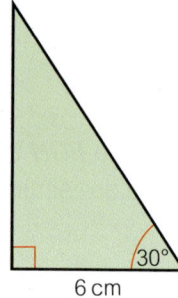

3 **P-S** Calculate the perimeter of an isosceles triangle with height 9.2 cm and base angles 39°.

4 **P-S / R** Ellie draws this triangle.

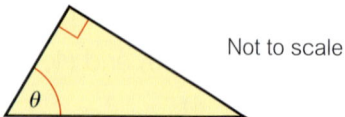

Not to scale

She works out tan θ = 1.
What kind of triangle has Ellie drawn? Explain.

5 **P-S / R** A kite has one right angle and one pair of opposite angles that are 106°.
Its shortest diagonal is 8 cm long.
What length is its longest diagonal? Give your answer to 3 significant figures.

6 **P-S** A small boat is caught in the beam of light from a lighthouse on a cliff.
The beam is at 23° to the horizontal.
The cliff top is 33 m above sea level.
The lighthouse is 8 m tall.
Find the horizontal distance of the boat from the lighthouse.
Give your answer to the nearest metre.

Q6 hint 'At 23° to the horizontal' means the angle between the beam and the horizontal is 23°.

113

7 **P-S / R** *ABCD* is an isosceles trapezium.

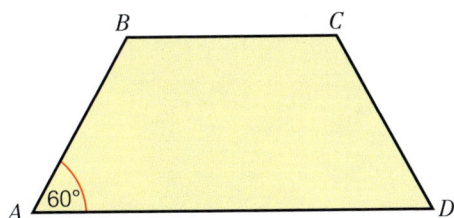

AD is parallel to *BC* and 6 cm longer.
BC = *AB*.
The perimeter is 30 cm.
Calculate the area of *ABCD*.

8 **P-S / R** Three similar triangles are joined to make a pentagon.

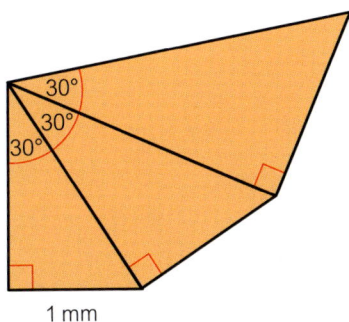

1 mm

Which is numerically greater, the perimeter of the pentagon or the area of the pentagon?
Show your working.

9 **P-S** *ABCD* is a kite. Its diagonals meet at point *E*.

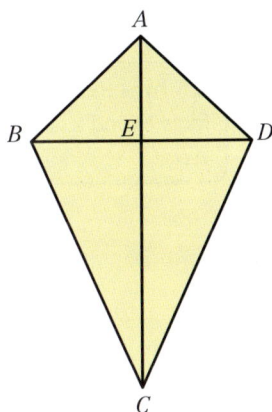

E splits *AC* in the ratio 2 : 3.
BD is 18 cm long.
Angle *ADE* is 60°.
What is the total area of the kite?

Reflect

10 In what ways have you used both Pythagoras' theorem and the tangent ratio together
in this lesson?

10.4 The sine ratio

- Use the sine ratio to work out an unknown side of a right-angled triangle

1 **R / P-S** A children's slide is 5.5 metres long.
It makes an angle of 30° with the ground.
What is the vertical height of the top of the slide?

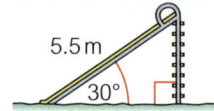

5.5 m
30°

2 **P-S** A ladder 6 m long is leaning against a wall.
The angle between the ladder and the ground is 72°.
What height does the ladder reach?

Q2 hint Draw a sketch.

3 **P-S** Work out the perimeter of this right-angled triangle.

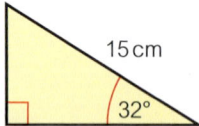

15 cm
32°

4 **R** In triangle ABC, angle θ and length x are marked.
Some students are given the values of θ and x and asked
to find the length of the hypotenuse.
Michael uses $\tan\theta$ and then Pythagoras' theorem.
Jean uses $\sin\theta$.
Do both methods work? Explain.

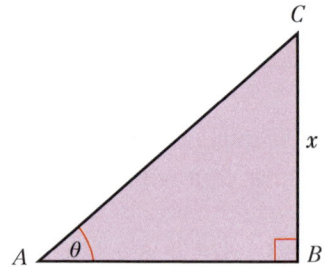

C
x
A θ B

5 **P-S** $ABCD$ is a parallelogram.
Find the length of diagonal AC, correct to 1 decimal place.

Q5 hint First use angle facts to find $\angle ACD$ and $\angle DAC$.

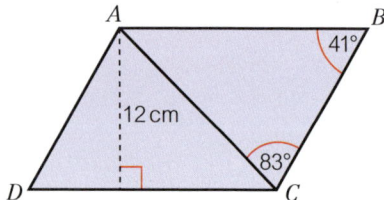

A B
41°
12 cm
83°
D C

6 **P-S** The diagram shows a seesaw.
The distance between the ground and the
centre of the seesaw is 84 cm.
The maximum angle between the seesaw and
the horizontal is 20°.
The length of the seesaw is 3.6 m.

3.6 m
20°
84 cm

To meet safety regulations, when the seesaw is at the maximum angle of 20°, the end of
each seat must be no less than 23 cm and no more than 150 cm from the ground.
Has the seesaw been safely installed? Give reasons for your answer.

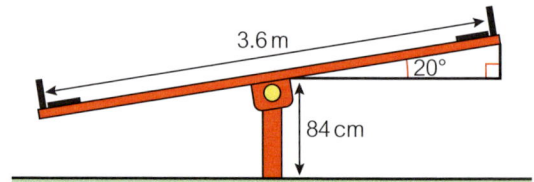

7 **P-S** A fishing lodge wants to build a new boat ramp.
The slope of the ramp must be 8° to the horizontal.
The total height of the bank is 2.8 m.

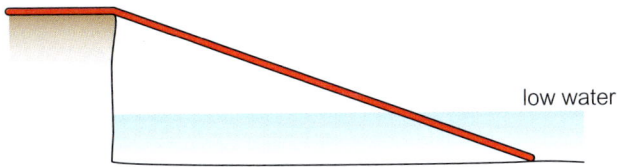

low water

a How long must the sloping section of the ramp be?
Give your answer to the nearest centimetre.

At low water, the depth of water at the ramp site is 1.2 m.

b What length of the ramp will always be under water?
Give your answer to the nearest centimetre.

8 **P-S / R** *ABCDE* is a regular pentagon. *O* marks its centre.
Work out its perimeter. Give your answer to 2 decimal places.

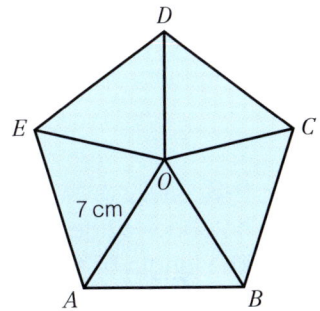

7 cm

9 **P-S / R** *ABCD* is an isosceles trapezium.
AB is 4 cm longer than *BC*.
AD is parallel to *BC* and is 8 cm longer.
The area of *ABCD* is 64 cm².
Find the perimeter of *ABCD*.

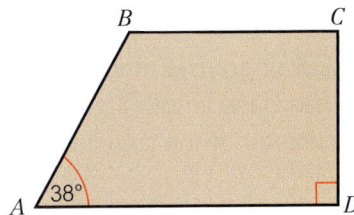

38°

Investigation

10 A right-angled triangle has one angle of 28°. One side is 6 cm long.

a What are the three possible triangles?

b What is the greatest possible area of the triangle?

c What is the greatest possible perimeter of the triangle?

d How do the area and perimeter change if the given side is 7 cm not 6 cm?

e How do the area and perimeter change if the given side is 8 cm not 6 cm?

f Is there a pattern? Predict the perimeter and area for 9 cm and then check it.

Reflect

11 In Q4, Michael and Jean use different methods to find the hypotenuse.
Michael uses $\tan\theta$ and then Pythagoras' theorem. Jean uses $\sin\theta$.
Which method do you prefer? Explain why.

10.5 The cosine ratio

• Use the cosine ratio to work out an unknown side of a right-angled triangle

1 **P-S** A roof is made from beams that make an isosceles triangle.
The sloping side of the roof is 8 metres.
The roof makes an angle of 30° with the horizontal.
Calculate the width of the roof.

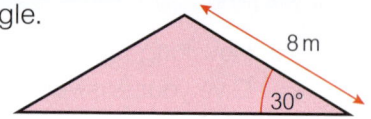

2 **P-S** A flagpole, AB, is supported by two ropes, BD and BC.
 a Find the length of BD.
 b Find the length of BC.

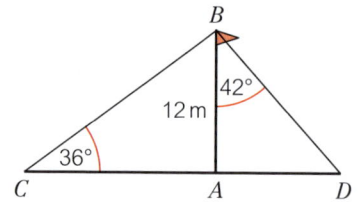

3 **P-S** Sally draws a straight line from one corner of her
notebook page to the opposite corner.
The length of the line is 22.9 cm.
Her line makes an angle of 56° with the bottom of the page.
What are the dimensions of Sally's notebook? Give your answer to the nearest mm.

4 **P-S / R** A parallelogram is made of two identical isosceles triangles.
Each triangle has base length 18 cm and base angles 43°.
What is the perimeter of the parallelogram?

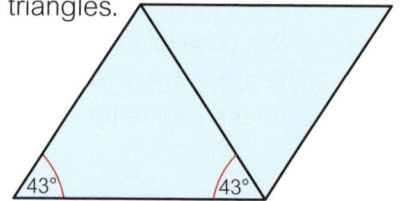

5 **P-S** The diagram shows the path of a ship that sails
20 km from P.

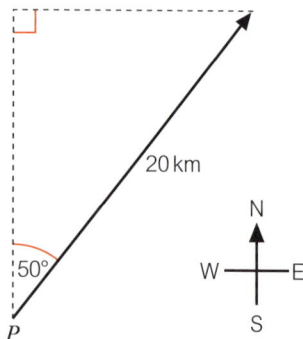

 a How far north has the ship travelled? Give your answer to the nearest metre.
 b How far east has it travelled?

6 **P-S** A plane flies on a **bearing** of 058° for 80 km.

    a How far north has it travelled?

    b How far east has it travelled?

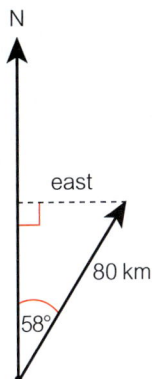

> **Key point** A **bearing** is an angle that is always measured clockwise from north and given as three digits.
> For example, an angle of 82° clockwise from north is a bearing of 082°.

7 **P-S** A ship sails for 50 km on a bearing of 130°.

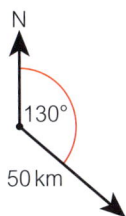

> **Q7 hint**
>
>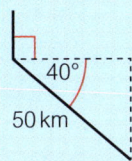

How far east has it travelled?

8 **P-S** A ship leaves port and travels on a bearing of 245° for 40.6 km.

    a How far west has it travelled?

    b How far south has it travelled?

9 **P-S** A speedboat travels for 45 minutes at 130 km/h on a bearing of 063°. How far north has the boat travelled?

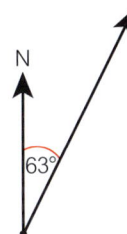

10 **P-S / R** A ship sails on a bearing of 324°.

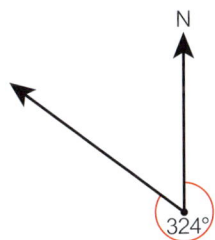

It travels 19 km north.
What is the distance it has travelled?

> **Reflect**
>
> **11** Explain why trigonometry is useful for solving bearings problems.

10.6 Using trigonometry to find angles

- Use the trigonometric ratios to work out an unknown angle in a right-angled triangle

1 **P-S** Sakina is planning to build a zip line.

It is going to start from a point 12 m above the ground, and will be 150 m long.

a What angle will the zip line make with the ground?

For a zip line to be safe, it needs to make an angle of less than 3.5° with the ground.

b How much does Sakina need to increase the length of her zip line by for it to be safe?

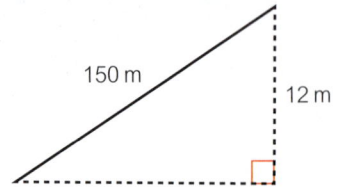

2 **P-S** Calculate the size of angle θ in this diagram.

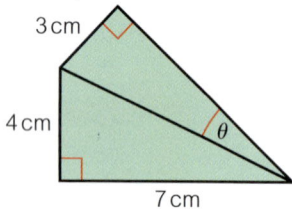

3 **P-S** A right-angled triangle has sides 8 cm, 10 cm and 6 cm.
Work out the sizes of all the angles in the triangle.

4 **P-S** In this triangle, BD is perpendicular to AC.

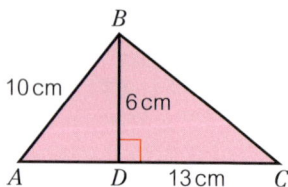

> **Q5 hint** First calculate the sizes of BCD and BAD.

Calculate the size of angle ABC.

5 **P-S** A hiker walks 5.4 km north and then turns and walks another 8.9 km east.

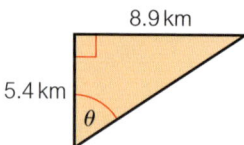

Calculate the hiker's bearing from his original position.

6 **P-S** A ship sails 30 km north and 50 km east.
On what bearing has it travelled?

7 **P-S** A ship sails 40 km west and then 60 km north.
What is the bearing of the ship from its original position?

8 **P-S** Work out the angle between AD and AC.

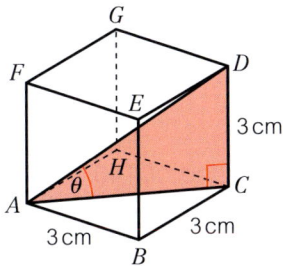

Q8 hint What other right-angled triangle is AC a part of?

9 **P-S** The diagram shows a cube of side length 7 cm.

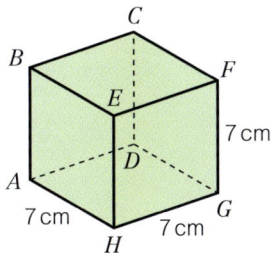

Q9 hint Try drawing and labelling all of the right-angled triangles in this shape first.

Calculate:
a the length AG
b the angle between AG and AF
c the length of the diagonal AF.

Investigation

10 a Draw a cube with side length 4 cm.
  b Work out the angle marked θ.
     Compare your answer with Q9.
  c Repeat for different sized cubes.
     What do you notice?
     Explain.

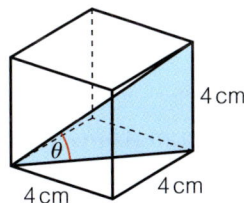

Reflect

11 In this lesson you calculated angles in 3D shapes.
What is the same and what is different about this compared to 2D shapes?

10 Extend

1 **P-S**   A drone is hovering 100 m above the ground.
The drone is observed by some people in a car as they look upwards at an angle of 15°.
30 seconds later, the people in the car had to look up at an angle of 70° to see the drone.
How fast was the car moving?
Give your answer in m/s and km/h.

2 **P-S**   A plane travels for 1.5 hours at 120 mph on a bearing of 050°.
It turns and continues for another hour at the same speed on a bearing of 140°.
At the end of this time, how far away is the plane from its starting point?

3 **P-S**   In this basketball court the basketball hoop is at the midpoint of AB.

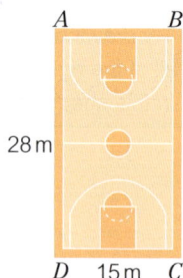

a Work out the distance from D to the basketball hoop.
The hoop is 3.1 m off the ground.
b Work out the angle between D and the top of the hoop.

4 **P-S / R**   The area of triangle CDE is 24 cm².
The length AG is 18 cm.
The length CE is 6 cm.
DH is an angle bisector for ADG.
$DA = DG$.
CE, BF and AG are parallel.
The height of the trapezium $ABFG$ is 6 cm.
What is the area of trapezium $BCEF$?

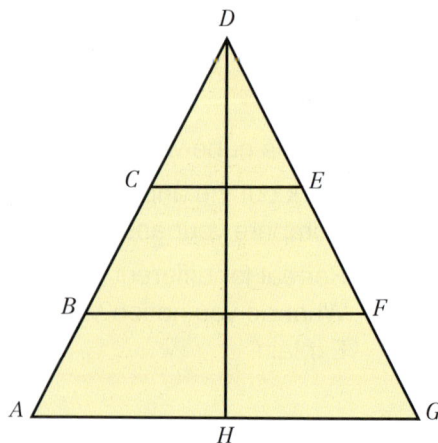

5   In a right-angled triangle ABC:
AB has length 5 cm
Angle ABC is 60°
Angle CAB is 90°.
a Use the tangent ratio to find AC and then Pythagoras' theorem to find BC.
b Use the sine ratio to find BC and then Pythagoras' theorem to find AC.
c **R**   Find two other methods you could use to find the perimeter of the triangle.
d **R**   Which method do you prefer and why?

6 **P-S** A regular hexagon has side length 6 cm.
Find the area of the hexagon.

Q6 hint **Q6 hint** What smaller shapes can you split it into? What do you know about angles in hexagons?

7 **P-S** A regular hexagon has side length $2x$ cm.
Find an expression for the area of the hexagon.

8 Sally has drawn a right-angled triangle where the tangent ratio of one of the angles is $\frac{5}{6}$.

   a Sketch the triangle, showing potential side lengths.

   b R Find three other triangles that would give a tangent ratio of $\frac{5}{6}$.

   c What is the size of the angle?

   d R Sally draws the angle accurately as an integer number of degrees.
Why would the tangent ratio not be exactly $\frac{5}{6}$?

9 **a R** Find the sine ratio for a right-angled triangle with an angle of 10°.

   b Find the sine ratio for a right-angled triangle with an angle of 20°.

   c Keep going up until 80°. Plot a graph of this, showing the angle size along the x-axis and the value of the sine ratio on the y-axis.

   d What do you think will happen at 90°?

   e Use your calculator to get the values up to 360°.

   f What do you think will happen after that? Check your prediction.

   g Repeat parts **a** to **f** for cosine and tangent. What is the same and what is different?

Investigation

10 **a** Find the size of every angle in this shape.

   b Use trigonometry to find the length of every side. Show your workings clearly.

   c Repeat, changing the original two labelled angles to any numbers you want.
What do you notice about your workings?
Is there a quicker way to calculate the side lengths of the rectangle without working out all of the sides in between?

   d Let the original two angles be x and y.
Compare the opposite heights of the rectangle.
What can you say about $\sin(x + y)$?
Is this always true?

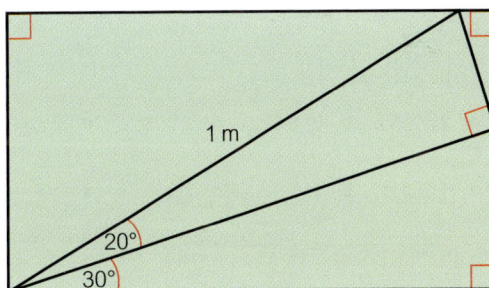

Reflect

11 In this unit you have looked at similar shapes and trigonometry.
How are similar shapes, trigonometry and ratio related?

ANSWERS

UNIT 1 Indices and standard form

1.1 Indices

1. a i 16   ii -32
   iii 64   iv -128
   b i Sign alternates as power increases.
   ii An even power of a negative number gives a positive answer. An odd power gives a negative answer.
   c Students' own answers.

2. Students' own answers, for example, $(-10)^3 = -1000$. The power should always be an odd integer.

3. a 39
   b $(5 \times 6 + 3)^2 = 1089$
   c The smallest answer is 39.
   d 564
   e 6 must change to 111.

4. a $3 \times (2 + 3)^2 = 75$
   b $(10 - (5 - 3))^2 = 64$
   c $2 \times ((6 - 2)^2 - 2) = 28$
   d $2(\sqrt{81} - \sqrt{25}) = 8$
   e $5(\sqrt{49} + 3 - 2) = 40$
   f $3 \times ((4 + 2) \times (6 + 8)) = 252$

5. 2^7 or 128

Investigation

6. a i $2^2 = 4$
   $2^2 + 2^2 = 8$
   $2^2 + 2^2 + 2^3 = 16$
   $2^2 + 2^2 + 2^3 + 2^4 = 32$
   $2^2 + 2^2 + 2^3 + 2^4 + 2^5 = 64$
   ii $2^2 = 4$
   $2^3 = 8$
   $2^4 = 16$
   $2^5 = 32$
   $2^6 = 64$
   b Increasing powers of 2
   c Same answers
   d $2^2 + 2^2 + 2^3 + 2^4 + 2^5 + 2^6 = 128 = 2^7$
   e $128 - 2 = 126$
   f $2^1 + 2^2 + 2^3 + 2^4 + 2^5 + 2^6 = 2^7 - 2$
   $2^1 + 2^2 + 2^3 + 2^4 + 2^5 + 2^6 + 2^7 = 2^8 - 2$
   $2^1 + 2^2 + 2^3 + 2^4 + \ldots + 2^x = 2^{x+1} - 2$

7. a 0
   b $\left[\frac{1}{8} \div \left(\frac{1}{4}\right)^2 - \frac{1}{4}\right] \div \left(\frac{1}{2}\right)^3$

8. a $2^7 \times 3^6$ b $3^5 \times 5^7$ c $2^8 \times 3^5$ d $2^{-2} \times 3^2$

9. B

10. a $\frac{5}{6}$ b $31\frac{1}{2}$ c $\frac{25}{288}$ d $10\frac{2}{3}$

11. $\frac{(3 \times 4)^2}{15} = \frac{3 \times 2^4}{5}$ or $\frac{(3 \times 4)^2}{15} = \frac{3 \times 4^2}{5}$

Reflect

12. Students' own answers.

1.2 Calculations and estimates

1. a i 4, 4   ii 8, 8   iii 16, 16
   b i Same answers.
   ii To find the square root of an even power of 2, halve the index.
   iii Students' own answers.

2. C

3. a $\frac{81}{25}$ b $\frac{81}{16}$ c $\frac{81}{16}$
   d $\frac{4}{25}$ e $\frac{4}{5}$ f $\frac{16}{25}$

4. Multiple answers, e.g. $\frac{16}{25}$ and its square root, $\frac{4}{5} = \frac{20}{25}$

5. Multiple answers, e.g. $\sqrt[3]{\frac{1}{64}} = \frac{1}{4}$, $\sqrt{\frac{1}{64}} = \frac{1}{8}$

6. a $2^3, 3^2, 4^3, 3^4, 6^5, 5^6$
   b It is more likely that a^b will be larger, as if both a and b are greater than 2 then a^b will always be bigger (as shown in part a).

7. a i 3   ii 3   iii 3
   b Students' own predictions.
   c i Under   ii Under   iii Under
   d Students' own predictions.
   e i 1   ii 1   iii 1
   f i Over   ii Over   iii Over

8. Students' own answers, e.g. $\frac{3.9^2}{\sqrt[3]{7.9}}$, $\frac{3.8^2}{\sqrt[3]{7.8}}$, $\frac{3.7^2}{\sqrt[3]{7.7}}$

9. a Multiple answers, e.g. $a = 8$, $b = 27$.
   b There are infinitely many answers, so long as the denominator is larger than the numerator. Provided this is true, cubing will always make the number smaller and cube rooting will always make it larger.

10. 10

11. a 2   b 2   c 2
    d 2   e 256

12. 2025

13. $0.16 = \frac{16}{100}$, and both 16 and 100 have exact square roots.

    $1.6 = \frac{16}{10}$, and 10 does not have an integer square root.

    $0.016 = \frac{16}{1000}$, and 1000 does not have an integer square root.

Reflect

14. Students' own answers, e.g.
    The power must be outside brackets to apply to the whole fraction.
    Squaring the numerator increases the size of the fraction, while rooting the numerator decreases it; they do the opposite when applied to the denominator.

1.3 More indices

1. a i $\frac{1}{100}$ ii $\frac{1}{100}$ iii Same answer
   b i $\frac{1}{1000}$ ii $\frac{1}{1000}$ iii Same answer
   c i The rule 'a power of a product equals the product of the powers' works for negative powers.
   ii Students' own answers.

2. 3 and 2

3.
$\left(\frac{1}{2}\right)^3$ =	$(0.5)^3$ =	2^{-3} =	$\frac{1}{8}$

   $(2 \times 4)^{-3}$ = $\frac{1}{512}$

   $\left(\frac{1}{8}\right)^0$ = 1

   8^{-2} = $\frac{1}{64}$

   $\left(\frac{1}{4}\right)^2$ = $\frac{1}{16}$

4. a 10^{-4} m   b 0.1 mm

5. a 10^{-1} b 10^{-2}
   c i 10^{-5} ii 10^{-10} iii 10^{-100}
   d No; $1.7 \times 10^{22} \times 10^{-100} = 1.7 \times 10^{-78}$ which is much less than one molecule.

6.
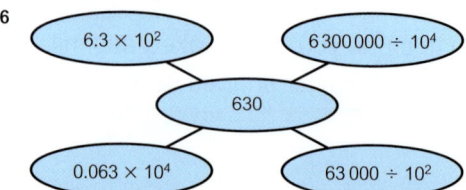

Diagram: 6.3 × 10² — 6 300 000 ÷ 10⁴ — 630 — 0.063 × 10⁴ — 63 000 ÷ 10²

7 **a** 7^{99} **b** 13^{60} **c** 10^{48} **d** 3^{90}

8 **a**

Name of organism	Length (m)	Width (m)
dust mite	0.00042	0.00025
bacteria	0.000002	0.0000005
virus	0.0000003	0.000000015

   b Dust mite   **c** Virus
   d Students' own answers, e.g.
   By using the prefixes, for example 1 mm = 1000 μm so
   0.42 mm > 2 μm > 0.3 μm.

9 0.0000001 mm

Investigation

10 **a** $5^{-6} + 1^2 - 3^{-4} = 0.987718321$
   b $1^{-2} + 5^6 - 3^{-4} = 15625$

Reflect

11 Students' own answers, e.g.
   I know that negative indices make numbers into fractions, so for
   the smallest answer, I wanted the largest numbers being made
   into fractions as that makes them the smallest.

1.4 Standard form

1 **a** 7.2×10^6 **b** 2.95×10^5 **c** 6.2×10^5
   d 1.7×10^{-5} **e** 3.2×10^{-2} **f** 3.5×10^{11}
   g 1.9×10^{12} **h** 2.4×10^{-8} **i** 3.2×10^{-11}

2 E 1.62×10^{-4}, C 1.65625×10^{-4}, B 1.69×10^{-4},
   D 1.691×10^{-4}, A 1.702×10^{-4}

3 **a** Bangladesh, Pakistan, India, China
   b 1.19×10^8
   c Roughly 7 times (6.63 times, to 3 s.f.)
   d 2.9566×10^9
   e 36% (to 2 s.f.)

4 **a, b**

Country	Population	Area (km²)	Population density
China	1 360 000 000	9 570 000	142
Hong Kong	7 110 000	1 050	6771
Iceland	317 000	100 000	3
USA	319 000 000	9 160 000	35
Vietnam	93 400 000	310 000	301

   c **i** Hong Kong   **ii** Iceland

5 $8.82 \times 10^5 : 1$

6 **a** 6.1536×10^{11}
   b Yes
   $9.6 \times 6.41 = 61.536$
   $= 6.1536 \times 10$ so $9.6 \times 10^7 \times 6.41 \times 10^3$
   $= 6.1536 \times 10 \times 10^{7+3} = 6.1536 \times 10^{11}$
   c No; the powers of 10 do not combine like this when adding.
   d Clare's working is correct.

7 **a** **i** $10^{-4} \times (6.75 + 4.25)$
   ii $10^4 \times (8.88 - 8.37)$
   iii $(3.9 \times 10^7) + (4.2 \times 10^7 \times 10^{-3}) = 10^7 \times (3.9 + 4.2 \times 10^{-3})$
   iv $(7.02 \times 10^{-3}) - (6.1 \times 10^{-1} \times 10^{-3}) = 10^{-3} \times (7.02 - 0.61)$
   b **i** 1.1×10^{-3}
   ii 5.1×10^3
   iii 3.9042×10^7
   iv 6.41×10^{-3}

8 3.7×10^{-7} m

9 **a** 1×10^9
   b An increase of 7.499×10^{10}, or 7500 times as many
   (roughly 10 000 times as many).

Reflect

10 When their power of 10 is the same, because that means that
   the numbers would start in the same place value column.

1 Extend

Investigation

1 **a** 3   **b** 10
   c 15, 21, 28, 36, 45, 55
   d The number increases by 3 then 4 then 5 then 6, etc.
   e 66
   f For cube numbers, the difference between the differences
   increases by 3 each time.

2 $10^6 \times (170 \times 10^{-9}) = 1.7 \times 10^{-1}$ m so it would be visible if the
   particles were end to end.
   Even if the particles were arranged in a disc, one particle
   deep, the diameter would be 1.13×10^3 particles and measure
   $1.13 \times 10^3 \times (170 \times 10^{-9}) = 1.9 \times 10^{-4}$ m across, so would
   also be visible.

3 3910 cm = 39.1 m (to 3 s.f.)
   This scale means that the model is a bit big. Making the Moon
   and Earth 1 cm apart would be more appropriate.

4 **a** A   **b** B   **c** B
   d B   **e** B   **f** A

5 No, there are no solutions between 1 and 100.

6 16 times

7 3

8 E.g. $4^2 = 3^2 + 7$

9 **a** If you divide 2^{16} by 2 you will get 2^{15} because there is
   one lot of 2 less.
   b $\dfrac{1}{3}$ **c** $\dfrac{1}{16}$

10 64

11 $\dfrac{2^9}{3}$

12 **a** 7.09×10^{14} km
   b 2.95×10^9 seconds

Investigation

13 **a** $12 = 30$ $17 = 101$ $20 = 110$ $64 = 1000$
   b $12 = 3 \times 10$ $17 = 1.01 \times 10^2$
   $20 = 1.1 \times 10^2$ $64 = 1 \times 10^3$
   c Students' own answers.

Reflect

14 **a** Standard form uses indices and it means that you can
   see where and how to apply the laws of indices to
   standard form.
   b Standard form is often used in scientific contexts as they
   often involve very large or very small numbers, and it makes
   the calculations more straightforward to write and work out.

UNIT 2 Expressions and formulae

2.1 Solving equations

1 a i $3g + 6 = 10g$
  $6 = 7g$
  $\frac{6}{7} = g$

  ii Students' own answers, e.g.
  I prefer Kerry's method because it makes it easier to see what is happening with the g.

 b Jake: LHS = 0.571, RHS = 0.57, so not equal.

  Kerry: LHS = $\frac{4}{7}$, RHS = $\frac{4}{7}$

  Kerry's solution is better because it is more accurate. Jake's solution is less accurate because it has been rounded.

2 $n \div 4 - 3 = 2$ or $\frac{n}{4} - 3 = 2$, $n = 20$, so there were 20 paintballs in the bag.

3 a $e = 4$ **b** $b = 6$ **c** $m = 2$
 d $m = 4$ **e** $p = 3$ **f** $n = 4$
 g $s = 1$ **h** $a = 2$ **i** $d = 3$
 j $z = 2$

4 a i $6 = 2x - 2$
   $8 = 2x$
   $4 = x$
  ii $-2x + 6 = -2$
    $-2x = -8$
    $x = 4$

 b Students' own answers, e.g.
  Subtracting $3x$ from both sides first is easier because it leads to fewer negative signs.

 c i $10 + x = 13$
    $x = 3$
  ii $10 = 13 - x$
    $-3 = -x$
    $3 = x$

 d Students' own answers, e.g.
  Adding $3x$ to both sides first is easier because it leads to fewer negative signs.

5 5 hours

6 a €4.86
 b Money is always given in decimal notation so you can compare easily.

7 6

8 a $x = -5$, perimeter = 36
 b No, because all the sides are equal. You can check by substituting.

9 $x = -13.25$, which means that some of the lengths on the L-shape are negative, which is not possible.

Investigation

10 a No, because equating any pair of two sides gives a different value of x each time.
 b Students' own answers for their triangle.

Reflect

11 a $\frac{3}{4}$ and 0.75 are equivalent so neither is more accurate than the other.

 b In general, a fraction solution may be more accurate (as in **Q1**), but it is not suitable when the solution is an amount of money or other quantity that needs to be written as a decimal (as in **Q6**).

2.2 Substituting into expressions

1 a i 5   **ii** 50   **iii** 11.4 (1 d.p.)
 b i 3   **ii** 11   **iii** 6.698 (3 d.p.)
2 a i 3.6 (1 d.p.) **ii** 6.4 (1 d.p.)
 b i 5   **ii** 9
 c They are not always equal.
3 a i 6   **ii** 20
 b i 6   **ii** 20
 c They are equal.

4 a 10 cm
 b i 6 cm   **ii** 5.85 cm
  iii 5.848 035 476 … cm
 c Yes; $\sqrt{200}$ cannot be written as an exact decimal.

5 a $20 = \dfrac{r \times 250}{100}$
 b $r = 8$, so the rate of interest is 8%.
 c $A = 425$, so his investment was £425.

6 a A5 $4a^2 - \sqrt{e} = 31$,

  B2 $(b\sqrt{d} + \sqrt{ai}) = -20$,

  C3 $\sqrt[3]{f} - 8c = 37$,

  D1 $\dfrac{hi}{3} + 3b^2c = -44$,

  E6 $\dfrac{b^2 + g^2}{h} = 5$,

  F4 $\sqrt[3]{dh} - 2c^2 = -46$

 b Card 7 with value 12 has not been used. Students' own answers. Expressions may include:
  $\sqrt{d} + i + g$, $2h^2 - cg$, $(bc)^2 - ae - (i + 1)$

7 Carlos is correct. If you multiply three negative numbers together, you always get a negative number, so $3x^2y$ and z^3 will both be negative for all values of x, y and z.

8 a 80   **b** 8   **c** 2   **d** -80
 e 100   **f** $\frac{1}{8}$ **g** $\frac{16}{5}$ **h** $-\frac{5}{6}$

Reflect

9 a Substitute in two 'easy' numbers to check whether the pattern works. If it does, try some different numbers in case it is a one-off.
 b You have not shown it is true for *all* values of the variables.

2.3 Writing and using formulae

1 a 80 m   **b** 92.5 m
2 a $\frac{1}{5}$ **b** $\frac{1}{3}$
3 a $P = 1.5a - 6$ **b** £18
4 a $F = ma$ **b** $a = \dfrac{v - u}{t}$
 c i 2 m s^{-2} **ii** 10 newtons
5 a $P = SU - (F + CU)$
 b i $P = 1.5U - 300$
  ii The selling price per unit minus the cost per unit.
  iii The fixed cost that must be paid no matter how many units are sold.
  iv No, because the fixed cost must always be subtracted. A positive y-intercept would mean the firm was making a profit even if it didn't sell anything.
 c i £82   **ii** £9.20   **iii** 31.5%
6 a $S = 2h - 1$
 b The y-intercept shows that if Afridi spends zero hours in the garden, he will find -1 snail. The gradient means that for every extra hour Afridi spends in the garden, he will find 2 more snails.
 c It is only based on two observation points, so not very accurate. Finding -1 snails is impossible.

Investigation

7 a $y = \frac{3}{5}x + 5$ **b** $y = \frac{3}{5}x + 8$

 c $y = \frac{3}{5}x + 3.2$ **d** $y = \frac{3}{5}x + 6.2$

 e The gradient stays the same but the y-intercept changes. If you add to the y-values, the y-intercept increases by the number you added. If you add to the x values, the y-intercept decreases.

Reflect

8 Find the equation of the line, in the form $H = mt + c$, where m is the gradient and c is the y-intercept.

2.4 Using and rearranging formulae

1 a i 68°F ii 212°F iii 32°F
   b i 15°C ii 100°C iii 0°C

   c $C = \frac{5}{9}(F - 32)$

2 a $x = \frac{p}{5 - k}$ b $x = \frac{10 - t}{m - 1}$

   c $x = \frac{17}{y - 4}$ d $x = \frac{mr}{r^2 - m^2}$

3 a $u = \frac{2v + ev}{6e - 1}$

   b 5

4 a i $a = \frac{F}{m}$ ii 8

   b i $m = \frac{F}{a}$ ii 3.5

5 a $x = \frac{y - 3}{2}$ b $x = \frac{t + 9}{5}$ c $x = \frac{v - 8m}{3}$

6 a $y = 5x + 12$
   b $y = -4x + 11$
   c $y = 3x + 9$

7 a $A = \frac{1}{2}(a + b)h$

   b i 9 cm ii 1 cm iii 30 cm

8 a $a = \frac{2d}{t^2}$ b 3.125 c 2

9 a $V = \frac{2}{3}\pi r^3$

   b $r = \sqrt[3]{\frac{3V}{2\pi}}$ c $r = \sqrt[3]{\frac{3V}{\pi}}$

10 a $T = \sqrt{P^2 - ag^2}$ b $a = \frac{P^2 - T^2}{g^2}$

   c $g = \sqrt{\frac{P^2 - T^2}{a}}$

   d P is not the subject, P^2 is the subject.

11 a $15y + 6 = 12x - 18$

   b $y = \frac{12}{15}x - \frac{24}{15}$

   c $x = \frac{15}{12}y + 2$

   d x must be larger because it is equal to a fraction of y that is greater than 1, plus 2. y is equal to a fraction of x that is less than 1, subtract a fraction that is greater than 1. Or:

   x is larger because $y = \frac{12}{15}x - \frac{24}{15} < x - \frac{24}{15} < x$.

Reflect

12 a You would only have needed to rearrange the formula once, rather than three times.
   b When you have lots of similar calculations, as in **Q1** and **Q7**, it is more efficient to change the subject first. When you are only finding one value of a variable, as in **Q4**, it is probably more efficient to substitute and solve the equation.

2.5 Index laws and brackets

1 a x^9 b x^5 c $x^{m + n}$
   d x^5 e x^4 f $x^{m - n}$

2 a i 1, 1, 1, 1, 1, 1
     ii They're all 1.
     iii When you divide a number by itself the answer is always 1.
   b i $\frac{x^5}{x^1} = x^4$, $\frac{x^5}{x^2} = x^3$, $\frac{x^5}{x^3} = x^2$, $\frac{x^5}{x^4} = x^1$, $\frac{x^5}{x^5} = x^0$

     ii $x^0 = 1$

     iii Any number to the power of 0 is 1.

Investigation

3 a i $\frac{3^2}{3^5} = 3^{2-5} = 3^{-3}$ and $\frac{3^2}{3^5} = \frac{3 \times 3}{3 \times 3 \times 3 \times 3 \times 3} = \frac{1}{3^3}$

     so $3^{-3} = \frac{1}{3^3}$ and $\frac{1}{3^3} < 1$

     ii $\frac{x^3}{x^4} = x^{3-4} = x^{-1}$ and $\frac{x^3}{x^4} = \frac{x \times x \times x}{x \times x \times x \times x} = \frac{1}{x^1}$

     so $x^{-1} = \frac{1}{x^1}$

     iii $\frac{y^8}{y^{11}} = y^{8-11} = y^{-3}$ and $\frac{y^8}{y^{11}} = \frac{1}{y^3}$ so $y^{-3} = \frac{1}{y^3}$

   b $x^{-n} = \frac{1}{x^n}$ is true for all values of x and all values of n.

   c, d Students' own answers.
   e When x is a positive integer, x^{-n} is a fraction between 0 and 1.
     When x is a fraction between 0 and 1, $x^{-n} > 1$.
   f When x is a unit fraction.
   g When x is a negative integer, x^{-n} is a fraction between -1 and 1.
     When x is a fraction between -1 and 0, $x^{-n} > 1$ for even values of n, and $x^{-n} < -1$ for odd values of n.

4 a x^6 b x^{20} c $x^{m \times n}$

5 a A7, B4, C6, D3, E5, F1, G2

   b $\frac{(x^a)^c}{x^b}$

6 a 3 b 32 c 9
   d 4 e -2 f -40

7 a $x^{-3} = \frac{1}{x^3}$ b $y^{-7} = \frac{1}{y^7}$

   c $p^{-1} = \frac{1}{p}$ d $z^{-8} = \frac{1}{z^8}$

8 a i $3x^{-2}$ ii $\frac{3}{x^2}$

   b i $6y^{-4}$ ii $\frac{6}{y^4}$

   c i $8y^{-7}$ ii $\frac{8}{y^7}$

   d i $\frac{p^{-4}}{3}$ ii $\frac{1}{3p^4}$

   e i $\frac{r^{-7}}{9}$ ii $\frac{1}{9r^7}$

   f i $\frac{q^{-10}}{5}$ ii $\frac{1}{5q^{10}}$

9 a $x^3 + x^2y$ b $x^3 + cx^2y$ c $x^3 + x^2y + cx^2y$
10 a $a(a^2 + b)$ b $ab(a^2 + b)$ c $a(a^2 + b + bc)$

11

x	$\div$	x^{-1}	$\div$	$\frac{1}{2}$
$\times$		$\div$		$\times$
2	$\times$	$4x^2$	$\div$	4
$\times$		$\times$		$\times$
x	$\div$	$\frac{x}{2}$	$\times$	x^2

Reflect

12 a When you multiply two expressions with the same letter raised to a power.
   b When you divide two expressions with the same letter raised to a power.
   c When an expression including a power is raised to another power.

2.6 Expanding double brackets

1 a $x^2 - 2x$ b $x^2 - x - 2$ c $x^2 - 4$ d $x^2 + 4$
2 a $6x + 38$
   b 6
   c $2x^2 + 19x + 19$
   d $2x^2 + 20x + 58$
   e $2x^2 + 2x - 14$
   f $4x + 18$

3 $n(n + 4) - 2(n + 7) = n^2 + 4n - 2n - 14 = n^2 + 2n - 14$
$(n + 2)(n - 6) + 2(3n - 1) = n^2 - 6n + 2n - 12 + 6n - 2$
$= n^2 + 2n - 14$
so $n(n + 4) - 2(n + 7) = (n + 2)(n - 6) + 2(3n - 1)$

4 a $\dfrac{2wz}{3}$ **b** $\dfrac{2b^2 + 2ab}{3}$

5 a Students' own answers, e.g. $l = 2a$ and $h = b$, or
$l = a$ and $h = 2b$

  b $lh = 2ab$, so any answers for l and h which have a product
of $2ab$ are valid.

6 a $x^2 + 3x$
  b $x^3 + 5x^2 + 6x$
  c **a** is but **b** is not, because the highest power of x is 3.

7 a $x^3 + 6x^2 + 11x + 6$
  b $x^3 + 12x^2 + 23x - 36$
  c $x^3 - x^2 - 14x + 24$

8 a $x^3 + 3x^2 + 3x + 1$ **b** $x^3 + 3x^2y + 3xy^2 + y^3$

9 a $y = (a - 2b)^2$ **b** $y = (T - 2x)^2$

  c $y = \dfrac{(kL - 2kx)^2}{5}$

10 a $k = mw^2$ **b** $e = \sqrt{1 - \dfrac{b^2}{a^2}}$

11 $\dfrac{12}{x(x + 2)(x - 2)} = \dfrac{12}{x} \times \dfrac{1}{x^2 - 4} = \dfrac{12}{x} \div \dfrac{x^2 - 4}{1} = \dfrac{12 \div x}{x^2 - 4}$

Reflect

12 The same: I still had to multiply every term in one bracket by
every term in the other bracket.
Different: My answers had more terms that could not be
collected and simplified.

2 Extend

1 $2(6a - 1) = 5a + 5$, $a = 1$

2 $x = 9.6$

3 a $2x(x + 2)(x - 2) = 4\pi(2y + 1)^3$
  b 500π
  c 32

4 a $m + n$
  b $(\sqrt{m} + \sqrt{n})(\sqrt{m} + \sqrt{n}) = \sqrt{m}\sqrt{m} + \sqrt{m}\sqrt{n} + \sqrt{m}\sqrt{n} + \sqrt{n}\sqrt{n}$
  $= m + 2\sqrt{m}\sqrt{n} + n$
  $= m + n + 2\sqrt{m}\sqrt{n}$
  c No; $\sqrt{m}\sqrt{n}$ would need to be zero, which is only possible if
one of m or n (or both) is zero.

5 LHS$^2 = mn$ and RHS$^2 = mn$ = LHS^2
Therefore the squares of both sides are equal. Since $\sqrt{mn}$,
$\sqrt{m}$ and $\sqrt{n}$ are all positive, neither the RHS nor the LHS
can be the negative square root of mn, and so RHS = LHS.
and so RHS = LHS.

6 a 2   **b** x **c** $12x$

7 a The powers must be the same.
  b $x = 5$
  c Yes. Since x is an integer, $2^{x + 3}$ will be an
integer power of 2.

8 $x = 4$ or $x = 2$

9 a $a^4b - 2a^3b^2$

  b $a^6b - 2a^7$

  c $\dfrac{3a^4}{b} + a^4$

10 a $x + 1$ **b** $\dfrac{2x}{9y^2 + 12y + 2}$

  c $\dfrac{1}{18xy^2 + 24xy + 8x}$

11 a 3^{2-x} **b** $4y^{2-x}$ **c** $4y^{2-x} + y$

Investigation

12 a **i** $x^2 + 2x + 1$ **ii** $x^3 + 3x^2 + 3x + 1$
  b They are the same.
  c 1, 4, 6, 4, 1
    1, 5, 10, 10, 5, 1
    1, 6, 15, 20, 15, 6, 1
    etc.
  d, e i $x^4 + 4x^3 + 6x^2 + 4x + 1$
  ii $x^5 + 5x^4 + 10x^3 + 10x^2 + 5x + 1$
  f The rth term in the expansion of $(x + 2)^n$ is the equivalent
term in expansion of $(x + 1)^n$, multiplied by 2^{r-1}.
For example, $(x + 1)^2 = x^2 + 2x + 1$
$(x + 2)^2 = x^2 \times 2^0 + 2x \times 2^1 + 1 \times 2^2$
$= x^2 + 4x + 4$
$(x + 1)^3 = x^3 + 3x^2 + 3x + 1$
$(x + 2)^3 = x^3 \times 2^0 + 3x^2 \times 2^1 + 3x \times 2^2 + 2^3$
$= x^3 + 6x^2 + 12x + 8$

  etc.

Investigation

13 a $a = 2, b = 3$
  b $a = 3, b = 2$
  c $a = 3$

Reflect

14 Students' own answers.

UNIT 3 Dealing with data

3.1 Planning a survey

1 a i Secondary
   b i Primary
      ii Survey – ask a random sample of people
   c i Secondary
   d i Secondary
   e i Primary
      ii Survey – give questionnaire to random
          sample of population
   f i Primary
      ii Survey – observation of random sample

2 a Any sensible answer, e.g. 10% = 150
   b i Biased – Year 10 students alone do not represent the
         whole population; every member of the population is not
         equally likely to be in the sample.
      ii Not biased
      iii Biased – only students who like what is currently on
           offer will be included in the sample.
      iv Biased – the food available in the canteen will not be
          included in the sample.
   c Primary
   d No, because it is only 3 students, so the sample size is too
      small to avoid any potential biases.

3 This sample is not representative of people who use the library
   at other times, and limits the responses to one group of users
   who are able to use the library on Thursday afternoons

4 a i Every patient visiting A&E of a UK hospital during
         unspecified time interval (possibly previous year).
      ii Not random because Saturday nights may not
          be representative of other times of day and other
          days of the week.
   b i Every person currently living in Denmark.
      ii Not random because not every person living in
          Denmark has an equal chance of being in the sample.
   c i Every teacher in a UK secondary school.
      ii Not random because not every teacher in a
          UK secondary school has an equal chance of
          being in the sample.
   d i Every teacher in a UK secondary school.
      ii Not random because not every teacher in a
          UK secondary school has an equal chance of
          being in the sample.

5 a 200 bags: a 10% sample would be 20 000 bags, but
      weighing this many – or even 2000 bags – would take too
      much time to be practical; if you found any anomalies in
      your data you would take a larger sample.
   b B (the nearest gram)

6 a Anonymous survey, as this gives everyone the opportunity
      to respond, and anonymity allows people to say what
      they really think.
   b 150

7 a A (5000)   b C (1 000 000)
   c B (6000)

8 When a firework is exploded it is destroyed and cannot be sold.
   A smaller sample size would be appropriate.

Reflect

9 If the population is very small, the number in the sample may
   be too small. If the population is very large or the thing being
   tested is destroyed in the process of testing, 10% is too large
   to be practical.

3.2 Collecting data

1 a Everyone in the population does not have an equal chance
      of taking part in the survey.
   b E.g. phone survey or internet survey.
   c C; no overlapping categories, grouped answers (easier to
      record and easier for people to answer), opportunity for
      amounts over £120.
   d E.g. people may not remember or may be unwilling to give
      the information.

2 a E.g.
      How old are you? Tick the appropriate box.
      ☐ 10–24 ☐ 25–39 ☐ 40–54 ☐ 55–69 ☐ 70+
   b E.g.

		Age (years)				
		10–24	25–39	40–54	55–69	70+
Amount spent per month (£)	0–40					
	41–80					
	81–120					
	121+					

3 a Restrictive, because not all possible options are included;
      expand the options to include bicycle, motorbike, boat,
      airplane, other.
   b Leading, because it suggests using car less because of
      cost; replace with, e.g., 'During the next year do you expect
      to use your car: less frequently, more frequently, with about
      the same frequency?'
   c Vague; replace with question about specific activities,
      e.g. 'At weekends which of these activities do you usually
      engage in: work, study, shopping, sport, reading, walking,
      watching TV, using a computer, cooking, clothes washing,
      other housework, other hobby?'
   d Leading, because it suggests the answer 'Yes'; replace
      with unbiased question, e.g. 'Does the bus service need
      to be improved?'
   e Restrictive, because not all possible options are included;
      expand the options and make response appear obviously
      subjective, e.g. 'Do you believe that the main cause
      of bad behaviour in lessons is: some students have
      general problems, the lesson is too long, the lesson is not
      interesting, the lesson is too hard, the lesson is too easy, the
      teacher is not strict, the class is too big, the classroom is
      not comfortable, an unknown factor?'
   f Leading, because it suggests the answer 'Yes'; replace
      with unbiased question, e.g. 'Should more people
      become vegetarians?'
   g Vague; replace with question about specific kinds of food,
      e.g. 'Which of these kinds of food forms the greatest part
      of your diet: fruit, vegetables, bread or cake or biscuit
      products, meat, fish, dairy products, pasta or rice?'

4 a Question A: too vague, needs specific time options.
      Question B: too vague, add some possible actions.
      Question C: leading question that encourages
      the answer 'Yes'.
   b Replace question A with question U.
      Replace question B with question Q.
      Replace question C with question W.
   c Students' own data collection sheet.

Investigation

5 Students' own answers

Reflect

6 You will have a good idea of the potential responses so
   you can make answer boxes to reflect what you expect to
   hear. Remember to add another box for options you have
   not thought of.

3.3 Calculating averages

1 E.g. −9, −7, −6, −6, −2
   or −10, −6, −6, −5, −3

2 1 g, 5 g, 5 g, 7 g, 9 g, 12 g, 17 g
   2 g, 5 g, 5 g, 7 g, 9 g, 12 g, 16 g
   3 g, 5 g, 5 g, 7 g, 9 g, 12 g, 15 g
   4 g, 5 g, 5 g, 7 g, 9 g, 12 g, 14 g
   5 g, 5 g, 5 g, 7 g, 9 g, 12 g, 13 g

3 a 8   b 18   c −2
   d 80   e 0.8
   f It increases or decreases the mean by the amount you
      added or subtracted, because you are shifting the whole
      data set so the mean will move by the same shift.

4 **a** 30.308
   b **i** 0.2, -0.2, 0.04, 1, 0.5
      ii 0.308
      iii 30.308
   c Yes; students' own answers.

5 98.8

6 **a** 500   **b** 498.75   **c** 502
   d The mean represents the data better; the mode is too high, as 10 of the 16 data values are lower than the modal value.

7 101 cm

8 **a** 8.5   **b** 79.25
   c 0.375   **d** 421

9 **a** 10 years 2.4 months
   b E.g. Using an assumed mean of 10 years.

10 **a** **i** $0 < L \leqslant 400$ **ii** $400 < L \leqslant 800$
   b **i** 770 miles   **ii** 3200 miles
   c You don't know what the actual lowest and highest values are.

11 **a** Table 1: $20 \leqslant b < 40$
      Table 2: $30 \leqslant b < 45$
   b Table 1: 80
      Table 2: 75
   c Table 1: 35.6
      Table 2: 37.8
   d Table 2. The range is more accurate because from Table 2 we know the highest value is less than 75 and so the estimate for the range is smaller. The modal class is more accurate because the class width is narrower. The mean may be more accurate, because the class widths are smaller and so the estimated values used to calculate the mean may better represent the actual data values in those classes.

Reflect

12 Students' own answers, e.g. when the data values are very large or very small, to simplify the numbers you are working with; when you have a very small number of data values. When the data is all close to one value. When numbers are simple or you are working with spreadsheets, it is probably no more efficient to use an assumed mean than to add up all the numbers and divide.

3.4 Displaying and analysing data

1 **a** Student B
   b Student A should have drawn a line of best fit. Student C's line of best fit is not very accurate – it has more points above the line than below it

2 **a**

Mass and height for 18 patients

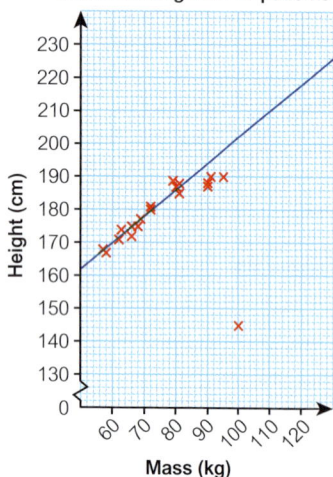

   b (110, 145)
   c **i** About 76 kg   **ii** About 162 cm
      iii About 217 cm
   d **i** Fairly reliable as it is within the range of the data.
      ii Not very reliable as it is just outside the range of the data.
      iii Unreliable as it is well outside the data range and is

much taller than most people's heights.

3 **a** 30 000 miles
   b 12 350 miles
   c $10\,000 \leqslant d < 15\,000$

4 **a** **Ages of people visiting two doctors' surgeries**

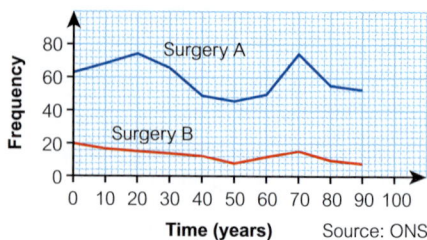

Source: ONS

   b $50 < a \leqslant 60$
   c Surgery B may have many fewer patients. The percentage of Surgery B patients visiting the doctor could be higher than for Surgery A.

Investigation

5 **a** Strong positive correlation
   b

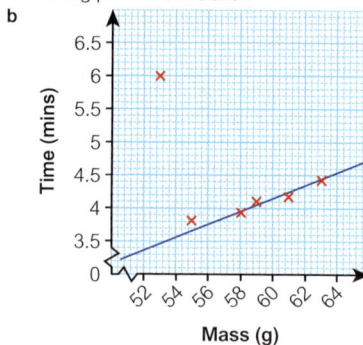

   c Mass 58.2 g, time 4.4 mins
   d No
   e It is far away from the line of best fit when there is an outlier.

Reflect

6 **a** Graph A
   b Stronger correlation means that predicted values will be more reliable because all the points are closer to the line of best fit, and the pattern in the data is stronger.

3.5 Presenting and comparing data

1 **a**

Population of Asia

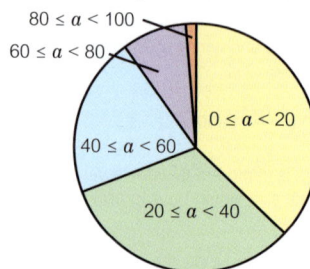

Population of Europe

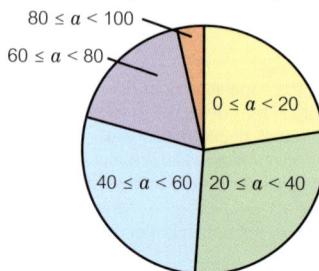

   b Student's own graph or charts, e.g.

129

Population of Asia

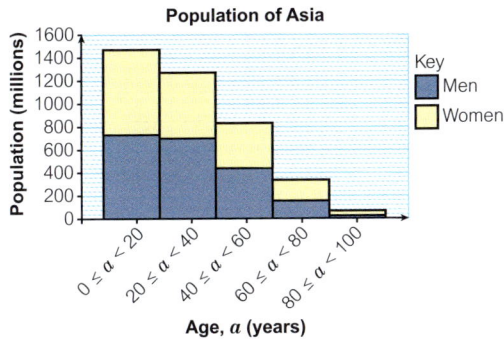

OR

Population of Asia

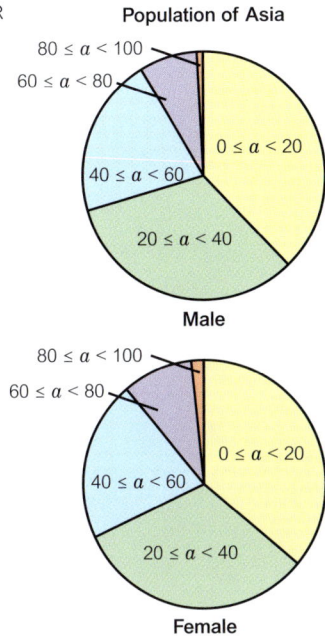

Male

Female

c Students' own dual bar chart, e.g.

Population of Europe

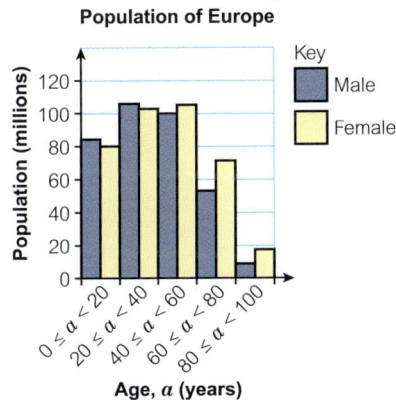

d Asia: $0 \leqslant a < 20$; Europe: $20 \leqslant a < 40$

e Asia: 30.9 years; Europe: 40.1 years

f Students' own answers, e.g.
A higher proportion of the population is aged under 20 in Asia than in Europe.
In Asia, there are more people aged 0–20 years than in any other age category.
In Europe, there are more than twice as many women over 80 as there are men over 80.

2 a For ages greater than 30, the higher the age, the lower the frequency of using the internet, both for social networking and for banking. That is, the older the age group is, the fewer people who use the internet for banking or for social networking.

b Between the ages of 20 and 30, the frequency of using the

internet for banking increases but the frequency of using it for social networking decreases. Many more 20-year-olds use the internet for social networking than for banking. The number of 30-year-olds who use it for banking is almost the same as the number who use it for social networking. The modal class for social networking is $20 \leqslant a < 30$, and for banking is $30 \leqslant a < 40$.

3 a **Employees earnings per year**

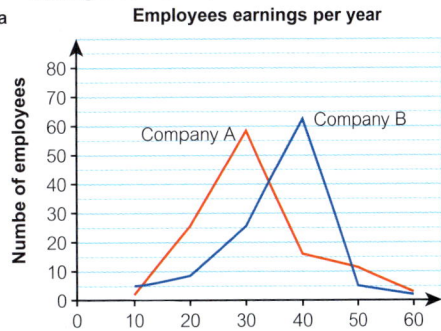

b The yearly earnings that the greatest number of people within the company have is lower in company A than in company B. The fact that the greatest frequency is lower in company A is also significant because the total number of employees is almost the same in both companies (107 in company A and 109 in company B). Not only is the most common amount earned per year greater in company B, but also a larger proportion of the company's employees earn it.

c Students' own answers.

4 a

Spanish test		French test
	1	2 9
9 8 8 6 3 1 0	2	4 5 8 9
9 8 8 7 6 4 2 2 0	3	0 3 5 5 6 7 8 8 8
8 5 0	4	0 1 7 8 9
0	5	

Key
0 | 2 means 20 marks

Key
1 | 2 means 12 marks

b i 13 out of 20 = 65%   **ii** 12 out of 20 = 60%

c No, because you don't know which results in each set are for which student.

5 a Students' own answers, e.g.

Three-legged race times

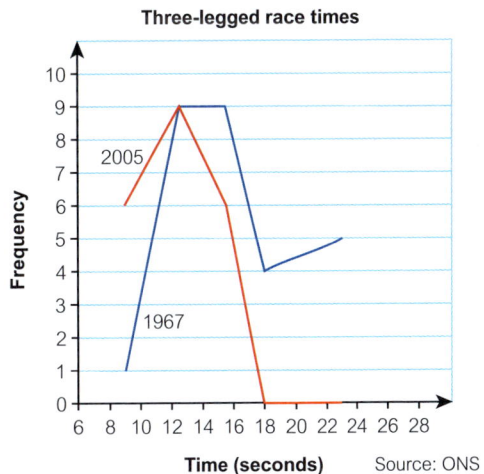

b The number of pairs of people who took between 11 and 14 seconds was the same in both years. People in 2005 were much faster, as no one took longer than 17 seconds in 2005.

Reflect

6 **a** Pie charts or compound bar charts

   b Grouped frequency table, dual bar chart or bar chart

   c Bar chart, line graph, pie chart or grouped frequency table

   d Stem and leaf diagram

   e Grouped bar chart or grouped frequency table

3 Extend

1 -3

2 24 years old

3 500 people

4 **a** They all know each other so probably have similar reasons for cheating.

   b Cheating is not OK, so people might not want to talk to Martin in case they get in trouble.

   c He is only looking at people that got caught, so his survey might be biased. People may not want to talk to Martin because they may be upset about getting caught.

5 **a** 800   **b** 640

   c 2007: 33.3, 2017: 33.6

   d On average, people did slightly better in 2017 than in 2007. In 2007, the greatest proportion of people got the highest scores, while in 2017, the largest proportion of people were in the second highest scoring group.

6 **a** 10   **b** 4

   c Students' own answers, for example, 4, 9, 5, 10.

   d Pie charts based on students answer to part **c**, e.g.

Station Street   **Park Crescent**

Key

$0 \leqslant L < 2$ $2 \leqslant L < 4$ $4 \leqslant L < 8$ $8 \leqslant L < 10$

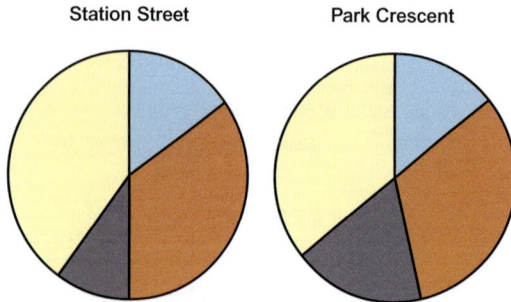

   e In both roads the modal class was $8 \leqslant L < 10$. In Station Street the class with the fewest letters was $4 \leqslant L < 8$. while in Park Crescent, the class with the fewest number of letters was $0 \leqslant L < 2$.

7 **a** We only know the percentages, not how many people are in each country.

   b

Percentage of people living on less than $1.90 per day

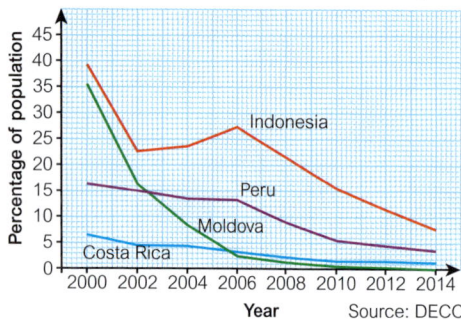

Source: DECC

   c Over time, the proportion of people living on less than $1.90 per day is decreasing in each of the countries shown. It is still highest in Indonesia but the gap between Indonesia and the others is closing.

Investigation

8 Multiple answers, e.g.

Length of worm	Frequency
$0 \leqslant L < 2$	3
$2 \leqslant L < 4$	1
$4 \leqslant L < 6$	10
$6 \leqslant L < 8$	7

Reflect

9 Students' own answers.

UNIT 4 Multiplicative reasoning

4.1 Enlargement

1 8 cm

2 **a** Large: 5.1 cm (1 d.p.), Small: 4.5 cm (1 d.p.)
  b 1.1 (1 d.p.)
  c The area scale factor comes from the length scale factor squared, because each side has been multiplied by the length scale factor.

3 Triangle A: height 3 cm, base 4 cm
  Triangle B: height 9 cm
  Triangle C: base 22 cm

4 **a** Scale factor 2, centre of enlargement (0, 0)
  b Scale factor 3.5, centre of enlargement (0, 0)
  c Scale factor $\frac{7}{4}$, centre of enlargement (0, 0)

5 **a** (0.1, 0.4)
  b (0.4, 2.2), (0.4, 0.7), (1.6, 0.7)
  c (0.4, 0.25), (1, 0.25) or (0.4, 1)
  d You don't know which vertex of triangle D is at (0.4, 1). Each vertex of triangle A requires a different centre of enlargement to take it to (0.4, 1).

Investigation

6 The centre of enlargement can be anywhere on the page. The scale factor can take any positive integer value.

Reflect

7 No, because a scale factor may be a fraction or a decimal.

4.2 Negative and fractional scale factors

1 1.6 cm

2 **a** Scale factor 2, centre of enlargement (−2, 2)
  b Scale factor $\frac{1}{2}$, centre of enlargement (−2, 2)

3 **a** Scale factor −2, centre of enlargement (7, 6)
  b Scale factor $-\frac{1}{2}$, centre of enlargement (7, 6)
  c E.g. enlargement with scale factor $\frac{1}{2}$ and centre of enlargement (7, 6) followed by 180° rotation about (7, 6)

4 An enlargement with scale factor −3 would turn the shape, as well as making it larger than the original.
  The inverse transformation is an enlargement with scale factor $\frac{1}{3}$.

5 **a, b, c**

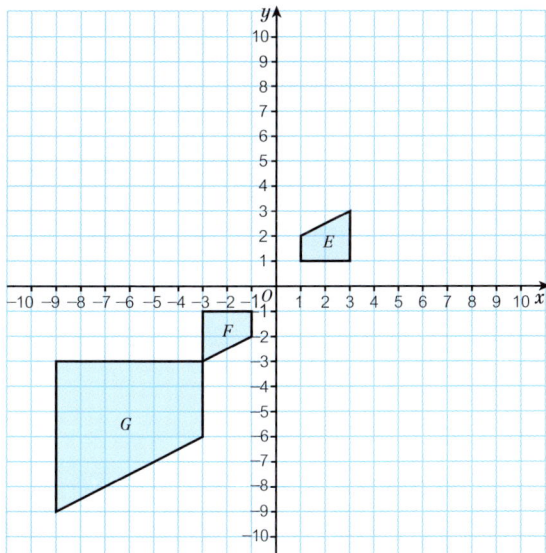

  d Enlargement, scale factor $-\frac{1}{3}$, centre of enlargement (0, 0)

6 (7, 3), (9, 3), (8, 7)

7 $\frac{9}{2}$ or 4.5

8 **a** Students' own answers, for example,
  1, 2. Steps 1 and 2 as in the question.
  3. Translate the new triangle by 1 to the right and 2 up, and then by 2 to the right. Colour these two new triangles red.
  4. Colour the space between the three smaller red triangles black.
  5. Enlarge triangle 2 (as created in steps 2–4) by scale factor $\frac{1}{2}$ using centre of enlargement (16, 4).
  6. Repeat steps 3 and 4 for triangle 2.

  b No, there are many different possible sets of instructions that will result in the three triangles shown.

  c Enlarge the third triangle by scale factor $\frac{1}{2}$ using centre of enlargement (21, 4). Then follow steps 3 and 4 of the method in part a with this triangle.

Investigation

9 Any value $\leq -\frac{1}{3}$ or any value $\geq \frac{1}{3}$

Reflect

10 The centre of enlargement stays the same, but the scale factor becomes the reciprocal of the original.

4.3 Percentage change

1 75 600

2 **a** 30 people
  b **i** 240 people   **ii** 84 people
  c **i** 54 people   **ii** 180%

3 **a** 10% = 37.5 so 100% = 375
  b 20% decrease
  c 0.8

4 **a** No; 13% of 146 million is different from 13% of 140 million.
  b 82.2%   **c** 58.9%

5 2.75%

6 **a** 4% more visitors   **b** 198 000 visitors
  c 174 000 visitors

7 The percentage changes are 28% for group A, 21% for group B and 31% for group C. So no, because the group that had no antibacterial spray administered had the greatest percentage change (well over the 20% threshold).

Investigation

8 **a, b** Students' sketches of the cuboids.
  c 48 cm³, 72 cm³
  d 50% increase; the same as the side length increase.
  e It is.
  f For two sides, the volume increases by 125%; for all three sides, it increases by 237.5%.

Reflect

9 If the numbers are simple multiples of 10% then it is easier to use the unitary method, but if the percentages are more complicated it is simpler to use the inverse multiplier method.

4.4 Compound measures

1 **a** 9.6 mph   **b** 15.36 km/h **c** 4.27 m/s

2 **a** 40 km/h   **b** 6.25 m/s
  c 550 mph   **d** 1.25 m/s
  e Because they measure the total distance divided by the total time. The athlete, for example, would not be running at a constant speed the whole time.

3 Alima

4 0.8 N/cm²

5 a Minnie shows the same gradient for walking home as walking to the shops; it should be less steep.
Dan shows only a short time at the shop; it should be longer than the walk there or back.

b

Mrs Smith's journey

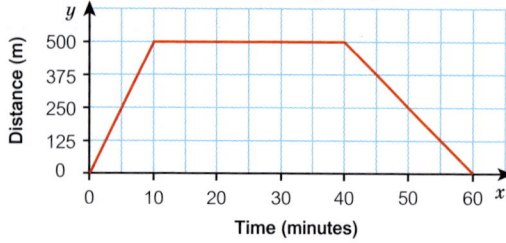

c 1 km

6 a

Ellie's journey

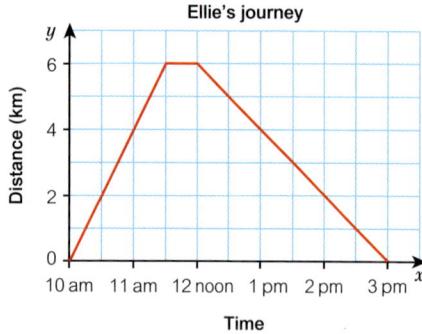

b 2 km/h

7 No. For example,
average speed of athlete = 10.2 m/s (1 d.p.) = 36.7 km/h (1 d.p.)
This is faster than Amir's remote-controlled car.

8 a C **b** A **c** 8.3 mph (1 d.p.)

9 0.92 g/cm³

10 486 kg

11 10.4 g/cm³

12 3136 N

Reflect

13 Yes, every speed is an average, unless you know that the object has been maintaining a constant speed.
Yes, they are also average measures because you do not know if an object has particularly dense areas or if more pressure is applied in one spot; you only know the total mass, volume, force or area.

4.5 Direct and inverse proportion

1 a 9 mistakes **b** 144 minutes

2 Small prints 86 pages per £1, medium prints 113 pages per £1, large prints 92 pages per £1. Medium is the best value for money.

3 a Inverse proportion **b** Direct proportion
c No proportion **d** Inverse proportion
e Direct proportion

4 40 people

5 Gardener's Gold (24.8p per litre of compost compared to 25p for Gardener's Best)

6 Yes. 400 × 28 = 11 200 words. 11 200 ÷ 450 = 24.89 pages.

7 a 2 g/cm³ **b** 2 g/cm³

  c $\frac{1}{2}$ **d** 2

  e i Directly **ii** Inversely

  f 7.5 cm³

8 a False **b** True **c** False **d** False

9 a 30 days **b** $10\frac{2}{3}$ days

Investigation

10 9019 km

Reflect

11 I looked to decide whether the quantities would both increase, or whether one would increase while the other decreased.

4 Extend

1 About 11.20 am

2 19 minutes (nearest minute)

3 1.76 m²

4 a B (polystyrene) will float in water.
  b B (polystyrene) and C (iron) will float in mercury.
  c No, because mass is proportional to volume so the density will stay the same.

5 a £4.2003 × 10¹²
  b 4 000 000 000 000
  c 19%

6 4.5 units in the x-direction

7 $\frac{x + y}{3.5}$

8 $\frac{2}{9}$ g

9 0.26 N/m²

10 13% decrease

Investigation

11 a Decreased by 9.5% (1 d.p.)
  b Decreased by 9.5%
  c Decreased by 9.5%
  d Multiple answers, e.g. increase by 10%, increase by 5%, decrease by 15%, increase by 3%, decrease by 1% (rounded)

12 a $\frac{8x}{9y}$ **b** $\frac{52x}{63y}$

Reflect

13 With ratio, you have to use fractions more, but it also involves multiplying and dividing to get your answer. When working with equations, you might add or subtract or use powers as well.

UNIT 5 Constructions

5.1 Using scales

1 **a** $24\,cm^2$ **b** 25 times
     c 400 times   **d** $1\,cm : 1\,m$
     e Abigail is incorrect because angles do not change size with the length of the lines.

2 **a** $1\,cm : 1\,m$
     b $6.1\,m$

3 **a** Student explanation, e.g. 1 cm represents 50 000 cm means that 1 mm represents one tenth of 50 000 cm = 50 000 mm
     b 50 000 m = 50 km

4 **a** $1:2\,000\,000$
     b Answers between 120 km and 160 km

5 Students' own scale drawings, e.g.

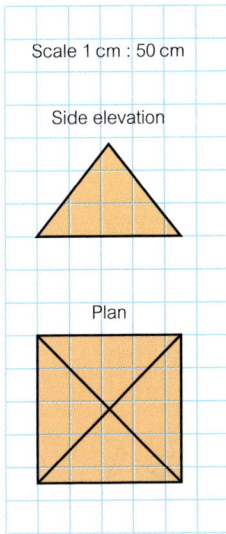

Scale 1 cm : 50 cm

Side elevation

Plan

6 Width $= 1\,\mu m = \frac{1}{1000}\,mm = 10^{-3}\,mm$

7 **a** $1:318\,550\,000$
     b Mercury: 15.316 mm, Venus: 37.997 mm, Mars: 21.281 mm, Jupiter: 438.926 mm, Saturn: 365.594 mm, Uranus: 159.234 mm, Neptune: 154.588 mm
     c 13.5 km
     d No, it is too large as the model would extend over 13.5 km. A much smaller scale is needed to show the model in a room.

8 5°

Investigation

9 **a** Scale of $1:n$ where $n > 771$ would work, e.g. $1:800$.
     b Scale of $1:n$ where $n > 1976$ would work, e.g. $1:2000$.
     c Answer depends on scale used in part **b**.
     For 1:2000, Burj Khalifa = 41.5 cm and Empire State Building = 22.2 cm, so difference = 19.3 cm.

Reflect

10 No. If there are no units, then it can be assumed that the same units are used in both parts of the ratio.

5.2 Basic constructions

1 **a** A circle
     b Circle of radius 10 cm drawn accurately

2 Fix a spike at the base of the goal post and attach a rope 8 feet long to it. Pull the rope tight and draw the semicircle formed by moving the rope.

3 **a, b**

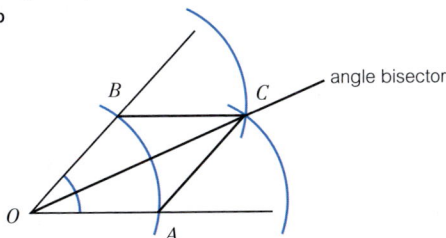

angle bisector

c You use the same radius for all the arcs, so all of these lengths will be equal.
d Rhombus
e Diagonal of a rhombus bisects the angle; diagonal of a rhombus is a line of symmetry.
f Kite
g Yes, because the diagonal of a kite bisects the angle; the diagonal of a kite is a line of symmetry.

4

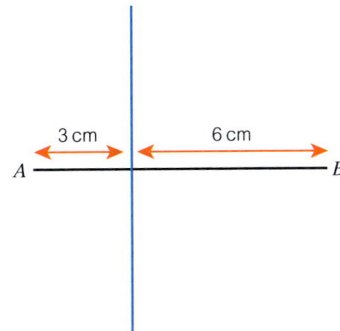

3 cm   6 cm
A   B

5 **a** Students' own constructions, e.g.

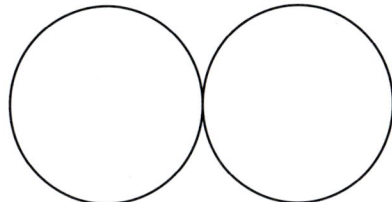

     b Students' own constructions, e.g.

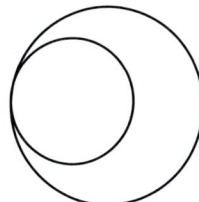

6 **a, b**

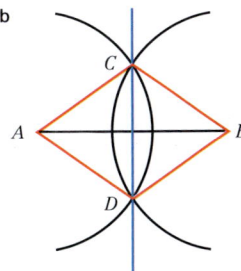

c You use the same radius for all the arcs, so as each point on a circle is an equal distance from its centre, all of these lengths will be equal.
d Rhombus
e Diagonals of a rhombus bisect each other at right angles.

7 **a–d**

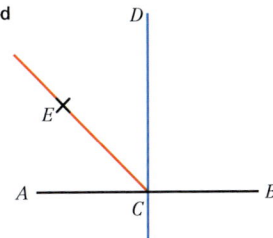

e Yes, because the position of C is fixed and angle ACD is always 90°, so E will always be 3 cm along the line at 45° to AB through C, no matter which point D has been chosen.
f 2.1 cm

8 a

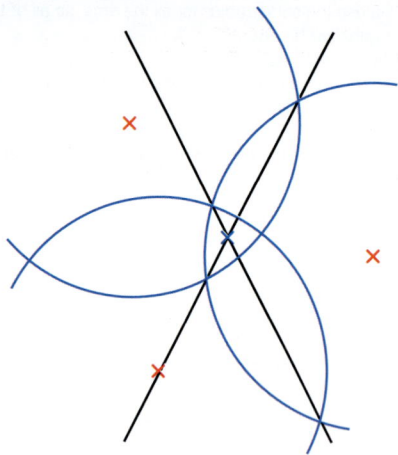

b No; it will always be closer to one of the dots because they are in a line.

9 a–d Regular hexagon constructed.

e Yes, because the straight-line distance from one mark to the next is the same as the radius, so six equilateral triangles are made, which fit exactly around the centre of the circle because $6 \times 60° = 360°$.

Investigation

10 a i, ii

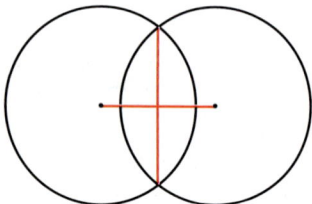

iii The two lines are perpendicular and bisect each other.

b i, ii

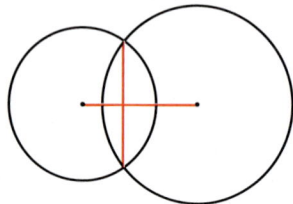

iii The two lines are perpendicular but they do not bisect each other.

c If they do not have the same radius, you will draw a perpendicular to the line but it will not bisect the line.

Reflect

11 Students' own answers, e.g.

Knowing that any point on a circle is the same distance from the centre helps me to know why I am drawing and using circles; knowing that I am using the diagonal of a rhombus to draw an angle bisector helps me to remember what the construction will look like.

5.3 Constructing triangles

1 a, b

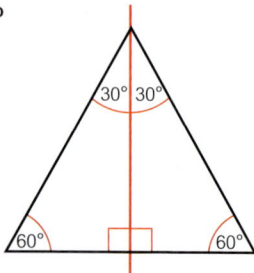

c, d Same as answers to parts **a** and **b**.

2 60° angle constructed

3 45° angle constructed by constructing a perpendicular and then bisecting the angle.

4 105° angle constructed, e.g. through use of 45° angle and 60° angle constructions.

5 Accurate copy of pattern constructed.

6 It still draws a circle that is inside the triangle and touching all of the sides. It does not touch the exact centre of each side.

7 Circle constructed that touches each corner of the triangle.

8 It still draws a circle that is outside the triangle and passes through all three corners. The corners are not evenly spaced around the circumference of the circle.

9 a Full size triangle accurately constructed.
b Right-angled
c Yes, because it is an enlargement of the first triangle, with scale factor 1.5.

10 45°, 45° and 90°

11 Accurate 5 cm square constructed.

12 a Students' sketches
b Accurate construction of a net of a regular tetrahedron, e.g.

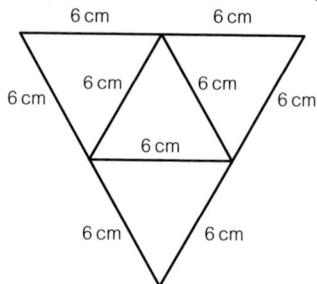

13 Students' own nets, e.g.

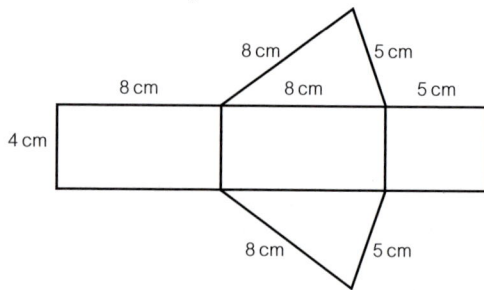

14 a Drawing in the diagonals of the hexagon creates six congruent triangles, each with two angles of $120° \div 2 = 60°$ and a third angle of $360° \div 6 = 60°$, so the six triangles are equilateral.

b

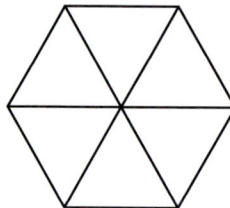

15

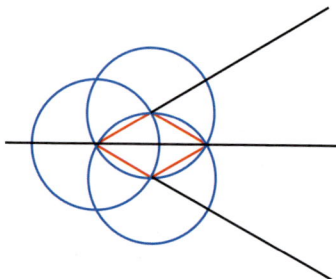

16 a Multiple answers, e.g. for a parallelogram with base 4 cm and height 3 cm:

1. Draw a 4 cm line segment AB and construct its perpendicular bisector.

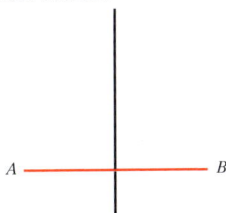

2. Mark a point C on the perpendicular bisector 3 cm from AB. Construct the perpendicular line through point C to give two parallel lines.

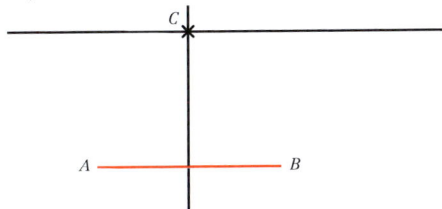

3. Join point C to point A. Set your compasses to the length of line segment AC and draw a circle with this radius centred on point B. Mark point D where the circle intersects the perpendicular from C. Join D to B.

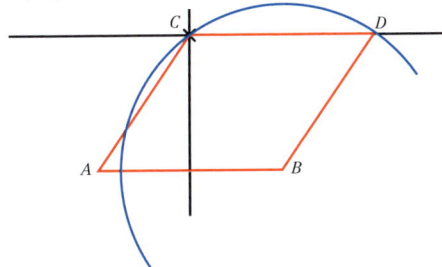

b Use the same method to construct a parallelogram with different base and height lengths, that multiply to give 12 cm², e.g. 2 cm and 6 cm.

Reflect

17 a 1. Construct a perpendicular bisector.
2. Construct a 5, 12, 13 triangle (or an enlargement).
b 1. Construct a right angle and then bisect it.
2. Construct a right-angled isosceles triangle.

5.4 Using accurate scale diagrams

1 Perpendicular at C constructed.

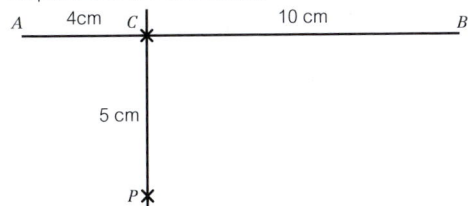

2 a Angle bisector of 80° constructed.
b Approximately 3.2 cm from each point to the angle bisector.
c Approximately 4.5 cm from each point to the angle bisector.
d The shortest distances from the points to the angle bisector meet it at right angles and are equal.
Any point on the angle bisector is equidistant from the two arms of the angle.

3 a 1 cm to 1 m
b Accurate scale drawing, e.g.

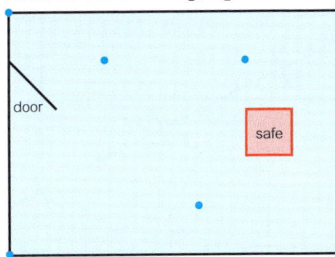

c, d Accurate lines and circles added to diagram.

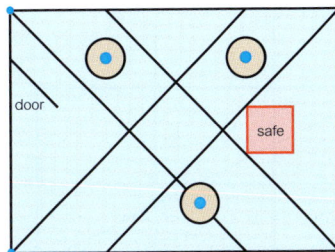

e Students' own answers, e.g.
Keep two on corners of the room, as no one can get near the safe without crossing one of these lines.

4 10.3 m

5 a 15.6 m (1 d.p.)
b Answer to part a uses height above Ashley's eye level, plus Ashley's height. But eye level is lower than height, e.g. perhaps 10 cm lower.

6 a

b 7°

7 Yes, because the height of the tent is about 2.2 m.

Investigation

8 a Never true: the lines cross at 67° (to the nearest degree).
b The lines always cross at 37° (to the nearest degree).

Reflect

9 It would have been very difficult. The scale drawing allowed me to quickly see all of the information in one place.

5 Extend

1 Yes, the sofa will fit through.
2 The sum of the two short sides is less than the length of the third side, so they will not meet.
3 a 1 cm   **b** 5 cm   **c** 3 cm
4 8 cm
5 756 cm²
6 Triangle with perpendicular constructed from A to BC. Distance 35.7 m.
7

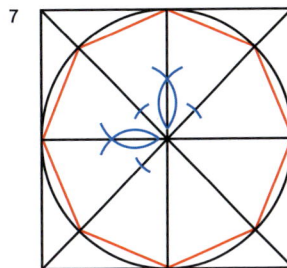

8 First, construct the perpendicular bisector (l) of BC.

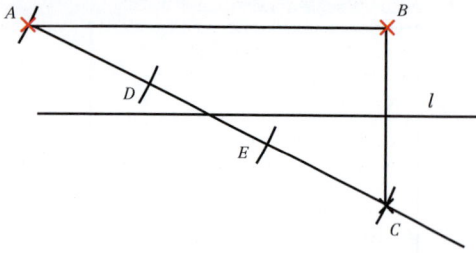

Then construct lines through each of points D and E that are perpendicular to l. These will divide AB into three equal parts.

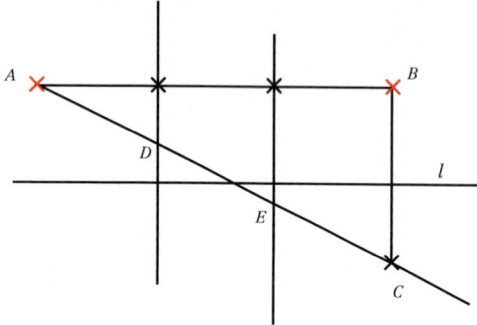

Investigation

9 a You get the same effect.
  b The inside circle cannot touch all of the sides, but the outside circle still works.
  c There are no patterns.

Reflect

10 Students' own answers.

UNIT 6 Sequences, inequalities, equations and proportion

6.1 nth term of arithmetic sequences

1 a

Pattern number	1	2	3	4	5
Number of white tiles	10	12	14	16	18
Number of black tiles	2	4	6	8	10

b i $2n$　ii $2n + 8$
c 30　　**d** 48
e $2n + 8 = 75$, $n = 33.5$, so he has enough white tiles to make the 33rd pattern.
$2n = 67$, $n = 33.5$, so he has enough black tiles to make the 33rd pattern.
Therefore, largest pattern he can make is the 33rd.

f

Pattern number	1	2	3	4	5
Total number of tiles	12	16	20	24	28

g $4n + 8$
h Adding the nth terms of the sequences of black tiles and white tiles gives the nth term of the sequence of the total number of tiles.

2 a, b

Term	1st	2nd	3rd	4th	5th
Square numbers	1	4	9	16	25
Triangle numbers	1	3	6	10	15

c $1 + 3 = 4$; yes
d $3 + 6 = 9$, $6 + 10 = 16$, $10 + 15 = 25$
e i $15 + 21 = 36$　　ii $21 + 28 = 49$
　iii $36 + 45 = 81$
3 a $n + 1$　**b** $3n + 4$　**c** $\dfrac{n + 1}{3n + 4}$
4 a $\dfrac{2n + 3}{2n + 6}$
b No; the terms are 0.625, 0.7, 0.75, ... There is no common difference.
5 a i 1, 4, 7, 10, 13　　ii 7, 12, 17, 22, 27
b $\dfrac{3n - 2}{5n + 2}$　**c** $8n$　**d** $2n + 4$
e $(3n - 2)(5n + 2) = 15n^2 - 4n - 4$

6 a

Term	1	2	3	4	5
$2n - 3$	−1	1	3	5	7

b

x	−2	−1	0	1	2
$y = 2x - 3$	−7	−5	−3	−1	1

c Same: nth term is the same as the equation for y. Bottom row of table is a sequence with common difference 2. Term numbers and x-values both increase by 1 each time. Both sequences include terms −1 and 1.
Different: Sequences start at different numbers. Term numbers are all positive, starting at 1. Some x-values are negative, starting at −2.
d Yes, the y-values form a linear sequence with common difference +2.
e Yes, $y = 2x - 3$ is in the form of the equation of a straight line $y = mx + c$, and the graph of $y = 2x - 3$ is a straight line with gradient 2 and y-intercept −3.
7 a True　**b** False　**c** False
d False　**e** True
8 First two terms are 7 and 2. The common difference is −5, so the 3rd term is −3, and after that all the terms are negative because they decrease by 5 each time.

Investigation

9 a i 2nd term　ii 2nd term　iii 3rd term
b The position of the first negative term is constant for two terms. When the first term is a multiple of 3, the position of the first negative term increases by 1, then stays constant until the term is the next multiple of 3.

c The position of the first negative term is constant for three terms. When the first term is a multiple of 4, the position of the first negative term increases by 1, then stays constant until the term is the next multiple of 4.
Check: 1, −3, ...; 2, −2, ...; 3, −1, ...; 4, 0, −4, ...

Reflect

10 In Q1, adding the two nth terms gives a linear sequence.
In Q3 and Q4, dividing one nth term by the other does not give a linear sequence.
In Q5 part **f**, multiplying one nth term by the other does not give a linear sequence.
So two linear nth terms do not always combine to give a linear sequence.

6.2 Non-linear sequences

1 a Arithmetic　　　　**b** Geometric
c Other (Fibonacci)　**d** Quadratic
2 You don't know what type of sequence it is, so the pattern could continue in many different ways (as in Q1).
3 a 10, 13, 16
b 12.25, 21.4375, 37.515625
c Multiple possible answers, e.g. 12, 19, 28 (2nd difference +2) or 13, 22, 34 (2nd difference +3).
d For parts **a** and **b** there was only one answer because you are adding or multiplying by a constant number. For part **c** there are infinitely many possible answers because you don't know what the 2nd difference is.

4 a

Position (n)	1	2	3	4
Term ($n + 2$)	3	4	5	6

b

Position (n)	1	2	3	4
Term ($n^2 + 2$)	3	6	11	18

c

Position (n)	1	2	3	4
Term ($n^3 + 2$)	3	10	29	66

d

Position (n)	1	2	3	4
Term ($n^4 + 2$)	3	18	83	258

5 The first sequence has the 1st differences the same, the second sequence has the 2nd differences the same, the third sequence has the 3rd differences the same and the fourth sequence has the 4th differences the same. The difference that is the same has the same number as the power of n.
6 a 50, $50\sqrt{5}$, 250
b Geometric, multiplying by $\sqrt{5}$ each time.
7 a 3, 9, 27　　　　　**b** Geometric
c Multiply by 3　**d** 2, 4, 8
e 4, 16, 64
f Geometric sequences can be made by using a^n as the nth term.
8 a Geometric　　**b** 0.5 or $\dfrac{1}{2}$
9 a $1.2n + 4.8$
b 36, 51.84, 70.56, 92.16, 116.64
c Quadratic
d i Geometric　　ii Geometric
10 a +2　　**b** +4　　**c** +4
d $2n^2$　　**e** $2n^2 + 5$
11 a $2n^2 + 7$　**b** $2n^2 - 7$　**c** $3n^2 - 7$
d $3n^2 + 1$　**e** $0.5n^2 + 1$
12 a 0, 1, 2, 3, 4　　　　　**b** $n^2 - 1$
c $\dfrac{n^2 - 1}{n + 1} = \dfrac{(n + 1)(n - 1)}{n + 1} = n - 1$, which is the nth term of the sequence 0, 1, 2, 3, 4

13 6

Reflect

14 If the highest power is 1, then the 1st differences will be constant. If the highest power is 2 then the 2nd differences will be constant. If the highest power is 3, the 3rd differences are constant, and so on.

6.3 Inequalities

1 **a** $x \leqslant 50$ **b** Yes

2 **a** $x > 2$

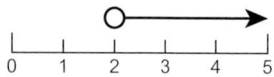

b $x > 20$

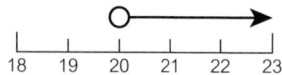

c $x < 5$

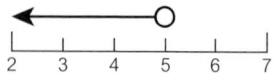

d $x > 27$

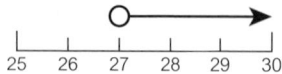

e $x > 6$

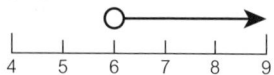

f $x < 3$

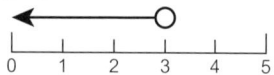

3 **a** Student's own answer, e.g. showing both solutions on a number line, or giving the same values that satisfy both inequalities, or by explaining that if $-2 > x$ then you can read this from right to left as 'x is less than -2'.

   b He divided by -2 and changed the direction of the inequality sign.

   c Students' own answers, e.g.
   I prefer Arthur's method because it does the same thing but in fewer steps.

4 **a** $x > -3$ **b** $x < -3.5$ **c** $x > -3$
   d $x < 12$ **e** $x < -12$

5 **a** $x < 6$

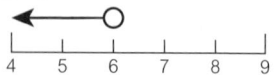

b $x > 6.4$

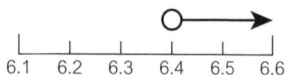

c $x < -7.5$

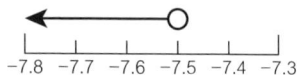

d $x < 3$

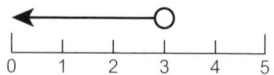

6 $1 < x + 3 \qquad x + 3 < 7$
   $-2 < x \qquad\qquad x < 4$
   $\qquad\quad -2 < x < 4$

7 **a** $-6 < x < 1$

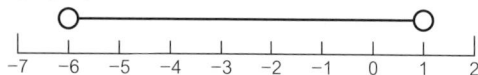

b $5 \leqslant y \leqslant 8$

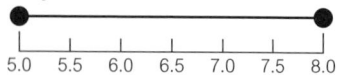

c $1 < y \leqslant 4$

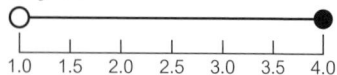

d $-4 \leqslant x < 8$

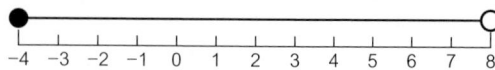

8 **a** $2 < 2x < 14$
   b $1 < x < 7$

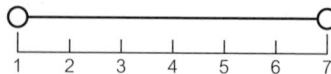

   c 2, 3, 4, 5 or 6

9 **a** $n \leqslant 2$

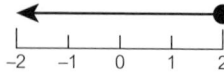

b $n > 3$

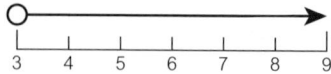

c $x < 8$

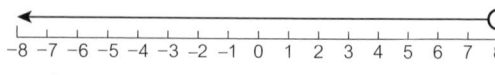

d $x \geqslant -6$

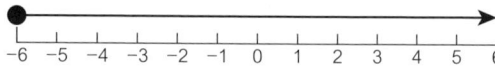

10 **a** $-2 \leqslant y < 3$

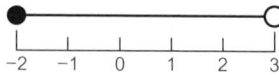

b $1 < x < 4$

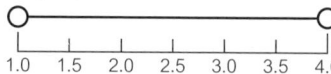

c $1 < n < 4$

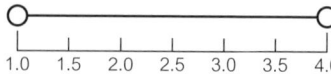

d $-2 < p < 7$

11 **a** $7 < 3x - 5 < 12$
   b $4 < x < \frac{17}{3}$

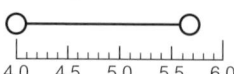

   c 5

Reflect

12 The methods are the same. You still use inverse operations. But if you multiply or divide both sides by a negative number when solving an equation, nothing changes; but if you do it when solving an inequality, you have to change the direction of the inequality sign.

6.4 Solving equations

1 **a** $x = 4.2$ **b** $x = 4.6$ **c** $x = 3.6$
   d $x = 4.5$ **e** $x = 4.2$ **f** $x = 2.7$

2 **a** 27   **b** 64
   c Because 39 is between $3^3 = 27$ and $4^3 = 64$.
   d, f

x	x^3	Comment
3	27	Too small
4	64	Too big
3.5	42.875…	Too big
3.4	39.304…	Too big
3.3	35.937…	Too small
3.35	37.595…	Too big

   e 3.3 is too small and 3.4 is too big, so the correct value must lie between them.
   g The solution is between 3.35 and 3.4. Both of these round to 3.4 to 1 d.p. and so any value between them rounds to 3.4 to 1 d.p.
   h $x = 3.391… = 3.4$ (1 d.p.)
   i It gives the correct solution, but it is not as quick as using a calculator.

3 **a** $y = 6.3$ or $y = -7.3$ **b** $y = 7.5$
   c $y = 4.1$ **d** $y = 4.6$
   e $y = 7.9$ **f** $y = 5.7$

4 **a** 6.2 cm   **b** 7.6 cm

5 4.7 cm

6 **a** $x = 7$ **b** $x = 4$ **c** $x = 6$ **d** $x = -2$

7 **a** $\dfrac{11x - 10}{10} = \dfrac{7x + 46}{8}$
   b $x = 30$ **c** $32°$ **d** $116°$

Investigation

8 **a** $x = 2.1$ **b** $x = 0.5$ **c** $x = -2.7$
   d You get three different solutions.
   e Yes, you still get three different solutions.

Reflect

9 The calculator method was better for Q1 and Q2 because it was quicker. The variable appears multiple times in the equations for Q3, making it impossible to rearrange to make y the subject and solve it.

6.5 Proportion

1 **a** Ratio of cost to number of days is constant:
      $27 ÷ 2 = 13.5$, $67.50 ÷ 5 = 13.5$, and so on.
   b $C = 13.5n$, where n is the number of days and C is the cost in £.

2 **a** $x = 148$ m, $y = 212$ yards, $z = 335$ yards
   b Distance in yards and distance in metres are directly proportional, so yards ÷ metres or metres ÷ yards is a constant.

3 **a** $48 : 162 = 8 : 27$
   b **i** 118.1 cm   **ii** 54.8 cm

4 **a** $R = 17.8P$ **b** 4450 South African rand
   c £36.52

5 **a** $y = 6x$ **b** $t = 2.4$

6 **a** All 36
   b Yes, because $xy = 36$, which is constant.
   c **i** No   **ii** Yes

Investigation

7 **a** 176.4 N   **b** 9.8 m/s²
   c **i** $W = 1.6m$ **ii** 22.4 N

8 **a** $P = \dfrac{1440}{A}$ **b** 48 N/cm²   **c** 2.5 cm²

9 **a** 5   **b** 125   **c** 4 or −4

10 78.4 m

11 **a** A – iii, B – ii, C – v, D – i
   b y is inversely proportional to the square of x.

Reflect

12 All equations where y is proportional to x^n are of the form $y = kx^n$.

All equations where y is inversely proportional to x^n are of the form $y = \dfrac{k}{x^n}$.

6 Extend

1 **a** **i** All x **ii** $x = -\dfrac{1}{5}$
      iii All x **iv** $x = 0$
   b **i** Identity   **ii** Equation
      iii Identity   **iv** Equation
   c Because they are only true for $x = 0$.

2 **a** **i** 1120 miles   **ii** 600 miles
   b 480 mph   **c** 7 hours 11 minutes

3 **a** Quadratic   **b** 7, 9, 11, 13, 15
   c 3, 12, 27, 48, 75   **d** Quadratic
   e $3n^2$ **f** $3n^2 + 2n + 5$

4 **a** 41.5   **b** −20
   c There are an infinitely many possible values of a and b.

5 **a** 5
   b Multiple answers possible, e.g. $38 - n$

6 Multiple answers, e.g. $3n^2$

7 242.28 (2 d.p.)

8 4

9 **a** Students' own answers, e.g.
      Length = $2a$, height = b.
      Need to have length × height = $2ab$.
   b No, because the length and height can be any two positive numbers that give length × height = $2ab$.

10 Multiple answers, e.g. $\dfrac{2x + 1}{5} \geqslant 5$

11 Multiple answers, e.g. $10 + 3x < 6x + 4 < 16 + 3x$

Investigation

12 **a** **i** 15   **ii** 24   **iii** 35
   b It is making a quadratic sequence.
   c It is still making a quadratic sequence, but the 2nd difference is not the same.
   d It makes a quadratic sequence with a 2nd difference of 4.

13 631

Reflect

14 Students' own answers, e.g.
   In sequences, I can see the pattern for the whole sequence much more clearly because I can tell what will happen in the sequence from the algebra. In proportion questions, I can write a formula to represent the relationship between two variables.

UNIT 7 Circles, Pythagoras and prisms

7.1 Circumference of a circle

1. a 3.978 873 577 cm
   b 3.141 592 654
   c Because π continues forever, we are only using a few decimal places of π.
2. a 3.4 cm
   b Windings gradually increase the diameter.
3. 14.0 cm (1 d.p.)
4. 74.6 km
5. a $\frac{5}{12}$ b $\frac{5}{12}$
   c i 44.0 cm ii 18.3 cm
6. a $r = 30.2$ mm b $r = 2.3$ cm
   c $r = 41.3$ mm
7. a 343.77°
   b The use of π means that the decimal digits go on for ever, and it is not possible to write an infinitely long decimal.
8. 10.2 cm
9. 0.5 cm
10. a Circle 1: 6π; circle 2: 8π; circle 3: 10π; circle 4: 12π
    b $2\pi(2 + n)$

Reflect

11. It has affected the accuracy when answers are given as a number, rather than in terms of π. These are less accurate because π continues forever so answers involving it have to be rounded.

7.2 Area of a circle

1. a 378.5 m² b 457 m
2. a 314.159 cm² b 310 cm²
   c 300 cm² d $314\frac{2}{7}$ cm²
   e The fraction gave the closest value to the calculator value while still being easy to work with.
3. a Manchester United 2.4 cm, Arsenal 1.8 cm
   b $2.3 billion

Investigation

4. a Circumference = 11.31 m, area = 10.18 m²
   b i It doubles.
      ii It increases by a factor of 4.
   c The circumference always increases by the same factor as the diameter does. The area increases by the square of that.
5. 31.4 m²
6. 49.1 m²
7. a $x = 120°$ b $x = 6.35$ cm
8. 1060.3 cm²
9. 2.8 m²
10. 502.7 cm²

Reflect

11. Students' own answers, e.g.
    I have used them to find parts of the area of a circle and to work with an approximation of π without a calculator.

7.3 Pythagoras' theorem

1. a 6.4 cm (nearest mm) b $\sqrt{41} = 6.403...$ cm
   c Part b, because $\sqrt{41}$ is an exact value, whereas part a depends on how accurately you can measure the line.
2. a i 5 cm ii 10 cm iii 20 cm
   b The hypotenuse values are all multiples of 5. The sides of all three triangles are in the same ratio.
   c 45 cm; $\sqrt{27^2 + 36^2} = \sqrt{2025} = 45$
3. a $7^2 + 24^2 = 49 + 576 = 625 = 25^2$
   b E.g. (14, 48, 50), (21, 72, 75), (28, 96, 100)
4. a Yes b Yes c No
   d No e No f Yes
5. Students' own answers, e.g. (10, 24, 26), (16, 30, 34), (18, 80, 82)

6. a Students' own answers, e.g. 16 cm
   b Overestimate: the angle is less than 90° so the side would be shorter.
7. a 5.4 b 8.2 c 6.7
   d 3.6 e 8.9 f 10 (exactly)
8. a 80 cm b 113.1 cm
9. a $6x = 360°$, so $x = 60°$
   b $x + 2y = 180°$, so $y = 60°$
   c Equilateral d 4.3 cm
   e 10.8 cm² f 65.0 cm²
10. 0.80 m
11. a 3 cm b 7.6 cm c 22.8 cm²
    d 36 cm² e 127.2 cm² f 84 cm³

Reflect

12. Students' own answers, e.g.
    I preferred using Pythagoras' theorem because the answer was more accurate.

7.4 Prisms and cylinders

1. a 112.5 ml/s
   b i 5318 ml = 5.318 l ii 47.3 s
   c £9.85
2. a The area is 2.65 times the capacity of the roller, so the roller will need to be filled 3 times (or filled once and refilled twice).
   b The roller may repeat areas.
3. a 78.5 cm²
   b i 78.5 cm² ii 78.5 cm² iii 78.5 cm²
   c It is always the same, because I just divide the volume by the height to find the area of the face.
4. a 180 cm³
   b i 360 cm³ ii 935 cm³ iii 1738.2 cm³ iv 1131.0 cm³
   c Hexagonal prism, because it is the closest to the circle without being larger than the circle.
5. Accurate drawing of semicircle with diameter 9.3 cm.
6. a 196.3 min b 5890
   c

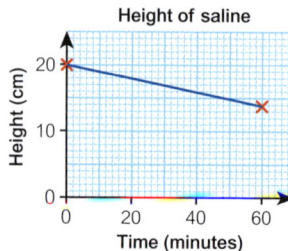

Height of saline

7. Shape B
8. a 4.5 cm b 0.09 cm
9. 2250 cm³; 2010.6 cm³. No it's too small.
10. a 9.95 cm b 10.30 cm
11. a i 289.5 g ii 1.93 g iii 0.0193 g
    b 19.3 mg/mm³

Reflect

12. The same: I am still working out the area of two shapes and some rectangles.
    Different: there is only one rectangle on the cylinder and its length is the circumference of the circle.

7.5 Errors and bounds

1. 1.25 g
2. a 40 g b 0.625 g
3. Nearest 100 kg
4. The number of packs of cards must be an integer, so there is no difference between < 425 and ⩽ 424.
5. 4.68 m/s
6. a 17.9 m, 18.2 m (1 d.p.)
   b 13.1 m², 13.6 m² (1 d.p.)
   c 198.0 m³, 207.3 m³ (1 d.p.)
7. No. 1500 × 10.5 cm = 15 750 cm < 15 800 cm
8. 1137.150 kg < M < 1263.150 kg

9 a 4 tubs

   b $1 < t < 5$ or $2 \leqslant t \leqslant 4$ or equivalent

10 a Lower bound: 1576.326 cm^2,
      upper bound: 1618.831 cm^2

   b Lower bound: 1.227 cm^2,
      upper bound: 1.307 cm^2

   c $0.078\% < P < 0.083\%$

Investigation

11 a $24.735425\,\text{m} \leqslant A \leqslant 24.845625\,\text{m}$

   b $24.7275\,\text{m} \leqslant A \leqslant 25.8375\,\text{m}$

   c $18.75\,\text{m} \leqslant A \leqslant 29.75\,\text{m}$

   d 25 m^2

   e The greater the accuracy level, the smaller the error interval.

Reflect

12 If the thing we are measuring takes discrete values then there is more than one way. If it is continuous then there is only one way.

7 Extend

1 139.5 cm

2 $x = 45°$

3 a 18.8 cm^2 **b** 15.6 cm^2 **c** 3.2 cm^2

4 a $\sqrt{2}$

   b **i** $\sqrt{3}$ **ii** $\sqrt{4}$

      iii $\sqrt{5}$ **iv** $\sqrt{6}$

   c $\sqrt{n+1}$

   d If the values were given as decimals, you wouldn't see that the number inside the square root is increasing by 1 each time.

5 70.52 cm^2

6 1128.38 cm^3

7 26.4 cm

Investigation

8 722 cm^2

9 a 57.3°   **b** 18 cm^3

   c 57.3°, 12.5 cm^2 **d** 57.3°

   e 2π

Reflect

10 Students' own answers, e.g.
Draw a picture and label it with the information.

UNIT 8 Graphs

8.1 Using $y = mx + c$

1 **a** **i** 90°   **ii** 90°

   b $y = -\frac{1}{5}x$

2 **a** 2   **b** $-\frac{1}{2}$

   c -1 **d** $\frac{1}{3}, -3, -1$

   e When two lines are perpendicular, their gradients multiply to -1.

3 **a** Parallel (same gradient)
   b Parallel (same gradient)
   c Perpendicular (gradients multiply to -1)
   d Perpendicular (gradients multiply to -1)

4 E

5 **a** $y = -\frac{1}{2}x + c$ **b** $y = \frac{1}{3}x + c$

   c $y = -2x + c$ **d** $y = 2x + c$

6 $y = -\frac{1}{3}x + 2$

7 **a** $y = \frac{1}{2}x + \frac{1}{2}$ **b** $y = -5x - 4$

8 **a** True   **b** True
   c True   **d** False

9 Students' own statements, e.g.
   'It is parallel to $y = 3x + 1$.'
   'It crosses the y-axis at $(0, 2)$.'
   'It goes through the point $(1, 5)$.'
   'It is perpendicular to $y = -\frac{1}{3}x - 5$.'

10 BC is $y = -10x - 15$; CD is $y = 0.1x + 5$;
   AD is $y = -10x + 5$

11 Fractions, because you can see the relationship between the gradients more clearly.

Reflect

12 They both need to have the y-intercept calculated in the same way. It is easier to find the gradient of a line parallel to a given line, as it is the same. When lines are perpendicular, the gradient must be calculated.

8.2 More straight-line graphs

1 B and E, A and C

2 The gradient of the first line is not 2, because y is not the subject of the equation.

3 **a** Parallel   **b** Neither
   c Parallel   **d** Neither

4 **a** $(8, 0)$ **b** $(0, 2)$
   c

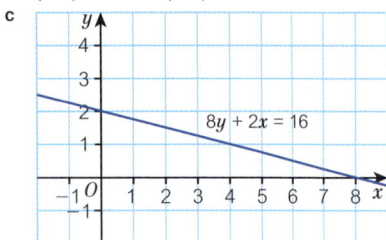

   d $y = -\frac{1}{4}x + 2$

   e 4

Investigation

5 **a** $-\frac{3}{2}$ and $\frac{2}{3}$

   b $-\frac{3}{2} \times \frac{2}{3} = -1$

   c $\frac{8}{10} \times -\frac{10}{8} = -1$

   d **i** $4x + 5y = 12$ **ii** $8y + 2x = 14$

6 **a** $x + y = -1$ **b** North-west

7 **a** $y = 0.025x + 1000$ **b** $y = -40x$

8 $y = -2.5x + 30$

9 **a** $x + y = 5$
   b $x - y = -1$
   c Because $x + y = 5$ rearranges to give $y = -x + 5$ and $x - y = -1$ rearranges to give $y = x + 1$, and so the gradients multiply to give -1.

10 $x - y = 5$

11 **a** $y = 2x$ **b** $y = 2x + 1$
   c $y = 2x + 3$ **d** All have gradient 2.

12 $y = 2x - 4$

13 **a** $y = 2x + 2$
   b $y = 2x + 2$
   c $y = 2x + 2$, because in both coordinate pairs the y-value is 2 more than double the x-value.
   d Substituting $x = 6$ into either expression gives the value 14.

14 Two

15 There is not enough information to know the equation of the line from one point.

16 **a** $y = \frac{1}{2}x - \frac{11}{2}$

   b It will be the same line, because the midpoint is part of the original line.

17 $y = -x + 2$

18 $y = \frac{1}{3}x + 1$

19 $\frac{3}{4}x + y = 4$ and $\frac{3}{4}x + y = 29$

Reflect

20 Any values would work but using 0 is the easiest as it gives an equation in only one variable, which is quicker to solve.

8.3 Simultaneous equations

1 **a**

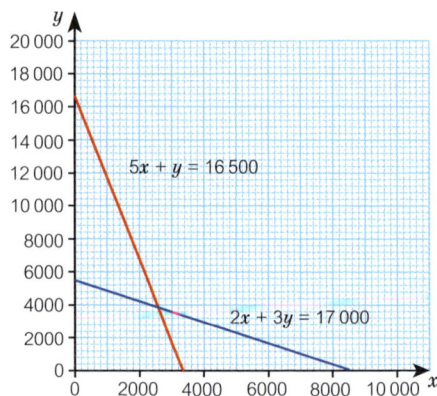

   b 20-second = £2500, 30-second = £4000

2 **a**

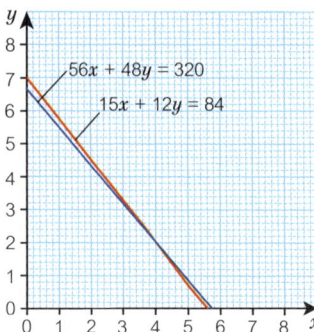

   b A burger costs £4, a drink costs £2.

3 **a** Dividing both sides of equation (1) by 2 gives $x + y = 10$.
   b 30
   c $3y = 30 - 3x$
   d $3y = 44 - 5x$
   e $30 - 3x = 44 - 5x$; $2x = 14$; $x = 7$
   f $y = 3$
   g $5x + 3y = 5 \times 7 + 3 \times 3 = 35 + 9 = 44$

h $x = 11, y = 1$

4 a $x + 9y = 343$ **b** $x + 6y = 235$

  c £36   **d** £19

5 a $x + y = 45$ **b** $60x + 80y = 3180$

  c

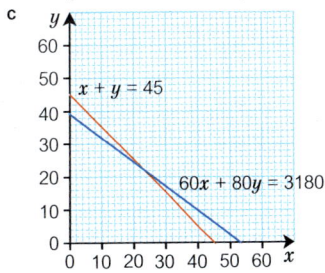

  d 21 water, 24 fizzy drinks

  e $x = 45 - y$, $x = 53 - \frac{4}{3}y$

  f $y = 24$

  g $x = 21$

  h Students' own answers

6 a

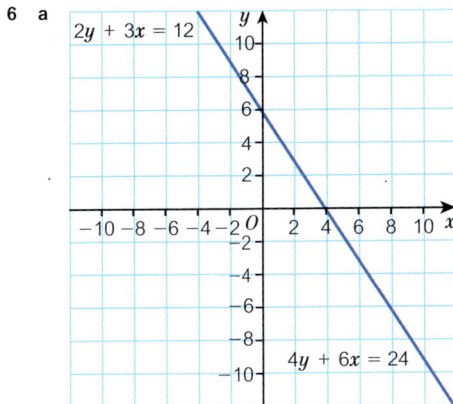

  b

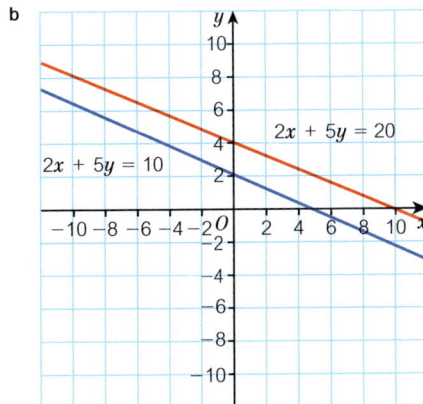

  c In part **a** they are the same line; in part **b** they are parallel.

  d There is an infinite number of solutions to part **a** and no solutions to part **b**.

7 a $x = -4, y = -7$ **b** No solution

  c $x = 2, y = 3$

  d Infinitely many solutions

  e No solution   **f** $x = 0, y = -3$

8 Students' own answers, e.g.

  a $y = 2x$ and $y = 2x + 1$

  b $y = 0.5x + 4.5$ and $x = -8$

  c $y = x$ and $2y = 2x$

Reflect

9 The graphs were linear, so their lines can only cross in one place, be the same line, or be parallel and never meet.

8.4 Graphs of quadratic functions

1 a

Speed, v (mph)	0	10	20	30	40	50	60
Skid, s (ft)	0	5	20	45	80	125	180

  b

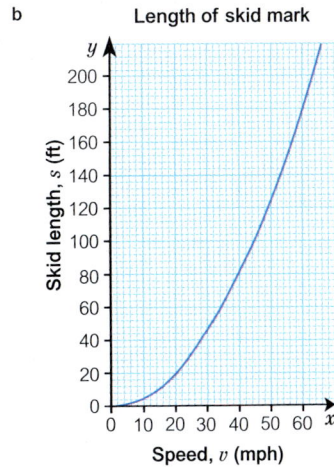

  c 44 mph

  d i 90 ft   **ii** 185 ft

2 a

Time, t (seconds)	0	1	2	3	4	5	6	7	8
Height, h (m)	50	70	80	80	70	50	20	−20	−70

  b

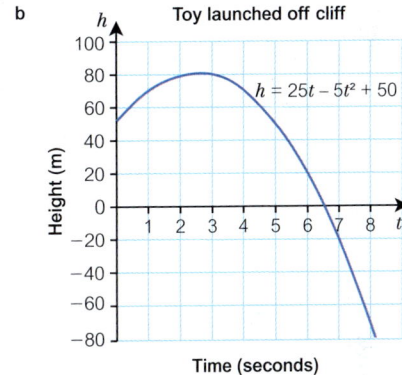

  c i About 81 m   **ii** About 6.5 seconds

3 a $A = x(10 - x)$ or $A = 10x - x^2$

  b

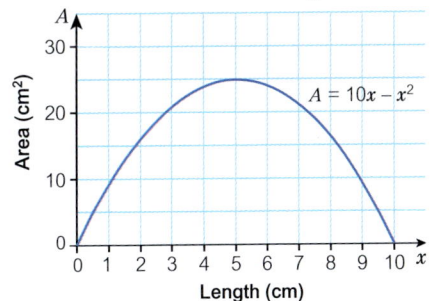

  c i 25 cm²   **ii** About 8.2 cm by 1.8 cm

4 a $y = x + 2$ and $y = x^2$

  b $x = -1, y = 1$ and $x = 2, y = 4$

  c $(-1) + 2 = 1$ and $(-1)^2 = 1$; $2 + 2 = 4$ and $2^2 = 4$

5 $x = 0, y = 1$ and $x = -2, y = 5$

6 a i

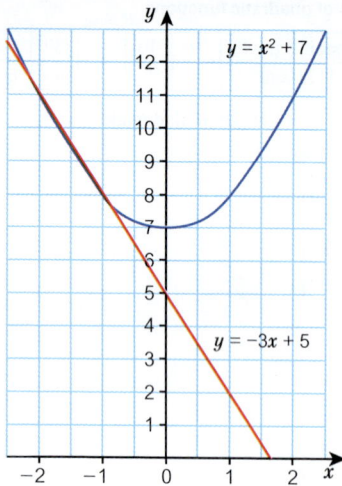

Graph showing $y = x^2 + 7$ and $y = -3x + 5$

ii

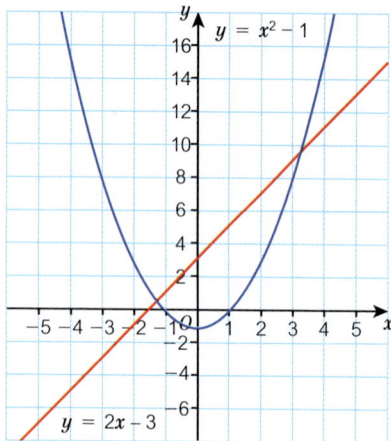

Graph showing $y = x^2 - 1$ and $y = 2x - 3$

b i $x = -2$, $y = 11$ and $x = -1$, $y = 8$

ii $x = 3.2$, $y = 9.5$ and $x = -1.2$, $y = 0.5$

Investigation

7 a Gradient is 2.

b Gradients are 4, 6 and 8.

c The gradients form an arithmetic sequence. In this case, the nth term is $2n$.

d Students draw some quadratic graphs with different equations and conclude that the gradients always form an arithmetic progression, which you can find the nth term for.

Reflect

8 If both equations are linear, there is either one solution, no solution or infinitely many solutions. If one equation is quadratic and the other is linear, there can be two solutions, one solution or no solutions, but there cannot be an infinite number of solutions.

8.5 More non-linear graphs

1 a

x	−3	−2	−1	0	1	2	3
y	−27	−8	−1	0	1	8	27

b

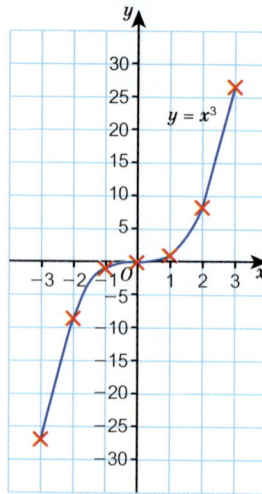

Graph showing $y = x^3$

c Rotational symmetry of order 2 about the origin.

2 a Students' estimated answers close to
  i 5.832   **ii** 1.912…

b i 5.832   **ii** 1.912…

c Calculator answers are more accurate; the accuracy of the value from the graph depends on the scale used, but will always be less accurate than the calculator.

3 a i $y = 2x^3$

x	−3	−2	−1	0	1	2	3
y	−54	−16	−2	0	2	16	54

ii $y = 5x^3$

x	−3	−2	−1	0	1	2	3
y	−135	−40	−5	0	5	40	135

b Students' graphs of $y = 2x^3$ and $y = 5x^3$ on the same axes

c Same: They have rotational symmetry of order 2 about the origin.
Different: $y = 2x^3$ and $y = 5x^3$ are steeper than $y = x^3$.

d They would both have rotational symmetry of order 2 about the origin.
$y = 3x^3$ would be 'squashed' towards the y-axis and $y = \frac{1}{2}x^3$ would be 'stretched' away from the y-axis compared to $y = x^3$.

4 a $y = -x^3$

x	−3	−2	−1	0	1	2	3
y	27	8	1	0	−1	−8	−27

b

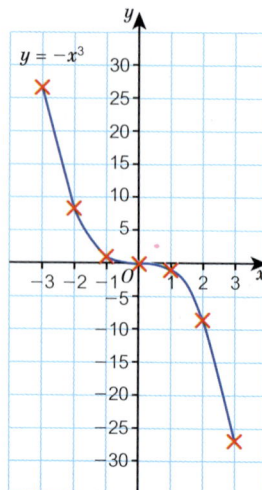

Graph showing $y = -x^3$

c Reflection in the y-axis (or in the x-axis)

d **i** 'Squashed' towards the y-axis

ii

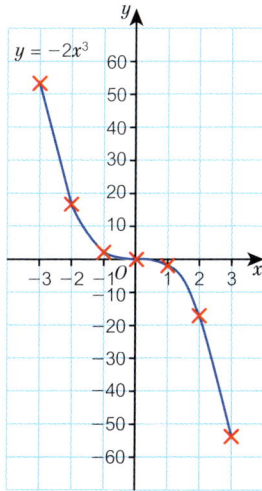

$y = -2x^3$

5 B is quadratic, C has two minimum points.

6 **a** $y = 6x^3$

b

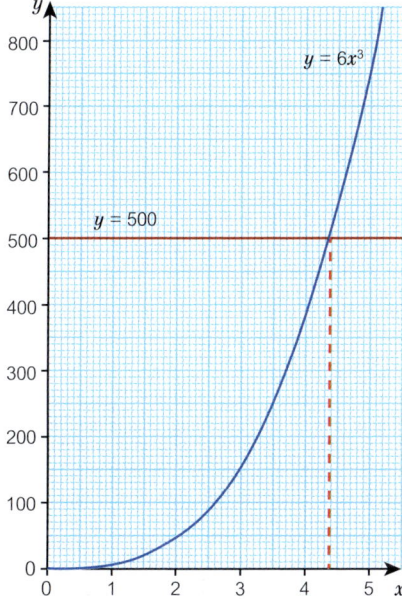

$y = 6x^3$

$y = 500$

c About 4.4 cm

7 **a**

x	0	2	4	6	8	10
x^3	0	8	64	216	512	1000
$A = 0.1x^3$	0	0.8	6.4	21.6	51.2	100

b

Air in ball

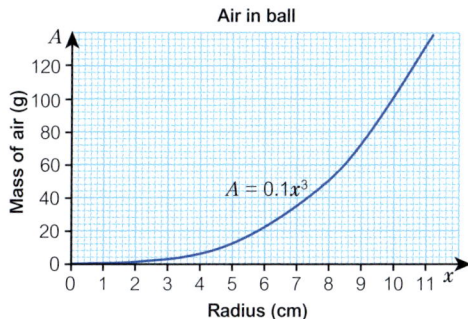

Mass of air (g)

$A = 0.1x^3$

Radius (cm)

c About 78 g   **d** About 6.7 cm

8 **a, d i**

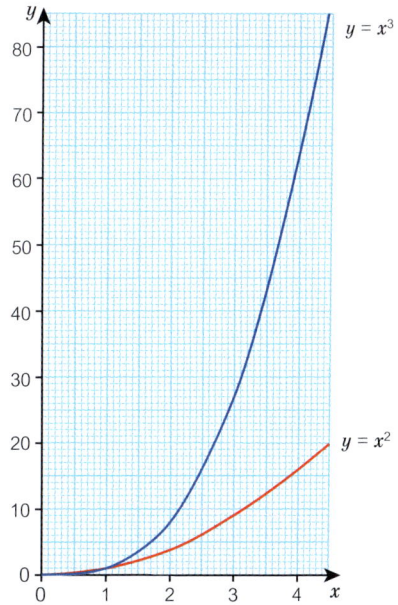

$y = x^3$

$y = x^2$

b Draw a line $y = 4$. The intersection of the curve $y = x^2$ with this line is at (2, 4) so the positive square root of 4 is 2; the other square root is −2, by symmetry.

c About 2.6

d **ii** About 3.7

e (0, 0) and (1, 1)

f $x^2 = x^3$ for $x = 0$
$x^2 > x^3$ for $0 < x < 1$
$x^2 = x^3$ for $x = 1$
$x^2 < x^3$ for $x > 1$

Reflect

9 **a** Cubic   **b** Quadratic
c Cubic   **d** Quadratic
e Cubic

8 Extend

1 $y = 2x + 4$ and $6y + 3x = 1$ or $y = 2x + 1$ and $6y + 3x = 4$

2 Yes, because the lines will always cross at exactly one point.

3 **a** $y = 3x + 10$

b E.g. $y = -\frac{1}{3}x + 8$ and $y = 3x + 13$

c Infinitely many   **d** (−22, 14)

4 E.g. $y = x − 5$

5 E.g. $4y + 10x = -8$, $8y + 20x = -16$, $16y + 40x = -32$

6 (4, 3)

7 $x = 4, y = 0$; $x = -4, y = 0$

8 **a**

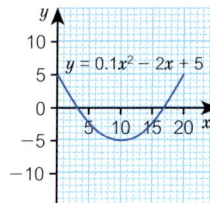

$y = 0.1x^2 - 2x + 5$

b x could represent the distance along the bridge, y could represent the height above the ground.

9 $y = 3x − 13$

Investigation

10 a   **i** $y = \frac{x}{2}$ **ii** $y = \frac{x}{3}$ **iii** $y = x$

    b

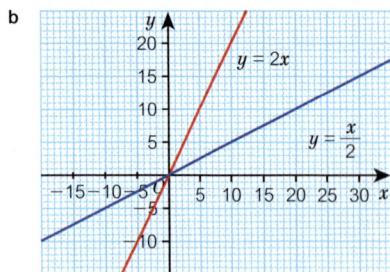

    c   **i**

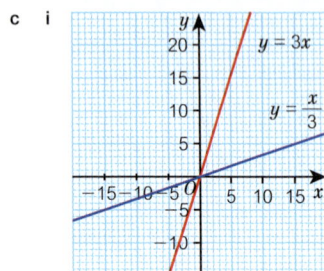

   ii, iii   The graph is reflected in the line $y = x$ to give the graph of the inverse function.

    d

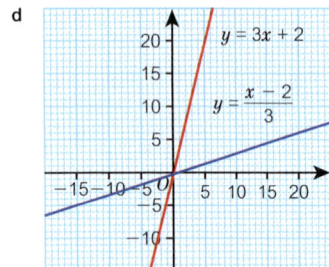

   e i, ii

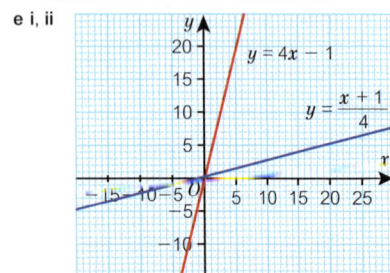

   iii, iv $y = \frac{x + 1}{4}$

11 a   The coordinates of the intersection points.

    b   This is the equation from part **a** with $3x$ subtracted from both sides, so will also have solutions corresponding to the coordinates of the intersection points.

    c   This is the equation from part **b** with 3 added to both sides, so will also have solutions corresponding to the coordinates of the intersection points.

    d $y = x + 3$

Reflect

12 Students' own answers

UNIT 9 Probability

9.1 Mutually exclusive events

1. **a** The coin can only have been made in one year.
   b **i** 0.3   **ii** 0.15   **iii** 0.35

2. $100\% - 4\% - 8\% = 88\%$

3. 0.375

4. $15:14:21$

5. **a** The probability of picking a red counter is less than 0.1 (but not zero). If there were 10 counters, then the smallest possible probability of picking a red counter would be 0.1, so there must be more than 10 counters.
   b 20

6. **a** $\frac{2}{5}$ **b** $\frac{3}{5}$ **c** $\frac{4}{5}$
   d They are not mutually exclusive: 2 is even *and* prime so it is counted twice.
   e Change the 2 to any other number.

7. No, because 36 is a multiple of 3 *and* a square number.

8. **a** True   **b** False   **c** False
   d False   **e** True   **f** True

9. Someone can be wearing both red *and* high heels, so the outcomes are not mutually exclusive.

10. Students' own answers, e.g.
    a 1, 3, 3, 5, 6, 8
    b 2, 2, 3, 3, 4, 4
    c 2 blue, 2 red, 3 blue, 3 red, 4 green, 4 green
    d 0

11. **a** Students' own answers, e.g.
    2, 3, 4, 6, 8 and 5, 7, 9, 15, 21
    b No. 'Prime number' and 'even number' are not mutually exclusive. 'Prime number' and 'square number' are mutually exclusive. 'Even number' and 'square number' are not mutually exclusive.

12. Students' own answers, e.g.
    a Getting a vowel and getting a consonant
    b Getting a vowel and getting an A

Reflect

13. So that you know whether for two events, A and B,
    $P(A \text{ or } B) = P(A) + P(B)$.

9.2 Experimental and theoretical probability

1. **a** $\frac{1}{13}$ **b** $\frac{1}{4}$

2. **a** No   **b** No   **c** Yes

3. **a** $\frac{1}{4}$ **b** 25
   c Probably fair because frequencies are close to 25. Spin more times to be more confident.

4. There might be more boys than girls, so each boy would have less chance of winning. Or vice versa.

5. **a** 0.0625
   b 14500
   c It is unlikely to be organic because only 10 out of 800 organic cabbages weigh 1.4 kg or more.

6. **a, b i, ii**

Colour	Probability	Prize	Expected number of wins in 200 games	Expected prizes in 200 games
red	0.2	50p	40	£20
blue	0.5	20p	100	£20
yellow	0.3	0p	60	£0

   b iii £40
   c £40 ÷ 200 = 20p so they should charge more than 20p.

7. Students' own answers, e.g.
   It is unlikely that the dice would only roll two different values in 5 rolls, so it is likely that the dice is not fair.

Investigation

8. **a** 0.5
   b–e Students' own answers
   f As the number of trials increases, the experimental probability gets closer to one value. For a fair coin, this will be 0.5. The experimental probability approaches the theoretical probability.

Reflect

9. As the number of experiments increases, the experimental probability gets closer and closer to the theoretical probability. But after any given number of trials, it is not very often equal to the theoretical probability.

9.3 Sample space diagrams

1. **a**

   b Students' own answers, e.g.
   'No, as the 3 appears twice and the 6 only appears once so the 3 is more likely.'

2. **a**

   b 1

3. **a**

   b 15
   c $P(\text{even}) = \frac{5}{9}$ and $\frac{5}{9}$ of 100 is 55.55... .
   70 is quite a lot higher than that, so the spinner is probably not fair.

4. **a** $\frac{1}{9}$ **b** $\frac{2}{9}$ **c** $\frac{4}{9}$ **d** $\frac{5}{9}$

5. **a** Game is fair as there are 4 possible outcomes (HH, TT, TH, HT), and 2 of these have two faces the same and 2 have two faces different.
   b Game is not fair because there are 9 possible outcomes, and only 3 of these have the spinners landing on the same number.

6. You are more likely get a total of 6 or more (14 possible outcomes) than a total of less than 6 (10 possible outcomes).

7. **a** $P(\text{odd})$ is only $\frac{4}{16}$
   b Jay
   c Students' own answers. e.g.
   1 point to Jay if the score is even, and 3 points to Mitra if it is odd, so that each player can expect 3 points from 4 rounds.

8 Multiple answers possible, e.g.

	4	4	4	4	4
6					
6					
6					
3					
9					

9 a The factors of 8 are 1, 2, 4, 8, so the only two ways are 2 on one dice and 4 on the other. (1 and 8 is not possible as dice only goes up to 6.)

  b There are $6 \times 6 = 36$ possible outcomes, and $\frac{2}{36} = \frac{1}{18}$

10 a Multiple answers possible, e.g. $a = 4$, $b = 5$, $c = 6$

  b $\frac{1}{8}$ **c** No

Reflect

11 Student's own answers, e.g. (for Q6)
'No, because a diagonal showed where the answers were equal to 6 and then I could just count how many squares would give an answer less than 6 or more than 6.'

9.4 Two-way tables

1 a **i** 0.73   **ii** 0.22
  b **i** 5
    ii 25 (rounding up for full packs of paper)
2 a **i** Dyfed-Powys   **ii** Humberside
  b **i** Yes, it has the lowest crime figures for burglary and for bicycle theft.
    ii Lots of places in the UK are not included in the list – they could be safer.
  c No, the probability is 2.16648×10^{-5}, or 21.6648 in a million. ('1 in a million' means that the probability is 1×10^{-6}.)
3 a E.g.

		M	O	U	S	E
Coin	Head					
	Tail					

  b Students own answer, e.g.
Jo's because it is quicker to fill in, as it only has the outcome you are interested in, and a choice of two cells.
  c $\frac{3}{10}$
  d Two-way table from part **a**, because it shows all the possible outcomes, and that there are 10 in all, of which 3 are 'head and a vowel'.
4 a

	Tea	Coffee
Men	6	1
Women	14	11

  b Yes, because the proportion of women who prefer coffee ($\frac{11}{25}$) is greater than the proportion of men who prefer coffee ($\frac{1}{7}$).
  c $\frac{11}{32}$ **d** $\frac{11}{25}$
  e In part **c**, you were selecting from all the men as well as the women, so the women who prefer coffee make up a smaller proportion of the total than when you are only looking at women.
  f 96
5 a 68   **b** $\frac{9}{20}$

c

	Hotdogs	Veggie burgers	No preference	Total
Year 7	4	0	8	12
Year 8	25	36	4	65
Year 9	3	0	0	3
Total	32	36	12	80

  d Year 8
  e There is not enough information on the other year groups. They could be in Year 7, Year 8 or Year 9.
6 Because 'even' and 'prime' are not mutually exclusive: you could record a score of 2 under either heading.

Reflect

7 The same: Both can show possible outcomes of two combined events, and you can calculate probabilities from each.
Different: Two-way tables can be used to record results from experiments or surveys.

9.5 Venn diagrams

1 a Because the intersection is not empty: 1 and 4 are square numbers *and* are less than 7.

  b $\frac{3}{10}$ **c** $\frac{3}{5}$ **d** $\frac{7}{10}$

  e False, because P(rolling a square number) + P(rolling a number less than 7) $= \frac{3}{10} + \frac{6}{10} = \frac{9}{10}$ whereas P(rolling a square number or a number less than 7) $= \frac{7}{10}$

2 a

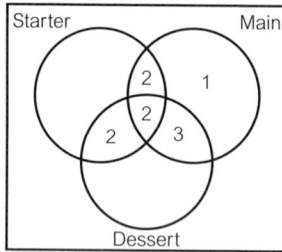

  b **i** $\frac{7}{10}$ **ii** $\frac{3}{10}$

Investigation

3 a **i** $\frac{2}{5}$ **ii** $\frac{3}{5}$

  b $\frac{2}{5} + \frac{3}{5} = 1$

  c There is no intersection between the circles in the Venn diagram.

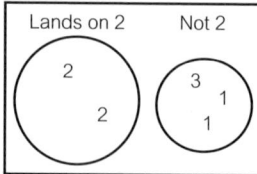

  d Probability of an event happening + probability of an event not happening = 1
  e You can subtract the probability of it happening from 1.
4 a **i** 1   **ii** 13
  b 20   **c** $\frac{3}{10}$
  d 3   **e** 10
  f $\frac{3}{40}$ **g** 4050 g
5 a 25   **b** $\frac{16}{25}$
  c $\frac{17}{25}$
  d You would be counting the people who were wearing both a hat and a coat twice.

Reflect

6 There would be no overlap between the circles.

9 Extend

1 Students' own answers, e.g.
49, 50, 51, 52, 53, 54, 55, 56, 57, 58

2 Every third number is a multiple of 3, and $1 \div 3 = \frac{1}{3}$

3 a

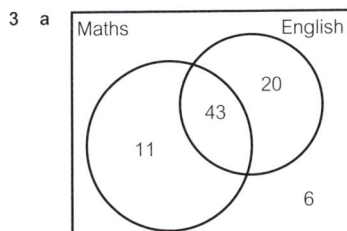

  b $\frac{43}{80}$

4 Attended the vampire party.

5 There are three events in Q4, which may all happen at once. Although a 3 by 3 two-way table could show data for three events, it has nowhere to record the outcome of all three happening at once.

6 Students' own answers, e.g. getting a score of exactly 2.

7 $\frac{2}{9}$

8 a Student's own answer, e.g. 2, 3, 4, 5, 6

  b $\frac{4}{25}$

  c Nat's statement that 'odd' and 'even' are mutually exclusive is correct, and so are 'odd, odd' and 'even, even'. But 9 of the possible outcomes are 'even, even', 4 are 'odd, odd' and 12 are 'one odd and one even' (in either order). So P(even, even) = 1 – P(odd, odd) – P(one odd and one even).

9 a Students may draw the line $y = x$ on the graph:

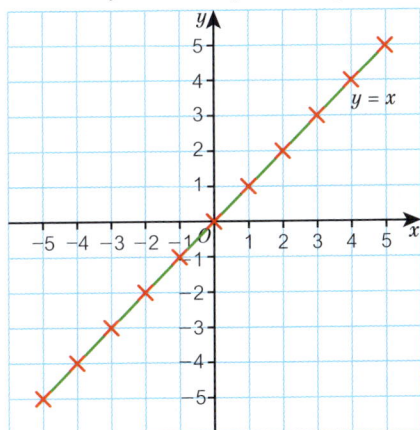

$\frac{1}{11}$

  b 121 points on the grid, of which 110 have $y \neq x$. As the grid is symmetrical, half of these have $y > x$.

So probability is $\frac{55}{121}$

10 a 44%   b 14%   c 54%

Investigation

11 Seven pieces of information, e.g. P(A and B and C), P(A and B), P(A and C), P(B and C), P(A), P(B), P(C).

Reflect

12 Students' own answers, e.g.
'He would expect this to happen 25 times. 40 is not too far away, so the coins might not be biased.' or 'This is 60% more times than expected, so the coins could be biased.'

UNIT 10 Comparing shapes

10.1 Congruent and similar shapes

1   a   Correctly constructed triangle
    b   Yes (ASA)
    c   You can change the side length, but the angles must stay the same.

2   Angle ABC = angle ADC
    Angle BAC = angle ACD (alternate angles)
    Angle DAC = angle BCA (alternate angles)
    $AD = BC$
    AAA and a side the same – must be congruent (AAS)

3   OC is a side of both triangles
    $OB = OA$ (both radii) so triangle ABO is isosceles
    Angle OBC = angle OAC
    Angle BOC = angle AOC
    As all angles are the same and two pairs of sides are the same, must be congruent (SAS or ASA or AAS or RHS).

4   a   Yes
    b   Yes; each exterior angle is equal to the base angle of the isosceles triangles; each side is the length of the base minus the length of the shorter side of the isosceles triangles.

5   $\frac{2}{3}$

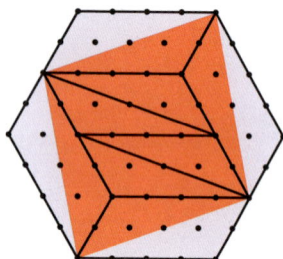

6   SSS, because you don't know the lengths of the vertical sides of the two triangles.

7   Yes (SSS). The opposite sides of a rectangle are equal so $AB = CD$ and $AD = BC$, and they share the third side, AC.

8   Sometimes, if the triangle is isosceles and the angle that is bisected is the one between the two equal-length sides.

9   a EG
    b   SSS, $EF = FG$, $EM = MG$, shares FM.
    c   They would not have equal side lengths.

10 No, because the angles that are the same size are between the two equal-length sides in triangle HIJ but not in triangle LKM, so they are not corresponding angles.

11 NOP and SRQ, OPN and RQS, PNO and QSR.

12 Not enough information: you would need the size of an angle, or the lengths of AB and CD or AC and BD.

13 a   True
    b   False (the angles could be in a different order)

Reflect

14 Yes, congruent shapes are also similar, with a scale factor of 1.

10.2 Ratios in triangles

1   a   Angle CDA = angle ABC = $(360° − (72° + 50°)) ÷ 2 = 119°$
        (opposite angles in kite are equal, angle sum of kite is 360°)
        Angle EFG = 119° (opposite angles in kite are equal)
        Angle HEF = 72° (angle sum of kite is 360°)
        Angle ABC = angle EFG, angle BCD = angle FGH,
        angle CDA = angle GHE, angle DAB = angle HEF
        All angles are the same, so $ABCD$ and $EFGH$ are similar.
    b $x = 12.9$

2   Yes, because the ratio of the lengths of corresponding sides is the same in similar shapes.

3   a   42 cm   b $\frac{2}{5}$

4   24 cm

5   Angle ABC = EFG; both are 110°. Angle BCD = FGH; both are 110°. Angle DAB = FEH; both are 70°. Angle GHE = angle CDA; both are 70°.

Investigation

6   a, b, d

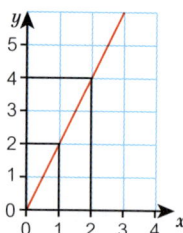

    c   The second rectangle is an enlargement of the first, scale factor 2.
    d   The diagonals form a straight line.
    e   It happens with all similar rectangles.
    f   It does not happen.
    g   It does work with other quadrilaterals but they may not be similar even if the diagonals form a straight line.

Reflect

7   Students' own answers

10.3 The tangent ratio

1   5.0 m

2   16.4 cm

3   52.0 cm (1 d.p.)

4   $\tan θ = 1$ = opposite ÷ adjacent, so two side lengths of the triangle are equal, i.e. it is an isosceles triangle. One angle is 90°, so the other two angles are both 45°.

5   11.2 cm

6   97 m

7   46.8 cm^2

8   Area = 3.56 mm^2, perimeter = 7.89 mm; perimeter is numerically greater.

9   350.8 cm^2

Reflect

10 The tangent ratio can be used to find the shorter sides of a right-angled triangle, which gives enough information to use Pythagoras' theorem to find the hypotenuse. So they can be used together to find the lengths of all three sides in a right-angled triangle.

10.4 The sine ratio

1   2.8 m

2   5.7 m

3   15 + 12.7 + 7.9 = 35.6 cm

4   Yes – Michael uses $\tan θ$ to find the adjacent side, AB,
    i.e. $\tan θ = \frac{x}{AB}$ so $AB = \frac{x}{\tan θ}$
    Then he uses Pythagoras' theorem to find
    $AC^2 = AB^2 + x^2$
    and hence the hypotenuse AC.
    Jean uses $\sin θ$ to find the hypotenuse AC,
    i.e. $\sin θ = \frac{x}{AC}$ so $AC = \frac{x}{\sin θ}$

5   14.5 cm

6   No; the seat is 146 cm (less than 150 cm) at its highest point, but 22 cm (less than 23 cm) at its lowest.

7   a   20 m 12 cm   b   8 m 62 cm

8   41.14 cm

9   36.9 cm

Investigation

10 a   The 6 cm side could be the hypotenuse, opposite the 28° angle or adjacent to the 28° angle.
    b   33.9 cm^2
    c   30 cm
    d   Maximum area is 46.1 cm^2, maximum perimeter is 35 cm.
    e   Maximum area is 60.2 cm^2, maximum perimeter is 40 cm.
    f   Maximum area and perimeter are always when the side is the opposite to the 28° angle. Perimeter increases by approximately 5 cm each time; no pattern with area. 76.2 cm^2 and 45 cm.

Reflect

11 Using $\sin\theta$ is more efficient.

10.5 The cosine ratio

1 13.9 m

2 a 16.1 m **b** 20.4 m

3 128 mm × 190 mm

4 60.6 cm (1 d.p.)

5 a 12 km 856 m **b** 15 km 321 m

6 a 42.4 km **b** 67.8 km

7 38.3 km

8 a 36.8 km **b** 17.2 km

9 44.3 km

10 23.5 km

Reflect

11 Bearings are measured as angles, and north and east are at right angles, so right-angled triangles can be drawn and trigonometry can be used.

10.6 Using trigonometry to find angles

1 a 4.6° **b** 46.6 m

2 21.8°

3 90°, 53.1°, 36.9°

4 118.4° (1 d.p.)

5 058.8°

6 059°

7 326°

8 35.3°

9 a 9.9 cm **b** 35.3° **c** 12.1 cm

Investigation

10 a Drawing of a 4 cm cube
   b $\theta = 35.26°$; it is the same angle.
   c The angle is always the same because the cubes are mathematically similar.

Reflect

11 The same: Right-angled triangles can be involved in both types of problems.
   Different: In 3D shapes, it can be more difficult to spot what right-angled triangles to use from the diagram.

10 Extend

1 Speed = 11.2 m/s = 40.4 km/h

2 216 miles

3 a 29.0 m **b** 6.1°

4 97.5 cm²

5 a $AC = 8.7$ cm, $BC = 10$ cm
   b $BC = 10$ cm, $AC = 8.7$ cm
   c, d Students' own answers

6 93.5 cm²

7 $10.39x^2$

8 a Multiple answers, e.g. 5 cm, 6 cm, 7.8 cm
   b Multiple answers, e.g. 10 cm, 12 cm, 15.6 cm or 20 cm, 24 cm, 31.2 cm or 40 cm, 48 cm, 62.5 cm
   c 39.8°
   d Because the exact angle corresponding to a tangent ratio of $\frac{5}{6}$ is not an integer, so rounding the angle to an integer number of degrees will alter the ratios of the sides slightly.

9 a 0.17 **b** 0.34

c

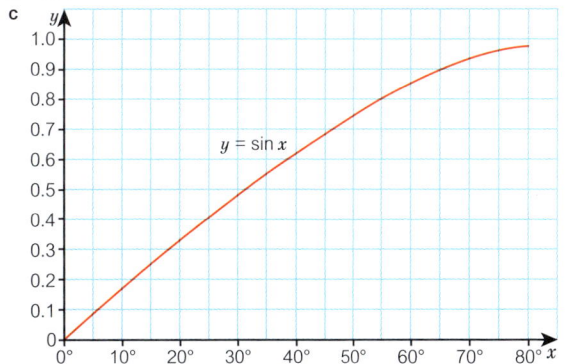

d $\sin 90° = 1$

e, f

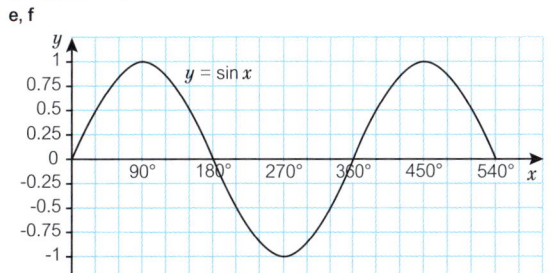

g The same: All the ratios repeat.
   Different: Tangent repeats every 180° but sine and cosine repeat every 360°.
   Tangent can be any number and there are places where it can't be calculated, but sine and cosine are always between 1 and −1.

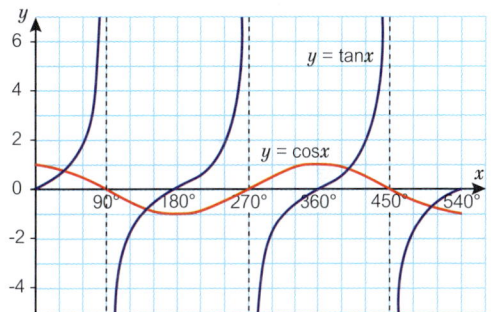

Investigation

10 a, b

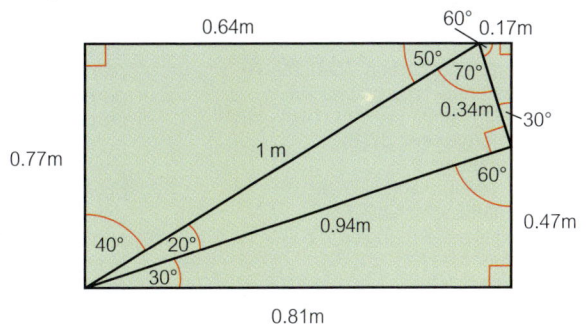

c You can find the length of the rectangle by multiplying the cosines of the two angles and the height by calculating the sine of the sum of the angles.
d $\sin(x + y) = (\sin x)(\cos y) + (\sin y)(\cos x)$
   This is always true.

Reflect

11 The ratio of side lengths in similar triangles is always the same. This is what trigonometry uses to calculate sides and angles.

Index